BOOKS IN A NUT SHELL

Selected Key Points
From Non-Fiction Books
On 8 Topics
In 8 Separate Chapters

By Stephen S. Battaglia

INTRODUCTION:

Have you ever had a conversation with someone and tried to remember information from a book you recently read? How embarrassed and irritated you must have felt when you couldn't remember that information as it was. What was the name of the book, and how can I retrieve that book to get the information. From time to time I have had the same problem. I do not have a photographic memory and as we age it appears to get shorter. So I decided some years ago to write a brief book summary of key points on each book I read that I thought was interesting, I wanted to remember or have easy access to the information.

After I retired I joined a discussion group of eight guys from our retirement community. We would meet every other Saturday and discuss financial and political information. This is what led me to writing my book summaries. I needed up to date information to include in these discussions. I would need to reread the books if they could be retrieved from our local library or on my Kindle.

When reading a book I'd highlight items in the book or bookmarked the items on my Kindle. When I completed the book the items would then be included in my computer under a folder titled, you guessed it, "Book Summaries". Well, years later these book summaries got to be quite extensive and useful and thought that I should put them in a book so others can benefit from these key point summaries. If the summaries sound interesting maybe one would want to read the entire book. Well that is it in a nutshell.

Remember these items are only what I thought were interesting points in the book. They are not all inclusive and it is not a summary of the book. Most of the items were taken directly from the book with little if any changes. The number of books got to be so extensive that I divided the material into eight sections of separate topics. So read on and keep this book handy for easy reference.

CHAPTER INDEX   PAGE

BOOKS IN A NUT SHELL

ANCIENT HISTORY

INDEX	PAGE

1. 1421 The Year China Discovered America
by Gavin Menzies

1. Khu Di was the first Ming emperor. Mongols under Kublai Kahn, the grandson of Genghis Kahn, ruled China in 1279. In 1352 the peasants of China revolted and took back the county with the cookie revolt.
2. Paper money invented by the Chinese in AD 806.
3. Tang Dynasty AD 618-907.
4. 1 nautical mile = 1.15 statute miles.
5. Dendrochronology- is the study of tree rings to establish the date of the tree.
6. Christopher Columbus's true legacy is not the discovery of America but the circulatory wind system of the Atlantic that goes counter clockwise.
7. Cotton represents 5% of the world crop. China is the leading producer of silk. Coconut is the most important nut crop and bananas originated in South East Asia.
8. There is a strong evidence of Chinese presence in old Mexican capital of Teotihuacan.

2. Barbarians to Angles   by Peter Wells

1. The Roman Empire was extinguished in the late 5th century. They could not expand after the 3rd century due to increasing use of mercenaries hired to guard their weakening borders in other territories.
2. In 27BC Augustus was named the first emperor of Rome. The Republic of Rome was established about 510BC.
3. Rome was the greatest power for about 8 centuries from 500BC. Wealthy men of the Roman government controlled all government positions. This was because they wrote the laws to favor them.
4. In 324 Constantine conquered the city of Byzantium that was changed to Constantinople and now changed to Istanbul. Constantine became the sole emperor of Rome.

5. Southern Britain was cleared of forest vegetation in the late Bronze Age and it never regained the woodlands. Roman armies under Claudius invaded Britain in 43 AD. In 410 Rome told Britain that they could no longer send troops to protect them.

6. Napoleon Bonaparte was crowned emperor of France on Dec.2,1804.

7. Dendrochronological analysis is the study of tree ring dating.

3. City of Fortune   by Roger Crowley

1. Venice, Italy had been conducting running fights with Croat ships or pirates for 150 years.

2. The Basilica of Saint Mark was designed by Greek architects after The Church of the Holy Apostles in Constantinople.

3. When Venetian merchants were expelled from Constantinople in 1190 the Pope started a new Crusade in 1198. This Crusade was called "Treaty of Venice" under Pope Innocent and ended the 4th Crusade in 1204. This divided the Roman and Byzantine Empires in Constantinople among the victorious parties. They were granted western Greece Corfu, Ionian Islands, and 3/8ths of Constantinople.

5. The object of the 4th Crusade was to repel Islam but in fact it advanced the spread of it.

6. The harbor of Serifos in the Aegean Sea was so rich in iron ore that it confused compasses of passing ships.

7. Christopher Columbus whose real name was Cristobal Colon primary objective crossing the Atlantic was to find a fresh stock of human slaves. There were more slaves in Genoa than any other city in medieval Europe.

8. Marco Polo was the first European to leave an eyewitness account of the cultivation of pepper in India and a study of the Silk Road through China.

9. At end of the 14 century the Mongol Empire had been fragmented and China had been replaced by the Ming dynasty.

10. Venice was a world class shipbuilding center where assembly line production, specialism, and quality control were enacted. Skill

separation was critical and poor work was punishable with dismissal. Skills were handed down through generations and guarded.

11. First maritime code was introduced in 1255.

12. On June 1416 the Venetians engaged the Ottoman fleet for the first time.

13. In 1511 the Portuguese conquered Malacca on the Malay Peninsula for the spices on the Spice Islands, and that squeezed the Venetian trade. The Portuguese went around the Cape of Good Hope to bypass the route taken by the Venicians and thus were able to undercut their prices.

14. Population in the 1200's were mostly sea faring individuals. This changed in the 1500 to manufacturing population due to the reduction of the ship traffic. The new business was glass of Murano, Italy, near Venice, importing of soda ash from Syria and sugar then moved from Syria to Cyprus.

15. Venice was the first European power to seriously interact with the Islamic world.

4. Decline and Fall of the ROMAN EMPIRE
by Edward Gibbon

1. The Roman senate was mentioned with honor till the last period of the empire. The senate of Rome lost all connection with the Imperial court and actual constitution.

2. Latin tongue was in use throughout the empire.

3. 275-285 AD- Diocletian divided the empire, the provinces and every branch of the civil as well as the military offices. He also increased the government and rendered it more secure. The empire was divided into four parts- East, Italy, Danube, and Rhine.

4. Among the Christians brought before the emperor was the grandson of St. Jude, the apostle who himself was the brother of Jesus Christ.

5. Theodosius, having himself the guilt of homicide, suggested that David, the man after God's own heart, had been guilty not only of murder but of adultery but should be also forgiven. Ambrose forgave David of his crimes.

6. The relaxation of discipline and the disuse of exercise rendered the Roman soldiers less able and less willing to support the fatigues of service, less willing to wear armor, and even got permission to not wear armor or helmets. The cavalry of the Goths, Huns, and the Alani wore armor and easily overwhelmed the Romans who did not wear armor due to its weight; all this was a significant cause of the fall of the Roman Empire.

7. 419-455 AD- The Roman princes were unable to protect their subjects against the public enemy as they were unwilling to trust them with arms for their own defense, imposed intolerable weight of taxes, and the universal corruption which increased the influences of the rich and aggravated the misfortunes of the poor.

8. The Italians after renouncing arms and after 40 years of peace were surprised by the formidable barbarians.

9. Valentinian the third was the last Roman emperor of the family of Theodosius.

10. Taxes were multiplied which distressed the public, the economy was neglected, and the rich shifted the unequal burden from themselves to the ordinary people.

11. 430-490 AD- With the extinction of the western empire, Odoacer was the first barbarian king of Italy.

12. The decay of agriculture was a factor in the decline of Rome. Losing food sources from Egypt and Africa, the people were diminished by war, famine, and pestilence.

13. 305-712AD- Christianity increased with the inclusion of the leaner and luxurious citizens of the Roman Empire and over the war like barbarians of Scythia and Germany who subverted the empire and embraced the religion of the Romans. Christian's, many of who were ecclesiastical, were dispersed as slaves in villages and successively labored for the salvation of their masters.

14. 449-582AD-It was stated that peace cannot be secured without armies and armies must be supported at the expense of the people.

15. In the space of four hundred years the hardy Gaul's, who had encountered the armies of Caesar, were imperceptibly melted into the general mass of citizens and subjects. The Western empire was dissolved and the Germans took possession of Gaul.

16. The Visigoths had resigned to Clovis the greatest part of their Gallic possessions but they did secure the provinces of Spain.

17. The Saxons achieved the conquest of Britain when Britain was separated from the Roman Empire.

18. The loss of strength of the Roman maritime province led them to be attacked by pirates of Germany.

19. The use of the Latin language was finally abolished.

20. Gaul and Britain were less adapted to agriculture but more adapted to cattle, flocks, and herds.

21. The name of Caesar was the second in command after the supreme title of Augustus.

22. In ten centuries of the Roman Empire not a single discovery was made to promote mankind.

23. The Ottoman's entered to the final destruction of the Roman Empire and this with the loss of Constantinople. The Ottoman's outnumbered the Christians in Constantinople by 50-1 and reduced the city to ruin.

5. Democracy for Beginners   by Robert Cavalier

1. In early Athens, Greece laws divided the country into grids all equal but only males could vote.

2. Aristotle, 384-322 BC, two forms of rule by many (everybody) or rule by property owners.

3. Alexander the Great was tutored by Aristotle. He conquered the world from India to Alexandria, Egypt. After his death his empire was divided into large kingdoms from which arose Italy and the Romans.

4. The Republics collapsed with the rise of the dictators- Caesars.

5. Augustine adopted the ancient idea that a goal of State is to provide peace, and the leaders and citizens think of the common good of all rather than their own good.

6. When Western Roman Empire collapsed the empires of the East continued as the Byzantium Empire with its seat in Constantinople- today's Istanbul, Turkey. Thus came the dark ages with not much writing.

7. Around 600 AD a new religion appeared under the prophet Muhammad. After his death in 632 AD Islam spread across the East and to Spain in the West.

8. Thomas Aquinas, 1225-1274, was a theologian at the Univ. of Paris. His ideal city is one ruled by a single wise man for the sake of virtue and the second best a mixed regime where laws do not conflict with human and natural laws.

9. Machiavelli- 1469-1527- Rulers survive and states become stable when things are done in any way that gets the job done. When it serves one's needs be deceitful. Be manipulative and vicious when it serves your needs but you can't be a cruel tyrant nor do you want the people to love you.

10. Unhealthy politics is when officials are elected by media campaigns that manipulate the voter and influence the outcome at whatever cost.

11. Reformation- 1517 by Martin Luther in his "95 Theses" from frustration over excesses of the Catholic Church and the selling of indulgences.

12. 1765 the Stamp Act in 1765 by the British parliament was a tax on all imports to the American colonies. Protest lead to the Boston Tea Party and the 1775 Lexington and Concord fighting- the American Revolutionary War.

13. Age of Enlightenment, a background of the French and American revolutions, led to the break with King George by the American colonies.

14. Under President Adams a Sedition Act of 1798 was passed holding newspapers accountable for "false, scandalous and malicious" attacks against Congress and the President.

15. Why do we disagree by parties- weighing evidence differently, differences in life experiences, and values and conflicts of values?

16. A large % of citizens including voters do not become informed to any significant degree on issues.

17. True public opinion is arrived at by discussion of the issues not that manipulated by the media or determined by the personality of the candidates.

18, Countries that only adopt a democratic constitution, without cultivating a sense of citizenship among their people, often fail at achieving a viable society.

6. Lords of the Horizons- History of the Ottoman Empire by Jason Goodwin

1. Islam has no priesthood. Koran is the law not the scripture.
2. The Byzantine Empire fell in 1327 to the Ottoman Empire.
3. The Turks were divided into tribes and never assimilated in an area. Osman who was born in 1280 and then followed by his son Orhan started the Ottoman Empire. Both ate and worked with their men.
4. In about 3000 BC horses were tamed.
5. The practice of accumulating money and creating a treasury was introduced.
6. In 1453 The Turks seized Constantinople from the Greeks and controlled the strait- the Black Sea to the Mediterranean.
7. In one thousand years, Constantinople was assaulted 29 times and repulsed 21 times.
8. In the 1520's, Sultan Suleyman of the Ottoman Empire introduced sign language for the deaf and dumb.
9. No born Muslin could be enslaved.
10. Ottoman Empire had no hereditary nobility. They lived for war and conquest. The governors were generals in the army. They were born to move and that made them warriors.
11. The Silk Road to China began at Bursa, Turkey.
12. A major down fall was that they thought it too expensive to build a navy to tackle the Christians (Crusades).
13. The Ottoman mustachio's were a symbol of faith and of their crescent moon.
14. 1574 was the turning pint of the Empire as all were tired of fighting and trying to hang on to power. With the capture of Cyprus it ignited the Holy League against the Ottoman's by Sain, Venice, Malta and the Italian states under the papacy.
15. In 1580 Murad III had the first plan for the Suez Canal but a rebellion stopped the plan.

16. The first 10 rulers of the Ottoman Dynasty averaged 27 years from Osman to Suleyman who was the last one and he died in 1566.

17. Previous Fratricidal law was that no relative male could rule and all were killed. This was broken in 1603 when the elders became successors.

18. Power slid from the sultans to their slaves.

19. Ottoman Empire was having trouble paying for their ever-expanding army. Revenue was drying up and overburdened its people.

20. In 1807 a Tilsit, Napoleon and the Tsar of Russia, divided up the empire of Alexander the Great.

21. In 1826 the Ottoman gunners having lost their clay pipes in the war created the first cigarette by rolling paper around their tobacco.

22. In 330 AD the Roman Emperor Constantine, after he lost Rome, found the new imperial city of Constantinople as his new imperial city.

23. 1069 was the date of the first Crusade.

24. The Black Death in Europe started in 1346.

25. In 1703 Peter the Great of Russia founded St. Petersburg.

26. The Ottoman Empire declared bankruptcy, mostly due to lavish spending and an over extended army with no funds to support it.

27. In 1923 Turkey was declared a Republic.

7. Mythology by E. Hamilton

1. Greek mythology begins with the Iliad about 1000 years before Christ.

2. Greek mythology is made up of stories about gods and goddesses.

3.The Dipper constellation also called the Great Bear does not set below the horizon.

4. Pindar the greatest lyric poet of Greece- 6th century. Other prose writers- Herodotus was the first historian of Europe.

5. About 250 BC, center of poets moved from Greece to Alexandria in Egypt.

6.The 12 Olympians -Greek and their Roman names, some were also named for the planets: Zeus-Jupiter, Poseidon- Neptune, Hades-Pluto,

Hestia- Vesta, Hera- Juno, Ares- Mars, Athena-Minerva, Apollo, Aphrodite- Venus, Hermes-Mercury, Artemis-Diana, Hephaestus-Vulcan.

7. The God of the grape vine- Dionysus also called Bacchus. Iris the Goddess is the Rainbow.

8. The Centaurs were half man and half horse. The Sileni were creature's part man, part horse, and walked on two legs.

9. Founders of Rome- Romulus and Remus.

10. What creature goes on four feet in the morning, on two at noon day and three in the evening- man: he crawls in early childhood, walks erect as an adult, and walks with a cane in old age.

11. Midas- synonym for a rich man. King Midas of Phrygian. Old Silenus, intoxicated wandered off from Bacchus and fell in a bed of roses of Midas. He was returned to Bacchus who gave him a wish. Everything he touches turned to gold. To cancel this wish he washed himself in the River Pactolus.

12. Valkyries – Val means slain.

13. Days of the week are named after Greek gods then changed to Roman gods: Thor- Thunder for Thursday, Tyr was the God of War for Tuesday, and Frigga - Odin's wife for Friday,

8. Sea of Glory by Nathaniel Philbrick

1. In late 1400's Chinese emperor Yung-lo sent a large flotilla that ventured to the east coast of Africa and the western seaboard of the America's.

2. Hudson's Bay Company dominated the Oregon territory. They surveyed the west coast of the Americas down to Mexico.

3. About 1838, Charles Wilkes undertook the expedition to discover the west coast and discovered Antartica.

4. Ferdinand Magellan first to circumnavigate the world. He called and gave the name to the Pacific Ocean that was, however, earlier founded by Balboa. In 1830 the Vincennes became the first U.S. naval vessel to circumnavigate the world.

5. On Wilkes voyage all officers were instructed to keep a daily journal. At the journeys end they would become the property of the U.S. Government.
6. Cape Horn in South America was named after the town of Hoorn in the Netherlands.
7. Hawaii, the youngest of the islands about 1 billion years old, is made up of five distinct volcanoes. Mauna Loa is the largest.
8. Hawaiian Islands were settled between 300-800 AD and New Zealand was discovered around 1000-1200AD.
9. An Englishman James Smithson left ½ million dollars in gold coins for the establishment for the increase and diffusion of knowledge, which is now the Smithsonian in Washington, D. C.
10. Herman Melville uses data from the US. Exploring Expedition in his masterpiece Moby Dick.
11. In June 1846, the boundary between the U.S. and British Canada were established at the forty-ninth parallel with the signing of the Buchanan-Pakenham treaty.
12. Gold was discovered in California in 1848.
13. Mexican War started in 1846.

9.   The Babylonians by Elaine Landau

1. 1792 BC, Hammurabi rules.
2. Over the years The Hittites, Kassites, and the Alamitos ruled Babylonian's and their territory.
3. Nebuchadnezzar II built the hanging gardens of Babylon, one of seven ancient wonders of the world, and reigned from 605BC until 562BC.
4. Siege of Jerusalem in 597 BC. Hebrews went to Babylonia as slaves and in 527BC were freed by Nebuchadnezzar II and returned home.
5. They imported all of their wood, as no forests existed in their territory that was in the desert of Africa.
6. The Babylonian's territory was invaded by Greeks, Arabs and the Turks. The Turks were eventually defeated by the British in WWI and renamed Iraq. Iraq became independent in 1932.

7. Alexander the Great made Babylon the capital of his empire. He was born in 599BC and took the throne in 558BC.
8. In 539BC Cyprus, the King of Persia, conquered the Babylonia and melted it into the Persian Empire.

10. The Borgias and their Enemies 1431-1519
by Christopher Hibbert

1. In 1305 distressed by the unrest and bloody disturbances in the city of Rome, French Pope Clement V 1305-1314 set up court in Avignon on the east bank of the Rhone.
2. Gregory XI another Frenchman and the last of the Avignon Popes moved the Curia back to Rome.
3. Emperor Constantine built the church of St. Peter's over the tomb of the first pope. Nicholas V moved the official residence from the Lateran to the Vatican Palace.
4. Pope Calixtus III organized a crusade that would free Constantinople from the grip of the Turks who had captured the city in May 1453.
5. Pope Sixtus IV was responsible for the Sistine Chapel and built by Giovannino de Dolci with the walls decorated with scenes of the lives of Moses and Christ.
6. In 1502 Pope Cesare appointed Leonardo da Vinci as his Architect and General Engineer. Leonardo painted the Last Supper in the convent of Santa Maria delle Grazie in Milan. Louis XII seeing this employed him as a military engineer.
7. Machiavelli wrote "The Prince".
8. Julius II unwilling to rely on mercenaries formed a papal army in 1506 known as the Swiss Guards and was a fighting force until 1825.

11. The Hundred Years War by Desmond Seward

1. Started about 1337 when Edward III of England claimed the throne of France and lasted until 1453 when the English finally lost Bordeaux.
2. Wool was the main export and jewel of England and the best part of their wealth.

3. At times the English were unable to pay angry mercenaries and forced to give up part of territory in the France area. Some of their funds came from pillaging the territory of all saleable gold and silver and capturing high placed individual as dukes, and ransoming them.
4. Charles V defeated Edward III and the Black Prince, and lost parts of then France.
5. War taxation was the spark that had set off the Peasants Revolt.
6. Joan of Arc was born about 1412 in a village called Domremy in Eastern Champagne, France.
7. England fought for and took land in various areas now known as France. France eventually fought back and took back the territory and driving the English out. They could not pay for the war on a foreign territory they tried to claim as their own.

12. The Life of Greece by Will Durant

1. Crete once with famous forests of cypress and cedar vanished. Now 2/3 of the island is a stony waste. It contains no great internal resources only commerce. Between Crete and the Greek mainland 220 islands dot the Aegean forming a circle around Delos called Cyclades.
2. In 1300BC the family owned Greek land. The father controls but cannot sell without all family members concurring.
3. Rise of Greece- 1000-480 BC: Babylonia gave Greece weights and measures, water clocks, and astronomical principles. Thales predicted the eclipse of the sun.
4. Trade between Mesopotamia and Greece created banking and coinage.
5. Every citizen of Sparta was trained for war and military service from 20-60 years old.
6. Periander, longest dictatorships in Greeks history- 625-585, established order and discipline, encouraged business, and checked exploitation in Corinth at that time the foremost city in Greece.
7. About 630 BC, Megara was ruled by Theagenes but was deposed by the rich. Revolution restored democracy where property was re-

confiscated from the rich, debts abolished, and interest paid to the wealthy had to be returned.

8. Pandora's Box- Prometheus left Epimetheus a mysterious box with instructions that is should under no circumstances be opened- Pandora opened and 10,000 evils fly out of it and a plague began.

9. Solon, in Athens about 580 BC, established law of wills, legalized and taxed prostitution, began government by written and permanent law, divided state land to the poor but only to those who would work the land, gave employment to the needy by extensive public works of aqueducts and roads. All financed with a 10% tax on all agricultural products. He retired at age 66 serving 22 years and remarked, " I grow old while always learning". Years later the aristocracy conspired to recapture power but plans were foiled and the leaders exiled.

10. Ephesus- founded about 1000 BC. Its temple here was the largest in Greece yet built and one of the 7 Wonders of the World.

11. Chios was a major wine industry in 431BC with groves also of figs and olives. Here Glaucus, about 560 BC, discovered welding iron. About 660 BC, Byzantium was built Island of Thasos noted for gold mines.

12. Pythagoras discovered trigonometry astronomy and music. First person to call the earth round but also geocentric in error.

13. Phocaeans of Ionia landed in now Marseilles and introduced the olive and the vine to France about 560BC.

14. Panhellenic games of Greece organized on a regular quadrennial event at Olympia in 776BC. Included five contests- broad jump, discus, spear hurling, 200-yard sprint, and wrestling.

15. Three orders of Greece architecture- Doric, Ionic and Corinthian. Greek architecture was entirely for religious buildings while Mycenaean was of general building. Finest buildings were the older temples of Paestum and Sicily all in Doric style.

16. In 512BC, Darius I of Persia over extended his territory and weakened his empire from Egypt, India, Mesopotamia, Palestine, etc.

17. Greece Golden Age 480-399 BC-Greek legislation is the basis of Roman law which provides the Western society's legal foundation. However, each party in a trial has his own lawyer and has to make in person the first presentation in his case.

18. Male citizens are subject to conscription during a war. However poorer citizens carry the brunt carrying the spears while the rich are clad in armor.

19. Without imported food the population would starve. This created the need for imperialism and a powerful shipping fleet.

20. Greek olives are used for eating, anointing, illumination, and fuel. It was its richest crop and the government imposed an export monopoly.

21. A class of women who entertain men dyed their hair yellow in the belief that Athenians prefer blondes.

22. The Parthenon was preserved through its use as a Christian church. After Turkish occupation in 1456 it was changed to a mosque.

23. Greek medicine was taken from the Egyptians and not changed until the 19 century.

24. Euripides about 410 BC was the first private citizen in Greece to collect a substantial library of books.

25. Pericles in 443 drew up a code of laws for the cities and Hippodamus, the architect, laid out the streets on a rectangular plan that is used today.

26. In 409BC, Hamilcar's son Hannibal, a Carthaginian, invaded Sicily then occupied by the Greeks. All this for control of the Mediterranean Sea route for shipping goods.

27. The Decline and Fall of Greek Freedom-399-322 BC-in 370 Athens was the greatest power in the eastern Mediterranean. Silver mines at Laurium were reopened. Banks received cash and valuables with no interest paid and lent money at high interest rates. This was the start of a banking system. Property amongst the middle class decreased who then took charge but the rich organized sexual encounters and political morality continued to decline. As the family size decreased the supply of citizens for military services suffered and outside mercenaries were hired to take their place.

28. Alexander the Great was born in 356 BC to Philip and Olympias (claimed descent from Achilles). And taught by Aristotle in his youth. When he won a war he distributed the spoils to his men. Jerusalem surrendered to him but Gaza fought until every man was killed. He united tribes as he conquered them. To bring in Persia he married the

daughter of Darius III, a branch of royalty. He died of over drinking at age 33 in 323BC.

29. The function of the state is to organize a society for the greatest happiness of the greatest number. Aristotle divided Greece into three types: Monarchy, aristocracy and democracy. No one form is better than the other and may be preferred under a given set of conditions. When the rich get the better of the poor or the poor of the rich neither of them will establish a free state.

30. Philip V in 215BC fearful of the growing power of Rome aligned with Hannibal and Carthage but Rome declared war on them and Rome began their conquest of Greece.

31. In 324 Antimenes of Rhodes organized the first known system of insurance and for a premium of 8% one could insure against the loss from runaway slaves. With little employment the poor turned to mercenary soldiering abroad. The government gave the destitute food and tickets to games. The poor organized themselves into unions but were overwhelmed by the power and cleverness of the rich.

32. The number seven- seven days of a week, seven planets, seven hill of Rome, seven wonders of the world, seven heavens, and seven gates of hell, The meaning of "Mazzol-tov" May your planet be favorable.

33. Like Solon, Nabis, a Syrian Semite of the people of Sparta, in 207 nationalized large estates, redistributed the land and abolished debt. After his assassination the revolution of the poor ended and so did Sparta.

34. An earthquake in 225BC destroyed Rhodes.

35. The basis of Judaism was religion. Entertainment and games were few, intermarriage with a non-Jew was forbidden so were celibacy and infanticide. In Caesar's time there were 7 million Jews in the Roman Empire. In 198 BC the Jews supported Antiochus and welcomed his capture of Jerusalem as liberation. Antiochus III needing funds for campaigns ordered the Jews be taxed at 1/3 of their grain crop and ½ the tree fruits. Jews who refused to eat pork or in possession of the Book of the Law were jailed or killed. In 164 BC under Judas the Jews won a decisive victory and now celebrated as Hanukkah.

36. Mechanics- Archimedes- screw machine and Ctesibius water pump. The Ptolemy's opened up a copper mine at Cyrus and Sinai, and controlled a monopoly of oil from plants like linseed, croton, and sesame. At Ptolemy's factory workers were slaves giving them low cost to undersell foreign trade of Greek handicraft. Ptolemy II introduced the camel into Egypt

37. Alexandria, Egypt stood, an ancient wonder of the world, the Lighthouse over 400 ft high. Completed about 179BC by Sostratus for Ptolemy II. It stood on the isle of Pharos and was destroyed in the 13th century.

38. Banking was a Government monopoly. A fifth of Alexandria was Jewish

39. The Rosetta Stone dated 196BC describes the coronation of Ptolemy V. Agriculture and industry declined until taken over by Caesar and Augustus made it a Roman province in 30BC.

40. Machiavelli-"There is no more ready corrective of conduct than knowledge of the past, and the soundest education and training for life of active politics is the study of history".

41. In less than 53 years Romans subjected the whole inhabited world to their sole government. Greece disintegrated from within.
No nation is ever conquered until it has destroyed itself- corruption, decay of morals, and decline of population, replacing citizen armies with mercenary troops, and exhausted natural resources. By 210AD all Sicily was controlled by the Carthaginians.

13. The Roman Empire by Don Nardo

1. 1000 BC- Roman primitives' tribes settled in west Italy.
2. 750 BC- Villages combined into a town called Rome.
3. 509 BC- A Republic was established by elected citizens and was now a democracy. Initially kings ruled in Italy.
4. 44 BC- Caesar was assassinated.
5. 27 BC- Octavian was named as Romans first emperor and confirmed by the senate with the title of Augustus. This began Roman's piece that lasted 2 centuries.

6. 5 BC- Roman's began conquering their neighbors and the power shifted to the military.

7. 13 AD- Augustus at 76 adopted Tiberius who at 55 became Caesar in 14AD.

8. 64 AD- While Nero was Emperor a fire destroyed a large portion of Rome.

9. 79 AD- Mt. Vesuvius erupted.

10. 79 AD- The Colosseum was inaugurated under Vespasian's son Titus. The Colosseum was about two ties the size of a football field holding about 60,000 spectators.

11. The fancy Roman feasts or dinners were of three courses- Appetizers-eggs to apples, main course- meats and vegetables with rich sauces, and the last course was dessert of mostly fruit. It was common for the guests to bring their own napkins that they used to take leftovers home (the start of the doggie bay).

12. 240 AD- Sassanians of the Persian Eire began invading the Roman towns.

13. 250 AD- The food supply declined, as the small farms could not compete with the large farmers. These farmers abandoned their farms to be assisted by the government.

14. 250 AD- the government was spending too much on the military while the people were over taxed. Order broke down as poverty increased.

15. 265 AD- The Roman military leaders took control and rebuilt their territory that they lost in the past years.

16. 300 AD- The Christian's were 5% of the population.

17. 312 AD- Constantine as Emperor entered Rome and established the "Edit of Milan" giving Christians freedom.

18. 361 AD- At and after Emperor Julian's rule all the future Emperors were Christians and not Muslims.

14. The Swerve by S. Greenblatt

1. 1417 AD, Poggio Bracciolini was the book hunter interested in manuscripts that were four or five hundred years old back to the

tenth century. He located copies throughout Europe traveling around to ancient castles, monasteries, churches, etc

2. Poggio served Pope John XXIII.

3. During the 5th century, the Roman Empire crumbled, cities decayed, trade declined, and the school system fell apart.

4. Johann Gutenberg, a German entrepreneur in the 1430's, invented moving type for printing.

5. When writing text and errors occurred they would scrape the ink with a razor and repair the spot with a mixture of milk, cheese, and lime a version of the current white out.

6. The greatest Roman Poet was Virgil and was 15 years old when Lucretius, the poet of "Nature of Things", died. Of him he said, "Blessed is he who has succeeded in finding out the causes of things".

7. The word paper comes from the word "papyrus" produced from tall reeds that grew in the marshy delta region of the Nile in Lower Egypt.

8. In 167 BC the Roman army routed King Perseur of Macedon and ended the dynasty that descended from Alexander The Great. Near that time the Greeks founded cities as Naples, Tarentum, and Syracuse.

9. Roman's first public library was formed in 40 BC by Pollio.

10. Notion of atoms originated in the 5th century BC by Leucippus of Abdera. Epicurus reasoned that all things are made of atoms.

11. There are no surviving contemporary manuscripts from the ancient Greek or Roman world. All that were found are copies mostly on charred papyrus fragments.

12. During this time there were high intellectual levels: Euclid- geometry in Alexandria, Archimedes – calculus and pi, Eratosthemes – calculated the circumference of the earth within 1%, and Galen revolutionized medicine. Some of these individuals called into question the Christian belief as a myth.

13. Charles Darwin on the origin of human species. His work on Galapagos Island and elsewhere were based on experimental and math science not ancient philosophical speculation.

14 Thomas Jefferson owned at least five Latin editions of "On the Nature of Things".

15. The War that Killed Achilles by C. Alexander

1. Tracing two extinct people of the Bronze Age- Greeks (Mycenaeans) and the Trojans (Hittites) of Anatolia
2. First rulers of Rome were the Anatolian's.
3. Achilles is Peleides son of Peleus. At Peleus wedding there was a dispute about who was the most beautiful among Athena's- Hera or Aphrodite. Aphrodite was crowned.
4. From the Iliad, judgement of Paris anointed Aphrodite as the most beautiful of the goddesses over Hera and Athene. His reward was Helen, later of Troy, as he states the most beautiful in the world and this was the cause of the Trojan War
5. The young Achilles was dipped in the river Sty's to render him immortal but when he was dipped his heel, ankle, did not get wet making him vulnerable in that area.
6. Achilles puts the Trojans to flight and chases them into the city Scaean. He is killed by Paris firing an arrow and guided by Apollo in his vulnerable body part to his ankle, the part of his body not in armor.
.

16. The Wisdom of History by Will Durant

Book #1
1. Lessons of history teach us that freedom is not a universal value but power and empire are. All is cyclical.
2. Lessons of history: we do not learn from history, Middle East is the graveyard of empires, religion and spirituality are the most profound motivators in human history, and rise and fall of nations is due to human decisions.
3. WWI started when on June 28,1914 Ferdinand of Austria was shot. War ended in 1918.
4. Hubris- Greek idea that downfall follows outrageous arrogance.
5. Freedom is not necessary as China has flourished without an idea of freedom. Order follows from the leader.
6. Common law came from Magna Charta in 1215.
7. First war appears to be when Hittites and Egyptians fought for dominance in the Middle East in 13th century B. C.

8. Nation of Israel rose and fell (1020-586 BC) in the collapse of the Egyptian Empire and the Trojan War. They were a major power in the 10th century B. C. as described in the book of Samuel. Assyrians and Babylonians conquered Israel and the Jews were taken off to Babylon. Jews returned in 538 BC.

9. Athenians had rights guaranteed by law-right to vote, and obligated all men to military service. As was the case when the United States was first formed.

10. Athens failure led Thucydides to conclude that democracy cannot rule an empire- democracy voters are fickle, distracted by silly issues, voters lack experience.

11. Alexander the Great had peace in the Middle East. He did not impose Greek values on the people but adopted their ways and customs. Once he died his generals carved up his empire.

12. Rome began as a small city on the Tiber River in 509BC. They did not believe in preemptive or undeclared wars. By 270 BC Italy was up to the Po River and gained Sicily about 3rd century BC.

13. U.S. Constitution based on Roman constitution made for small city –states. Italy by 70BC was corrupted by concentrated of wealth in the Senate. The only way to get elected was to spend lavishly for political favors with wealthy businessmen's money. Small farmers were almost gone by the 1st century BC.

14. Terrorism was linked to the Middle East throughout the Roman Empire. Rome never solved this problem. Jews were protected and not required to worship the Roman emperor as a god. Not so to the Christians.

15. Middle East problem strained the military and financial resourced of the empire of Rome. Empire collapsed in the 4th and 5th centuries AD. Caused by collapse in morality of the people, food source, military became bloated and inefficient, taxes on the middle class, distraction in the Middle East, and loyalty to Rome disappeared due to lack of finances to pay for all.

16. After WWI the Ottoman Empire was shorn away and Jerusalem was captured. The Armistice dated Nov. 11, 1918 divided the Ottoman Empire- Britain got Palestine and Iraq, and the Greece got Constantinople.

17. Freedom has never existed in the Middle East. . France and Britain could not force democracy on Syria, Iraq or Palestine.

18. Napoleon's preemptive war against Russia was his downfall.

19. Genghis Kahn "emperor of all men" worriers on horses with armor and helmets. In 1221 he ruled central Asia and part of Persia (Iran).

20. Thomas Jefferson was the third US president in 1801 and the first to commit troops in as commander-in-chief.

Book #2

21. Rome began as a small city by the Tiber River in 509BC

22. US constitutions based on Rome-both made for small city- states

23. Small farmers almost gone in Italy by the 1st century BC

24. Rome annexed Jerusalem. In 70 AD Jerusalem was captured and the Jewish temple was destroyed.

25. Over 200 years the Roman Empire was a superpower that brought peace and prosperity to the world. They collapsed in the 4th and 5th centuries AD. Rome first intervened in the Middle East in the 2nd century BC and fell from power in the 3rd Century AD. Tried everything but nothing worked.

26. Byzantium name followed Constantinople was changed to Istanbul.

27. Muhammad was born 570 in Mecca and died in 632. His son-in-law and cousin, ALI, created a division between Sunnis and Shiites.

28. Crusades began in 1096 and continued until 15th century. First crusades captured Jerusalem and then the Muslims were massacred en masse.

29. After WWI Italy got southern Anatolia and southern Asia Minor, France got Syria, Britain got Palestine and Iraq, and Greece got Constantinople.

30. Freedom never existed in the Middle East.

31. French revolution began in May 1,789. Napoleon was fighting on many Russian.

32. Father of Communism is Karl Marx, a German. He stated that workers destroy capitalism that oppresses them with the lowest possible wages.

33. China and Russia never chose freedom in their long history.

34. First emperor to unite China- Ch'in Shih Huang, 221 BC, and built 7000 terracotta soldiers to guard him in death.

Book #3

35. Genghis Khan and Alexander learned that authoritarian rule and not democracy is the destiny of the Middle East. Khan was born about 1155. The eastern name for the Mongols is Tatars- the devil's horsemen.

36. In the year 1789 Geo. Washington took office and the French Revolution began.

37. United States became the only nation to be founded on principles. People became citizens by accepting these principles.

38. Thomas Jefferson was the 3rd president in 1801. He and Adams died on July 4, 1826. In 1803, Jefferson purchased the Louisiana Territory from France for $15 million. He sent his aid Lewis and Clark to find a path to the west. Sacajawea was their Indian guide.

39. 1836 Houston annexed territory by beating Santa Anna at Battle of San Jacinto. Mexico sought to block the annexation and they fought from 1846-8. US gained Texas, Arizona, New Mexico, and California from this conflict.

40. God is mentioned 4 times in the Declaration of Independence but not in the Constitution.

41. Lincoln inaugural address was in March 1865. Lee surrendered on Palm Sunday 1865.

42. Suez Canal opened in 1869. 1898 US went to war with Spain and annexed Puerto Rico and the Philippines.

43. French and British failed in the Middle East but the US thinks they are immune to the laws of history. Birth of the Middle East is about 3000BC. History teaches us that conquerors of foreign countries are often not welcomed as liberators.

The earliest empires in the Middle East were Asyria, Persia and Egypt.

17. Turkey by Luis Baralt

1. Size- about that of Texas and Oklahoma combined.
2. One quarter of its borders are on three bodies of water- Black Sea, Mediterranean and the Aegean Sea.
3. Turkey's largest city is Istanbul.
4. In the 8th century BC, Byzas founded Byzantium.
5. In the 2nd century AD it was conquered by the Roman Empire.
6. The Huns controlled this territory in the 8th century BC. Islam religion dominates.
7. The Roman Empire in the 3rd century AD was divided into three territories- Gaul & Britain, Danubian, and the territories of Italy, Africa and the East.
8. In 324 AD Constantine I, the Roman Emperor, conquered Byzantium and it became the New Rome. The city was renamed Constantinople and May 11, 330.
9. After 1129 years the Byzantine Empire ended in 1453 and was renamed Istanbul. The city then converted from Catholicism to Islam.
10. In 1453 the Ottoman Turks conquered Constantinople.
11. In 1923 the Republic of Turkey changed the capitol from Istanbul to Ankara.
12. Turkey under the Ottoman Empire sided with Germany in WWI.
13. The Fundamentalist took control of Iran in 1979.
14. The territory of Turkey is 40% forest, about 45% is agriculture, a world leader in grains and cotton, and they have very little oil.
15. Islam is the religion of Turkey where 98% are Muslims.
16. Muhammad was born in 570AD and died in 632. He had two daughters. One of the daughters was married to Ali who became head of the Shite Branch. Muhammad's father-in-law, Abubaku, became the main Islam branch of the Sunnis.
17. Turkey mostly consists of Sunni's while Iran is mostly Shite's.
18 .The Koran came from the writings of Muhammad.

BOOKS IN A NUT SHELL
HISTORY

INDEX   PAGE

INDEX

1. A Peoples History of the United States
by Howard Zinn

1. Columbus- half of the population who came to the new world died, murdered, etc.

2. Bering Strait land bridge closed about 25,000 years ago.

3. When Columbus arrived there were about 25 million Indians in North America.

4. First slave ship to North America landed in Jamestown on August 20, 1619 as the first settlement from a Dutch ship. First the Dutch then the English dominated the slave trade.

5. By 1800, 10-15 million blacks had been transported as slaves to the Americas. The first blacks were brought into Hispaniola in 1503.

6. By 1770, the top 1% of property owners owned 44% of the wealth.

7. Seven Years War or the French and Indian War 1763, England was victorious over France and expelling them from North America.

8. The United States coined by Governor Morris did not mean Indians, blacks, women or white servants.

9. Men signing the constitution in 1787 were lawyers and slave owners. At that time the Supreme Court selected the President.

10. In 1790 most of the 4 million Americans lived within 50 miles of the ocean. By 1840, 4.5 million crossed the Appalachian Mountains removing most of the Indians.

11. 1818 American acquisition of Florida by the Seminole War when they seized the Spanish forts. The Spanish were forced to sell Florida and most went to what I now Cuba.

12. Mexico won its independence by defeating Spain in 1821. This included what is now Texas, New Mexico, Utah, Nevada, and Arizona. In 1836 Texas broke off from Mexico.

13. June 1864, Congress passed a low granting equal pay to Negro soldiers.

14. In1883 the Civil Rights Act of 1875, outlawing discrimination against Negroes using public facilities, was nullified by the Supreme Court.

15. 1853 move towards price agreements, mergers, and monopoly when New York Central RR was a merger of many railroads.

16. Conscription Act of 1863, rich could avoid military service by paying $300 or by a substitute.

17. Pittsburgh in 1877 had 33 iron mills, 73 glass factories, 29 oil refineries and 158 coalmines.

18. Railroad construction done by 3,000 Irish and 10,000 Chinese over 4 years working for $1 or 2 per day. The two major lines started from East coast and went to Utah in 1869. The U.S. Army then wiped out Indian villages on the Great Plains for farmers to move in.

19. Andrew Carnegie was a telegraph clerk at 17, then secretary to the head of the Penn. RR, then broker in Wall Street selling RR bonds and was soon a millionaire.

20. Crises of 1893-closed 643 banks and 16,000 businesses.

21. 1880-90 all forms of oil and cotton accounted for 90% of US exports, 70% being oil and next was cotton.

22. 1898 Cuban rebels fought the Spanish conquerors and won independence. 1901 via the Platt Amendment passed by Congress gave the U.S. the right to intervene for the preservation of Cuban's independence.

23. 1898 peace treaty with Spain turning over to the U.S. -Guam, Puerto Rico and Philippines for $20 million.

24. 1907 a financial collapse and panic.

25. T Roosevelt and Taft were Trustbusters.

26. After the declaration of war, WW I, only 73,000 volunteered and with that Congress instituted the draft.

27. 1905- only the upper 10% enjoyed a marked increase in real income.

28. 1920- women won the right to vote- 19th amendment.

29. 1929- highest 5 % received about 1/3 of the income.

30. 1933- production fell by 50% and about 25% were out of work.

31. 1945-WWII unions rose- CIO and AFL.

32. Between 1900 and 1933 U.S. intervened in Cuba 4 times, Nicaragua twice, Panama 6 times, Guatemala once, and Honduras 7 times.

33. 1935 -50% of U.S. cotton and steel were sold in Latin America.

34. 1947- U.S. supplied weapons and military advisers to the Greek civil war and the right wing government in Athens.

35. Between 1947 and Dec. 1952, 6.6 million persons were investigated and no cases of espionage were uncovered.

36. Senate reported one hundred of the largest contractors who held 68% of the military contracts employed 2,000 former high-ranking officers of the military,

37. 1953 CIA overthrow the government of Iran, in 1954 CIA overthrew the legally elected head of Guatemala from military bases in Honduras and Nicaragua.

38. U.S. companies controlled 80 to 100 % of Cuba's utilities, mines, cattle ranches, and oil refineries, and 50% of their RR.

39. Invasion violation re Charter of Organization of American States "No state or group of states has the right to Intervene directly or indirectly, for any reason whatever, in the internal or external affairs of any other state."

40. 1953 -1.6% of the population owned 80% of the corporate stock and 90% of corporate bonds.

41. 1910 -90% of blacks lived in the South. By 1965 50% blacks lived in the North. By 1965 mechanical pickers harvested 81% of the cotton.

42. 1954 the U.S. was financing 80% of the French war in Indonesia with 300,000 military personnel, arms, etc.

43. Rubber and tin from Malaya and Indonesia are their principal source of exports from Southeast Asia. They import rice, iron ore and coal.

44. Gulf of Tonkin episode was a fake, the officials of U.S. lied when McNamara said, "the U.S. destroyer Maddox underwent an unprovoked attack". The CIA engaged in a secret operation attacking North Vietnamese coastal installations.

45. By the end of the Vietnam War 7 million tons of bombs were dropped on the country which was twice the total dropped in WWII.

46. 1960- 36% of women worked for paid wages

47. 1969- women were 40% of labor force

48. Court actions to do away with abortion began in 1968 and 1970.

49. 1973- Roe v Wade prohibit abortions in last three months of pregnancy and for health reasons.

50. Watergate- secret fund of about $500,000 to be used against the Democratic Party for leaking false news to the press, forging letters, and stealing campaign files.

51. ITT willing to give $1million to overthrow the Allende Gov. in Chile.

52. Hartford- ITT merger settled out of court in a secret arrangement where ITT gave $400,000 to Republican Party.

53. 1971 milk subsidies were stopped.

54. CIA operative told reporter- assassination plots against Castro of Cuba and other state heads, and gave African swine fever virus into Cuba in1971 via army base in Canal Zone to anti-Castro Cubans.

55. Opposition to Vietnam had brought the abolition of the draft.

56. 129 banks with foreign branches in 1974 with $155 billion deposits.

57. Panama Canal saved American companies over $2 billion a year while U.S. collected $150 million and paid Panama $2.5 million. We maintained 14 military bases in the area.

58. 1903 US engineered revolution against Colombia and set up the Republic of Panama giving U.S. military bases control of the Panama Canal in perpetuity.

59. American companies depended on poorer countries for 100% of their diamonds, coffee, platinum, natural rubber, and cobalt.

60. Most foreign aid is military and by 1975 the U.S. exported $9.5 billion in arms.

61. Per IRS figures of 1974 the very rich paid 26.9% in taxes while the oil companies paid 5.8% in taxes-

62. CIA instructed Iran Savak on torture techniques. In 1979 the U.S. embassy in Teheran was taken over by students to remove the shah and held 52 hostages.

63. Pres. Reagan- cut benefits to the poor, lower taxes for the wealthy, increase the military budget, and worked to destroy the revolutionary movements in the Caribbean.

64, Statistics showed that the armed forces of the world were responsibly for two-thirds of the gases depleting the ozone layer. The U.S. delegation of the Earth summit objected and suggested defeat of the pending law.

65, Reagan years- unemployment grew in 1982 by 30 million while 16 million lost medical insurance, elimination of free school lunches to more than 1 million, lowered tax rate of the rich from 70% to eventually 28%. By 1986 $70 billion was lost every year via increase of Federal debt, income of the top 1% increased by 77% from 1977 to 1989 while others had no gain.

66, Fearing Soviets, the U.S. spent over $1 trillion building up nuclear and non-nuclear forces. All this by creating a fear in the minds of the public. All this with the help of the words of the CIA saying that the Soviets were increasing spending 4-5 % each year when it was only 2%.

67. Under Pres. Reagan, Star Wars initiated for a shield over the U.S. After billions spent all failed. However, it was declared a success by Caspar Weinberger who lied and had results faked.

68. SA Sandinistas Marxist gave land to peasants, spread education, and health care to the poor. Reagan insisted a Communist threat and worked to overthrow the Sandinista Government.

69. Congress made it illegal to support directly or indirectly, military of paramilitary operation in Nicaragua. Reagan ignored the law and funded the contras secretly.

70. 1986 story that confirmed that weapons were sold to Iran. Reagan lied and said the shipment was a few token antitank missile (2,000). Reagan and Bush were involved in the Iran contra affair.

71, War Powers Act- "President shall consult with Congress before introducing military into conflicts.

72. U.S. invaded Panama in December 1989 with 26,000 troops.

73. Before the Gulf War the U.S. sold weapons to both Iran and Iraq.

74. Reagan gave military aid to the dictatorship of El Salvador.

75. 1990 -84% favored a surtax on the wealthy. This Provision was dropped in a budget compromise.

76. Pres. Eisenhower said "Every gun that is made, every warship launched, every rocket fired signifies a final sense of theft from those who are hungry and are not fed, those who are cold and not clothed.

77. Tax changes in 1995 gave the richest 1% over $1 trillion and now owned over 40% of the nation's wealth.

78 Under Pres. Reagan housing subsidies for the poor was reduced from 400,000 to 40,000.

79. Clinton raised the tax on the superrich from 31% to 37% and corporate taxes from 34% to 35%.

80. The Kurds were killed by the Iraq's with gas supplied by a firm in Rochester, New York. The CIA funded Iraq to fight Iran.

81. Pres. Bush policy- tax cuts for the rich, oppose all environmental regulations, and planned to Privatize Social Security.

2. A Splendid Exchange- by W. Bernstein

1. Octavian's forces defeated those of Anthony and Cleopatra at the battle of Actium in 30BC.

2. First rounding of the Cape of Good Hope by Diaz and Vasco de Gama.

3 .Stable countries are trading countries. After Actium, trading between Rome and Asia took off.

4. Camels, who originated in North America, were first prized for their milk in 6000BC. About 1500BC they were used for silk and incense trade in Asia. They store water throughout their body not in their hump and drink up to 50 gal of water in one setting.

5. Refrigerated ships started in the late 19th century.

6. Ricardo's Law of Comparative Advantage- better to do what you do best and import the other items rather than attempting to become independent.

7. Smelting started about 3500BC – process to make pure metal by removing other items by heating. About 2800 BC, bronze ratio was maximized of copper to tin about ten to one.

8. The Suez Canal completed under Darius the Great- 5th century BC and eventually silted up.

9. Athenian's ambitions triggered the Peloponnesian War and paved the way for Alexander the Great conquest of Greece, Egypt and west Asia.

10. The Red Sea was infested with pirates. All travel in the Indian Ocean was dictated by the Monsoon winds- south in the winter, north in the summer.

11. Roman Empire was drained of its gold and silver to pay for its luxuries leading to its decline. She consumed more than she produced.

12. Rule of law in the desert and on lands where tribes exist that an attack on one tribe is an attack on all.

13. Law of Islam- forbade stealing from fellow believers but not from infidels.

14. In 1095 Pope Urban II called forth the First Crusade to regain the Holy Land.

15. In the 13th century Genghis Khan conquered all of central Asia.

16. In 1500 the Chinese Emperor issued an edict that vessels with more than two masts were a capital offense and were destroyed. In 1595 any ocean going vessel was included.

17. Turks and Egyptians had been fighting over Jerusalem for decades before the arrival of the Christians.

18. Epidemics first stated in 2000BC in the Old Testament. The Athenian plague of 430BC killed ¼ of its army.

19. 205BC Eratosthenes deduced the earth was a sphere and calculated its size.

20. Treaty of Tordesillas about 1492 divided the world into two halves- Portuguese and the New World to Spain.

21. About 1602 Dutch East and West India Companies (VOC & WIC), were said to have conducted the First World War to control spices in Asia, sugar in Brazil, and slaves and gold in Africa. All transactions were financed by the Dutch. Success or failure depends not on size but advanced political, legal, and financial institutions.

22. The Strait of Hormuz entering the Persian Gulf was a key trading location off of the Agian Sea.

23. Before 1700 global commerce revolved around armed trading that sought to preserve monopolies in fabled commodities from exotic locations.

24. Coffee in about 1680 a Turk, Zkolschitzy, began selling the drink on the street, door to door, and later rented a house that became the first Viennese café.

25. Cotton was grown in India and converted to cloth by cheap labor. Manufacturing destroyed the Indian textile industry before cotton and spices were king. Remember Holland imported everything, they were the world's wealthiest nation on a per capita basis.

26. In 1790 about 1/6 of the total population in the new world, America, were slaves.

27. In 1650 the English cleared Barbados and planted sugar cane that supplied 2/3's of their consumption. Later, they converted to rum from the waste product molasses. Shortly falling sugar prices, tariffs and depleted soil ruined the plantations.

28. 80% of the slaves went to Brazil although most died from the trip or the hard work to make sugar.

29. War of 1812- Napoleon forbade his allies to trade with England. British then forced all traffic heading to Europe to stop first in Britain and that disrupted the flow of American cotton.

30. Dutch in Indonesia were the first to smoke opium in 1600's when they added a few grains to imported tobacco. China first outlawed opium imports in 1729. Opium made up over half of British trade and mostly to China.

31. Before the income tax in the twentieth century, import duty financed 90% of the American Government.

32. 1914 was the opening of the Panama Canal and the final curtain on the age of sail vessels.

33. Free trade and tariffs depend on the time of developments of products, travel, and negotiations. Between 1880 and 1914 when tariffs were erected, the steam engine made for a much cheaper shipping cost. This more than made up for the import tax and the total world GDP increased. Cheap labor, agricultural competition, and new products have an effect.

34. 1950 farmers made up 35% of population, in 1980 they make up about 1.5%.

35. Oil- world production of oil is about 80 million barrels and the US use about 20 million of which ¾ or 12million must be imported. The Strait of Hormuz and the area around Malacca are

key shipping routes for oil, the closure of either would cause chaos around the world. Pres. Carter stated that an attempt by an outside force to gain control of these areas would be regarded as an assault on the US. One could also include the Suez Canal.
36. Free trade in a developed country helps skilled workers and hurts low skilled labor.

3. A VOYAGE LONG and STRANGE
by Tony Horwitz

1. Columbus landing and the Pilgrims arrival occurred a thousand miles and 128 years apart.
2. Maine was once called "Land of Bad People" because there were Indians there.
3. First English colony in New England was Fort St. George in Pelham, Maine.
4. Greenland has no arable soil and three quarters of its surface is sheet ice. Norsemen settled and in about AD 1000 discovered America- Labrador, Newfoundland, Nova Scotia.
5. Columbus had a son, Ferdinand. Columbus was born about 1451 in Genoa, Italy.
6. Vikings refers to Norsemen who went on raids. Most stayed home in Scandinavia.
7. In 1492 Granada, Spain fell and was the last Muslim outpost in Europe. All Jews had to convert or leave Spain.
8. The trade winds in the Atlantic moved counter clockwise in a giant circle and helped explores return to Europe.
9. Columbus landed on an island and called it San Salvatore or Holy Savior. He never did set foot on what is now U.S..
10. Sand and coral islets are called cays.
11. Natives in San Salvatore rolled leaves called tobaccos. The Europeans got hooked on it and became the most profitable export.
12. Columbus landed on an island he called La Isla Espanola. Now named Hispaniola and divided between Haiti and the Dominican Republic.

13. Since the disease from the Spanish killed most of the African inhabitants they shipped large numbers of Africans to replace the workers on the island.

14. In 1795 Spain ceded the colony of Hispaniola to Napoleon.

15. America is named after Amerigo Vespucci and first appeared on a map in 1507 By Waldseemuller.

16. Ponce de Leon reached a wooded territory and called it La Florida after the "Feast of flowers" because it was Easter time in Europe. This marked the first recorded landing by a European on the now U.S. soil in 1513.

17. At one time about 30 million indigenous people roamed the Plains of America. By 1900 only about 1million still existed in North America.

18. In 1830 the Indian Removal Act forced the surviving tribes to move west of the Mississippi.

19. The Algonquian's Indian tribe called the Great Water – Misi Sipi we know as Mississippi.

20. The first Protestant refuge in North America was established by English Pilgrims at Plymouth in 1620.

21. The French shipped home sassafras and tobacco. The name nicotine comes from the then ambassador to Portugal, Jean Nicot.

21. In the late eighteenth century, the Spanish occupied and built what is now the French Quarters of New Orleans.

22. In 1763, British won control of Florida and most Spanish families fled to Cuba.

23. In 1565, 56 years before the Pilgrim feast at Plymouth, the Spanish performed a thanksgiving mass and celebration.

24. Walter Raleigh named his American domain Virginia in honor of Elizabeth the Virgin Queen. John White's daughter Eleanor Dare gave birth which was the first Christian born in Virginia and was named Virginia.

25. In 1602 Bartholomew Gosnold landed in an area where the sailor's caught so much fish that he called in Cape Cod. From there he landed in a vine draped island and named it after his daughter calling it Martha's Vineyard.

26. Sarah Josepha Hale of New Hampshire wrote "Mary Had a Little Lamb".

27. During the Civil War, Abraham Lincoln proclaimed the last Thursday of November 1863 as Thanksgiving.

28. The word succotash is derived from an Algonquian word meaning "mixed"- beans, corn, and meat.

29. California is believed to derive its name from Calafia, queen of the tall black, Amazons.

4. China Inc by Ted C. Fishman

1. By 2010 about ½ of all Chinese will live in urban areas.

2. In 2003 GDP of China was $1.4 trillion when the U.S. was at $10 trillion plus and the world GDP was about $36 trillion.

3. China economy must grow better than 7% to meet those entering the job market.

4. China is pulling in more investment dollars than the US and that was $53 to $40 billion in 2003.

5. They make about 40% of all furniture sold in the U.S. The U.S. lost about 30% of the furniture work force.

6. China's trade volume is number three behind the U.S. and Germany, and it is ahead of Japan.

7. Shanghai was the site in 1921 of the first meeting of the Chinese Communist party. In 1949 the Communists seized the country. At that time commercial life stopped.

5. Civilization- the Best and the Rest   by Niall Ferguson

This book reviews areas of civilization to study how they grew and collapsed- science, competition, property, medicine, consumption & work. Book's key point is to understand what made their civilization expand so spectacularly in its wealth, influence, and power.

1. Current population is about 7% of all human beings that ever existed.

2. Dark Ages- fall of Rome and the 12th century Renaissance did not qualify as civilizations.

3. Black Death- 1347-1351 reduced the population of world in half. Bubonic plague caused by the flea born bacterium. Poor sewage in Europe was a good cause of its continuation. In China the city

collected excrement to use as fertilizer to help disease from spreading.

4. Printing press and paper (money, toilet paper) invented in China about 11th century. Blast furnace was invented in 200 BC- in China.

5. Zheng He, China's Navy Commander in the 1400's, had the largest Navy until WWI. Eventually he was forced to destroy all of the ships with over 2 masts by the imperial leader for fear of losing his people to other worlds.

6. 1557 Portuguese were ceded Macau peninsula of the Pearl River delta.

7. First Emperor of China 221-210 BC was Qui Shihuan.

8. 1640 Japanese policy of strict seclusion from outside world. By 18 century 95% of diet was cereals. No meat was in diet. This accounted for the gap in height structure averaging 5'2" vs Europe 5' 7".

9. In 1842 China ceded Hong Kong to British and was forced to open ports for trade. This started the opium trade that was first rejected by China but forced upon them. British traded opium for silver.

10. Crusades to the Holy Land- 9 from 1095 to 1272.

11. Niccolo Machiavelli's book, "The Prince", stated and encouraged power at all cost.

12. Ottoman fall- rising cost, no tax source, high borrowing cost, high interest cost to European bondholders.

13. State of Israel- May 1948.

14. About 70% of Science and Engineering students are women.

15. Democracy - rule of law, individual freedom, private property, constitutional government.

16. In England 45% of the property is owned by nobles, 20 % by church, and 5% by the crown.

17. Why didn't South America establish like the U.S? .- Power was too concentrated in the hands of the Spanish, the people had no administrative responsibilities, Simon Bolivar was a dictator, no rule of law, and no property rights. In the U.S. at the same time 75 of property was individually owned.

18. In 1650 Indian population in both North and South America accounted for 80% of the population. By 1825 that population was down to 4%.
19. Between 1500 and 1760 2/3 of migrants to America were slaves.
20. On the eve of WWI British Empire covered about ¼ of land surface.
21. In 1850 the average life expectancy at birth was 28.5 years. By 2001 it was 66.6 years.
22. Napoleon Bonaparte died on the island of St. Helena in 1821. He tried to win with iron and steam, and was defeated by commerce and finance.
23. 1848 France abolished slavery, as did British in 1833.
24. World's first soccer match- 1872 between Scotland and England on St. Andrew's Day- result tie 0-0.
25. By 1913 the United States was the world's #1 industrial economy. If the entire rail were laid end to end it would circumvent the earth 13 times. In the U.S. the unemployment rate in 1938 was 12.5%.
26. WWII- Germany was defeated by British cracking the German codes, Russia's manpower slaughtered German soldiers and American capital flattened the German cities.
27. Dungarees were named after cloth from Dongri in India.
28. Nov. 9, 1989, East Berliners were able to leave for the West.
29. U. S. household savings in 2007 was below zero and also drawing down their equity in their home. Total private and public debt was more than 3 ½ time's GDP.
30. Final breakdown in the Roman Empire began in 406 when Germanic invaders crossed the Rhine into Gaul and then Italy.
31. In Paul Kennedy's 1987 book, "The Rise and Fall of the Great Powers", he states that when a state overextends itself it runs the risk that the potential benefits from external expansion may be outweighed by the great expense of it all.
32. All civilizations collapse are associated with fiscal crises as well as wars, sharp imbalances between revenues and expenditures as well as difficulties with financing public debt. The Ottoman Turks debt service rose from 17 to 50 % by 1877. In the US in the space of 10 years the federal debt doubled from 32 to 66% in 2011. Half

of the Federal debt is in foreign creditors with most in the hands of China.

33. Interest payment of U. S. debt is at 9% will increase to 20% by 2020 and 36% by 2030.

34. What could go wrong with China's expansion- real estate or stock market bubble, social unrest (0.4% of households own 70% of the country's wealth), and finally antagonizing its neighbors as they use their own people to work other countries mines and other buildings.

6. COLDER WAR by Marin Katusa

1. U.S. dominated due to its energy and currency issues.

2. Soviet Union collapsed in 1989.

3. 1996 Yeltsin joined by Putin who moved from St Petersburg. Yeltsin installed Putin as Federal Security Services successor to the KGB in 1998.

4. Russia's energy, as an exporter, is enhanced by any disruption of energy production outside of Russia especially in the Middle East.

5. Control of world's reserve currency now in U.S. and can dictate terms of trade, move price of commodities, and extract a fee when money passes. Britain once held that control but lost it after WWII.

6. British invaded Tibet and fought two wars in Afghanistan to create buffer zones against Russia.

7. Control oil and you control money.

8. In 400BC Chinese drilled for gas and oil, and used bamboo pipelines over short runs.

9. Today's petroleum era began in 1846 at Baku in Russia. 13 years later Titusville, Pa was the first successful oil well at 70 feet and produced 25 BPD. Internal combustion engine in 1876 enhanced oil production.

10. In 1949 U.S. went from net oil exporter to net importer.

11. Soviet's lost the Cold War due to failure of its energy infrastructure and the drop in world oil prices, and not Reagan's saber rattling in 1989.

12. Money invented at same time in China, India, and Mediterranean. Coins introduced about 700-500 BC.

13. Paper money originated in China about 6th century and on one of Marco Polo's travels he brought back some of that money.

14. Britton Woods conference in New Hampshire, where the U.S. became currency center away from Britain. Britain was in debt to the U.S. who exported food and military components to all Europe during the war.

15. Aug 15, 1971 Nixon closed the gold window ending convertibility of dollars into gold secure and protect our oil from Saudi Arabia. Nixon negotiated a deal where we would protect them against Israel and other Mid-Eastern states, and protect their oil fields. Saudis would then make oil sales in US dollars and invest surplus oil proceeds in U.S. Treasuries.

16. Putin resigned from the KGB in 1991 to finish his University PhD. His thesis was that Russian economic success depends on properly exploiting energy resources.

17, U.S. spent $5 billion in Ukraine to persuade and then destabilize them. They then supported a coup against the elected government. The Coup in Ukraine created a revolution to overthrow a democratically elected president.

18. 1954 Khrushchev handed the Crimean Peninsula to Ukraine. Putin thought Ukraine was a money pit and wouldn't mind leaving it for someone else.

19. Why confront another nation with soldiers when you can build cooperative relations that will serve your interests so much better in the long run.

20. Putin worked to corner the uranium market. Russia controls about 40% of the global enrichment capacity and their down blending facilities. They have deals to build 21 nuclear power plants around the world.

21. Russian produced 6 million bpd of oil in 1998 and increased that to 10 million bpd in 2009. By 2012 they produced 13 % of the world's oil when the world consumed 85 million bpd and 55 bpd were traded internationally.

22. In 2009, Rosneft, a Russian company, gained 30% stake in Exxon Mobil in the US, Gulf of Mexico and Canada. From 2002 and 2010 Russia's share of the European oil market grew from 29-34%.

23. U.S. in 2005-imported 60% oil consumption by 2013 it dropped to 32%.

24. Druzhba is the longest pipeline in the world carrying 1 million barrels of Russian oil per day across Belarus to refiners in Poland, Germany, Slovakia, and Hungary.

25. European Union relies on Russia for 1/3 of its natural gas. In Poland and Romania it is almost 100%.

26. U.S. has 65 nuclear plants – 100 reactors, for about 20% of the total energy. We mine about 4 million of our total needs of 9 million pounds.

27. U-235- 3-10% commercial nuclear plants, 20% research, 20-90% submarines, and 90% for weapons. Russia supplies over 40% of world's enriched uranium mostly to power plants.

28. Russia picked up mining operation in Australia, Canada, Kazakhstan, South Africa, and even the U.S. They will produce more uranium each year than all American mining companies combined. Putin's goal is to corner the conversion and enrichment markets. They would then control pricing and availability.

29. Sunnis- Mohammed's father in law, Shiites -Ali Mohammed's son in law. Mohammed died in 632 AD.

30. In 1935 Iran chose the U.S. for oil help. In 1941 Mohammad Reza Pahlavi appointed a government congenial to British and the Americans. An election removed the shah with the help of the CIA who organized and funded demonstrations against the democratically elected head- Mosaddegh to reinsert the shah. The U.S. then encouraged an invasion of Iran by Iraq. The U.S. supported with money and weapons.

31. In 1995, U.S. imposed sanctions on Iran as it suspected them of developing nuclear weapons. Harsher sanctions were imposed in 2006.

32. China is supplied with 15 % of its energy by Iran.

33. Iran was part of the Ottoman Empire from the 16th century until WWI.

34, Kurdistan of 25 million people is the largest ethnic group in the world without a sovereign homeland. British originally promised them a country.

35. In 2003, at the 2nd Gulf War, the Kurds joined Sunni's.

36. Aldous Huxley- "That men do not learn very much from the lessons of history is the most important of all the lessons that history has to teach".

37. U.S. mistake in supporting the Mujahideen. Which gave way to an armed Osama Bin Laden's rebel group of al-Qaida.

38. Afghanistan- landlocked country ruled by medieval warlords with no oil or natural gas but does have substantial minerals. The area has been known for years as "the graveyard of empires.

39. Afghanistan lies in the path of the Silk Road and is the path of a Russian proposed pipeline to carry oil and gas from the Caspian Sea and Central Asia to the Arabian Sea without passing through Russian territory.

40. The U.S. supported the Taliban who were Sunnis and a counter balance to the Iran Shite neighbors. They also supported the Trans-Afghanistan pipeline in our effort to get oil. So with Pakistan we funneled weapons and money to the Taliban to help defeat the Northern Alliance. The Taliban were known to have close ties to Al-Queda.

41. Pakistan told BBC the U.S. was preparing military action against Afghanistan in October.

42. Assad and Syria- the US funded selected anti-Assad insurgents. Assad is close to Iran and Russia.

43. Syria is involved directly or indirectly in nearly every conflict in the Middle East. The Russians do not want to lose control of the area as it would undermine Gazprom's dominance of the European gas market but would allow cheap Qatari gas to flow via Syria to the Mediterranean.

44. CIA is operating in Turkey to help allies, chiefly Saudi Arabia determine which anti-Assad forces are the good guys to receive arms and material.

45. About 50% of Israelis are descended from Jewish immigrants from Russia and Eastern Europe. Israel uses natural gas to produce 20% of its electricity.

46. U.S. oil imports- 22% in 1970 and 36% in 1973.

47. Saudi citizens- 60% are under the age of 20 and 40% are unemployed. They are unhappy that U.S. is cutting back on their oil. Could be problem in the future as they currently park their oil money in US treasuries.

48. After WWII Britain mired in debt. The U.S. had huge holdings of gold from exporting food and other goods to the countries at war.

49. In 1970 the US manufacturing capacity was at 23%. Today it is at about 12 %. Investment markets are creating bubbles as in the dot-com stocks and real estate.

50. When Qaddafi began encouraging Arab and African nations to abandon the dollar and instead use a new currency the gold dinar he was pushed out of office with the assistance of the U.S. and NATO.

51. Iran has 39 oil tankers sailing off radar or turned off their onboard transponders.

52. 2009 China passed the U.S. to become Africa's biggest trading partner at about $200 billion. China gets 1/3 of its oil from Africa. In 2010 China agreed to build three oil refineries in Nigeria at a cost of $23 billion.

53. Russia and India are close to a major energy alliance.

54. China oil imports- Iran 9%, Saudis 19%

55. Russia wants to replace the petrodollar and it will happen but when?

56. In 1946 most autos were from the U.S. now only 12 are.

56. 2013 the US spent $643 billion on military over 1/3 of the world's total, and 20% for the U.S. federal spending.

57. Foreigners hold over $5 trillion in U.S. Treasury securities and CD's, which is about 47% of the total.

7. Collapse   by Jared Diamond

1. Factors for environmental collapse: Environmental damage, climate change, hostile neighbors, and society's responses to environmental problems.

2. Western Roman Empire was beset by barbarian invasion and fell about 476 AD.

3. Glacier National Park in Montana had 150 glaciers in the late 1800's and now has about 35. Present rate of melting they will be non-existent in about 2030.

4. Water quality impaired due to erosion, road construction, forest fires, logging, and fertilizer runoff. Montana was in the top 10 in

U.S. state per capita income now it is 49th due to the decline in extraction industries as logging mining, oil, and gas.

5. Easter Island with its 20 to 70 feet tall statues weighing about 10 to 270 tons was discovered in April 5, 1722 by a Dutch explorer. Settlement of the island was in about 900 AD. The Island was completely deforested.

6. Tree ring dating is called dendrochronology.

7. The first humans to reach the Americas living as hunter-gatherers arrived in the U.S. southwest by 11,000 BC.

8. Mayan cities were rediscovered in 1839 by John Stephens. In 1527 the Spanish started to conquer the Mayan's. Bishop Diego de Landa destroyed all the Mayan writings in an effort to eliminate paganism. Corn constituted about 70% of the Mayan diet. Its population peeked in about 900AD. Deforestation and hillside erosion was one of the main reasons for their moving when the population growth outstripped its resources.

9. Viking means "raiders". They grew out of trading and open sea routes to rich peoples need as fur, silver, and gold. The raids began on June 8, 793 AD with the attack on a monastery in northeast England.

10. Iceland was heavily damaged by the heavy destruction of trees and vegetation.

11. Greenland Norse diet was wild animals as caribou and seals. They ate very little fish. Heavy deforestation soil erosion affected their demise along with hostile Inuit's.

12. Australia and New Guinea were first settled around 46,000 BC. Both lands were joined back then.

13. Japan population lives on about 20% of the land. Their forests are protected and growing. In 1635, Japanese were forbidden to travel overseas and also forbidden from leaving coastal waters. All Portuguese were expelled from Japan. Coal was used in place of wood and everything efficient is being used.

14. Countries like Germany, Denmark, Switzerland, France, and other western European countries have expanded their forested areas as did Japan.

15. Rwanda and Gurundi are the two most densely populated countries in Africa. The Hutu's militias imported weapons and prepared to exterminate the Tutsi's of Rwanda. High population

densities and worse starvation were associated with more crime. This is one pressure form of genocide.

16. Hispaniola, a Caribbean Island, is divided into two countries with a 120-mile border, Haiti and the Dominican Republic. Originally both parts of the island were heavily forested. Today only 1% of Haiti and 28% of the Dominican Republic is still forested. Christopher Columbus arrived in Hispaniola in 1492 but Native Americans previously settled the island about 5,000 years before. Haiti achieved independence in 1804.

17. China has about 1/5th of the world's population. It is the largest producer of sulfur oxides ozone- depleting substance into the atmosphere. With fertility control their population growth will be 1.3% in 2001. They consume 1/4th of the world's coal (¾ of their energy comes from coal), and are the second largest producer and consumer of pesticides. China's forest only covers 16% of their land area as compared to Japan at 74%. Factories have closed due to water shortage. They are the largest producer of tobacco and there are about 350 million smokers. Logging was banned in 1998. At one time they had the largest shipping fleets but most were dismantled.

18. Australia exports mining goods but they are using up their forests and fisheries faster. Sheep farming ruined the land. Rabbits and fox were introduced from Europe. Rabbits plague the land and consume about half the pasture vegetation. They are the largest producer of wool and the largest exporter of Coal. Only 20% of the land is forest. They once had the tallest trees now most have been cleared. It has been over fished almost to extinction. The future is bleak and will lead to a declining standard of living with the deterioration environment.

19. Mining is a major problem of water pollution. This includes digging up land for minerals where chemicals are used and either left or moved out of the way. These chemicals include cyanide, mercury, and sulfuric acid that all are toxic. The government is not requiring insurance bonds for these projects for environmental damage. Lobbyists are paid to get the laws relaxed.

20. President Bush does not believe the scientists on global warming. Companies have little interest in the environment unless required by the government.

21. Seafood consumption in China has doubled in the last decade. ¾ of the world population will be living within 50 miles of the seacoast by 2010. Failure to regulate the fishing industry is leading to some fish becoming extinct.
22. Collapse of societies evolves swiftly from its peak population numbers, wealth, and power. Reason: overuse of resources and consumption, waste production with environmental problems, all approaching the limits of resources.

8. Founding Brothers   by Joseph Ellis

1. July 1804 Burr and Hamilton dueled. Burr shot and mortally wounded Hamilton. At that time Burr was the second ranking official in the federal government and Hamilton was treasury secretary.
2. In the 1800 election after a tie Burr and Jefferson went to 36 ballots in the House of Representatives before the voting went to Jefferson.
3. 1790 financial plan for recovery of public credit. Problem of passing this plan was a provision of the assumption of state debts by the federal government led by John Madison. In negotiations, it was agreed that the capitol would be on the Potomac River now Washington DC. A ten-year residency preceded this in Philadelphia. This was the Assumption Bill.
4. Late 1700's the U.S. was a tangled mess of foreign and domestic debt and in a needed to restore public credit. As an example, Virginia's land class was in heavy debt to British and Scottish creditors who were compounding interest on loans faster that the profits on tobacco and wheat.
5. Madison was the first secretary of state.
6. In 1608 John Smith first discovered the Potomac water's, which was named by the Algonquin Indians "Petomeck" meaning "trading place".
7. The Civil War began in 1861. Virginia at that time contained about 1/5 of the nation's population and 1/3 of its commerce.
8. The Constitution imposed restrictions on the Congress's power to end the slave trade but said nothing about abolishing slavery itself. Slavery was an economic precondition of prosperity and no

white man would perform the tasks required to drain the swamps and clear the land.

9. Northwest Ordinance, July 1787, forbade slavery in the territory north of the Ohio River.

10. Washington assumed the presidency in 1789. Prior to that and the Constitution of 1776, Washington's image was everywhere- officer in the Continental Army and Constitutional Convention. He voluntarily surrendered the presidency after two terms thus setting the precedent that held firm until 1940 and later reaffirmed in 1951 with the passage of the Twenty-second amendment. John Adams was his VP.

11. Of the first six presidents only Adams had a male heir.

12. Jefferson would not let himself get involved in policy making decision of the Adams administration lest it compromise his role as leader of the Republican opposition.

13. It is said that history shapes presidents and not the other way around.

14. Washington and Adams were committed to neutrality at all cost. They negotiated with France when there were French Privateers in the Atlantic and Caribbean.

15. Jefferson wrote Madison when Adams was president- "As to do nothing, and to gain time, is everything with us. In order for the Republican's agenda to win, the Federalist agenda needed to fail, also- never interferes when your enemies are busily engaged in flagrant acts of self-destruction".

16. In 1800 Adams signed the Treaty of Mortefontaine officially ending hostilities with France. In 1803 under Jefferson, the U.S. purchased the Louisiana Territory and doubled the size of the national domain.

17. Adams- the five Pillars of Aristocracy are beauty, wealth, birth, genius and virtues. Any of the first three could overtake any one of the last two.

18. Adam- Britain will never be our friend till we are her master.

19. Both Adams and Jefferson died on the same day July 4, 1826.

20. American Revolution ended with Napoleon's defeat at Waterloo in 1815.

9. Ghost Wars: CIA, Afghanistan & bin Laden
by Steve Coll

1. On July 12, 1941Pres. FDR created CIA- Coordinator of Information
2. There is only one route between USSR and Kabul, the Salang Highway, and Russia must control to keep a grip on Afghanistan.
3. Mujahedin best fighters and fundamentalists.
4. Pres. Reagan expanded US aid to Afghan Guerrillas in March 1985.
5. During 1985, 5 million Americans traveled overseas and 6,000 died, 17 from terrorists.
6. Congress allocated about $500,000 for Afghan covert operations in fiscal 1986.
7. A. Azzam preached against the US and would start the Hamas group in 1986. Importantly, Prince al-Faisal and Saudi intelligence became important supporters.
8. Gates of the CIA said the Soviets would not withdraw from Afghanistan.
9. Afghan task force director Frank Anderson suggested that the CIA should get out of the country when the Soviets did.
10. CIA unveiled a covert plan to cut off the main supply line between
Kabul and Jalalabad was the only route between the two cities.
11. The US became involved in Afghan politics and had betrayed American principles McWilliams argued.
12. Policy sought Nejibullah ouster to promote moderate government.
13. The CIA collaborated with Pakistani intelligence.
14. Under American law, Pressler Amendment, the CIA's conclusion automatically ended American military and economic assistance to Pakistan.
15. By early 1991, the Afghan policies pursued by the State Department and the CIA was in open competition with one another. But they had different clients.
16. Saudi officers were assigned to expelled bin Laden from the Saudi territory mainly do the fact that the U. S. was out to kill him.

17. On Jan 1, 1992, the CIA's legal authority to conduct covert action in Afghanistan ended. The Soviet Union had formally dissolved.

18. CIA did hot work inside the American legal system and were under the National Security Act of 1947. They were prohibited from spying on American's or using intelligence it collected abroad for criminal prosecutions in American courts.

19. The new Islamists found money and guns not in Tehran but in Saudi Arabia. The White House and the CIA were reluctant to confront the Saudi's.

20. The Saudi charities and religious ministries aided the Taliban's rise during 1995-6.

21. Unocal offered a new pipeline in Afghanistan.

22. In Jan. 1996, the CIA opened a new office to track Osama bin Laden, first of its kind to track a single terrorist.

23. NSA tapped into bin Laden's telephones and he eventually eliminated all phones. He granted an interview in Khartoum and stated, "I thought people were supposed to be innocent until proved guilty". At that time, Security Advisor Berger knew of no intelligence showing that bin Laden had committed any crime against Americans.

24. Bin Laden was expelled from Saudi Arabia for antigovernment agitation.

25. American's were the main enemy of Muslims worldwide bin Laden told British journalist. This was the beginning of war between Muslims and the U.S.

26. The CIA worked with Massoud against the Taliban. CIA would supply money and arms to assist. Massoud was also afraid that the CIA was working with the Taliban to get the Unocal pipeline underway.

27. The CIA supplied about 2600 stinger missiles to the Taliban. Once the Soviets left, the CIA wanted them back.

28. The Taliban opposed Iran and its Shiite creed and in a sense allied with American interests.

29. Pakistan, Saudi Arabia, and U.A.E. anointed the Taliban as Afghanistan's legitimate government.

30. The CIA was founded by President Truman to prevent another Pearl Harbor.

31. In 1990 bin Laden sought to persuade the Saudi royal family to lead a jihad against Saddam Hussein's Iraq. It was denied and invited the American military to wage the war.
32. A classified doc in Sept. 1998 warned of a strike on an American airport.
33. History showed that Afghanistan could never be ruled by one faction and should be a coalition.
34. Much support to bin Laden came from Saudi sources even in 2000.

10. INDELIBLE INK: Birth of America's Free Press
by Richard Kluger

1. Pres. Roosevelt said "Essential human freedoms- speech, expression, worship, want and fear.
2. U.S. was the first nation to monumentalize liberty of speech and the press as a fundamental right of its people.
3. The first slander laws took effect in 1275 under the reign of Edward I.
4. Under James I to defame another's reputation would be punishable by fine, imprisonment or the amputation of the ears. Libeling robs a man of his good name.
5 Reporters Without Borders rated U.S. 46th out of 180 nations for the erosion of press freedom. This was due to the aggressive prosecution of whistleblowers with pressure on reporters to disclose courses of information in the public interest but embarrassing to government officials.
6. In the 16th century England secular and religious officials were fearful of the printed material as a goad to social unrest. Press control began in 1529 with Henry VIII's issuing a list of 100 banned books.
7. In 1610 Henry Hudson sailing under the Dutch flag named the new land New Netherlands (now New York). He traveled 150 miles north up this river (now the Hudson River) to a tributary now the Mohawk River.
8. After the English Civil War of 1650 with the military dictatorship under the Stuart dynasty speech and writing was curbed.

9. The new Stuart dynasty in British moved in 1664 to displace the Dutch presence through a bloodless conquest. It was not a crown colony but a proprietorship and named after the Charles II brother James the Duke of York now New York. Reverted to a royal holding in 1685.

10. The Dutch recaptured New York but in 1664 the British naval forces recaptured the area and King Charles presented the territory to his brother James the duke of York.

11. Martin Luther's iconoclastic postings in 1517 lead to the Protestant Reformation.

12. In 1719 every governor was told that a license was needed to print matter as books, pamphlets, etc.

13. A local law imposed a 6% ceiling on loans to stamp out usury and doing business became easier in New York.

14. Progress was made via trade-based revenues and not from higher taxes on big landowners.

15. Smuggles easily circumvented the Indian Trade Act of 1720 law. This law set who could sell to the Indians and what they could sell to them.

16. Molasses Act- impose a duty on colonists for buying molasses and sugar imported from non- British territories as the French West Indies. Thus giving the British colonial planters a pricing advantage.

17. In 1722 Albany was the second largest settlement in the New York colony.

18. A commission in1725 was formed to relocate the boundary of New York and Connecticut agreeable to the then Governor Burnet.

19. Ever since Britain had established a colonial presence in America, the crown had assigned the power to grant land titles to either royal governor it appointed or to proprietors it gifted outright like William Penn.

20. Under question was "could a citizen be convicted to question or criticize in any way truthfully or falsely or by distortion of the government's conduct".

21. The British Stamp Act in 1765 a revenue measure had a serious impact on colonial America and a threat to printers' livelihoods.

22. In September 1776 the British troops seized New York City from George Washington who hastily retreated his little army.

22. From the court cases against Zenger and his Journal helped to implant in the Public mind that open protest against an imposed and arguable unjust government was both a social necessity and a civil right.

24. The first amendment to the Bill of Rights stated "Congress shall make no laws abridging the freedom of speech or of the press or the right to peaceably assemble".

25. Pres. John Adams tried to pass the Alien and Sedition Act of 1798 which held it a crime to publish "false, scandalous, and malicious writing" against the government and its chief.

26. The Branzburg v. Hayes the Supreme Court decision in 1972 decision to deny reporters no more right than any other citizen to withhold information sought by prosecutors. But it allowed the states and Congress to pass "shield" laws granting reporters the privilege of not having to disclose confidential sources. Only Wyoming did not pass the shield law.

11. Iron Curtain: The Crushing of Eastern Communist by Anne Appelebaum

1. The Berlin Wall was built in 1961.

2. Gulag refers to the system of mass forced labor camps. Stalinism and Totalitarianism are used interchangeable.

3. In 1939 the Soviet Union and Nazi Germany signed the Molorov-Ribbentrov Pact dividing up countries as Poland before World War II.

5. The Polish state existence was in 1918. The river Vistula runs through Poland.

6. After the war, ¾ of Germany's industrial complex was dismantled and 80% went to Russia.

7. Hitler's invasion of the Soviet Union began in June of 1941.

8. Pre WWII, USSR sold oil and grain to Germany, and Germany sold weapons to USSR.

9. The first Soviet invasion of Poland was in 1939 and the second was in 1944. 20% of the Polish people did not survive WWII.

10. The German occupation of Poland was to destroy Polish civilization.

11. W. Churchill first used the term "Iron Curtain" in a speech at the end of the war in May 1945.

12. The Truman Doctrine- "support free people who are resisting attempted subjugation by armed minorities or by outside pressure".

13. Berlin Blockade- in June 1948 Soviet Union cutoff electricity as well as road, rail, and barge access to West Berlin.

14, The Black Madonna of Czestochowa and the Blessed Virgin of Ostra Brams are icons in Poland.

15. The beginning of the strongest sensitivity and memory of children lies between the 5th and 7th year.

16. In the 1980's East Germany had the largest police state, Poland the highest church attendance, Romania the most drastic food shortage, and Hungary the highest living standard.

17. Mussolini's words "You cannot make an omelet without breaking the eggs".

18. In August 1920 "The miracle on the Vistula", the Pole's defeated the Red Army.

12. Lost and Found in Russia   by Susan Richards

1. By 1993 40% of Russians were living in poverty opposed to 1.5% in the late Soviet period.

2. When the system changed 60-70% of the state enterprises were privatized and corruption grew with money moving out of the country.

3. Guaranteed jobs caused people not to think.

4. In the last year of Communism life expectancy was 68 years. By 1995 that figured dropped to 58.

5. Cyanide used to separate ore from rock-poisoned desert and water where mining was in use.

6. In 1581 the Cossacks subdued the Mongols and conquered Siberia.

7. Tunguska explosion of 1908 flattened 800 square miles of forest.

8. Seven tycoons controlled 50% of the Russian economy.

9. Three quarters of Russian business is conducted by barter.
10. Russia's financial crash of 1998 was caused by lack of taxes being collected.
11. Pythagoras is credited with being the first to start exploring natural harmonics in a systematic way.
12. Russian fairy tale of Baba Yaga is the witch who kidnaps children and cooks them for her supper.
13. Putin introduced a flat rate income tax,
14. Crimean War of 1854-55 involved Russia, France, Britain and Turkey. The greatest of the caravan routes from China ended in Crimea Russia.
15. Catherine the Great wrested Crimea away from the Turks in 1789. She dreamt of reviving the Byzantine Empire with Constantine as the emperor.
16. Gazprom supplies Europe with 2/3 of its gas imports through Ukraine.

13. Moyers on Democracy   by Bill Moyers

1. Abraham Lincoln government expenditures were mostly for roads, bridges and railroads. Created land grant colleges.
2. Plutarch's warning that an imbalance between rich and poor is the oldest and most fatal ailment of all republics.
3. The top one percent of households have more wealth that the bottom 90%.
4. Peace Corp started in about 1960-61 in the Kennedy /Johnson era.
5. Military power serves empire rather than freedom.
6. Under Johnson the Joint Chiefs of Staff said it would take 1 million fighting men and ten years to win in Vietnam.
7. Grant and Eisenhower graduated from West Point. George Washington commissioned Thaddeus Kosciuszko to build the original West Point fortification.
8. Woodrow Wilson was the only president to earn a PhD.
9. In 1993 1/3 students graduate in debt today about 2/3 do. Interest on loans pre 2001 was 27% for private loans and about 7% of Government loans.

10. In the 1900 century the most profitable export to China was opium shipped by the British in India. America needed money but had no opium to sell and encouraged Turkey and Persia to grow opium. Now we pay Turkish peasants not to grow opium.

11. U.S. homicide rate is ten times as Europe or Japan.

12. Income gap between rich and the poor is the widest since records started over 40 years ago. Extreme variance undermines democracy.

13. Mark Hanna was the first political fund-raiser and was on behalf of William McKinley who raised 10 times the money that Jennings Bryan did. The money was raised from banks, insurance companies, railroads and industry trusts.

14. A bribe? Gingrich and Lott got $13 million in soft money from the tobacco industry and they got a $50 billion tax credit.

15. In 1940 the average male teacher earned 3.6% more than other college educated individuals. Now they earn 60% less. In 2003 U.S. ranked 24 out of 29 in advanced countries in math and 15 of 27 in reading.

16. In 2005 CEO's get about 262 times the wage of average workers. Wealthy individuals are the least tax audited and about 8 times lower.

17. In 1966 Fred Friendly resigned from CBS because they would not show the Senate Hearing on the Vietnam War. In 1967 he helped start PBS with no commercials.

18. Theodore Roosevelt warned a century ago of the subversive influence of money over public policy.

19. 1966 Congress passed the Freedom of Information Act.

20. 2/3 of media are monopolies.

21. The infamous Sedition Act of 1798 sought to quell and make it a crime to publish false, scandalous and malicious writings about the government or its officials.

22. US monies to public broadcasting is about $1.50 per person compared to about $50 in other countries.

23. Adam and Eve had two sons Cain and Abel. Cain a farmer and Abel a shepherd. Both vied for God's favor. Cain was jealous as God selected the lamb instead of Cain's farms fruit. He kills his brother for this. All conflicts today are and were driven by religious motives or memory of same.

24. The Tarzan's yell by Johnny Weissmuller was made by three men including a hog caller.

14. On China by Henry Kissinger

1. Territorial claims of the Chinese Empire stopped at the water's edge; Song Dynasty (960-1279) let the world in nautical technology.
2. Ming dynasty, 1405-1433, Admiral Zheng He set out in fleets to India and even reached the west coast of the now America's.
3. In the 1820's China produced 30% of the worlds GDP exceeding Europe, and the United States combined.
4. Confucius name was actually Knog Fu-zi (551-479). He believed in harmony not power.
5. Chinese protocol for overloaded ships was kowtow or complete prostration with forehead touching the ground three times.
6. China did not export its ideas but let others come to seek them.
7. Western test maxims by victories in battle where Sun Tzu of China test victories where battle have become unnecessary- defeat without fighting.
8. Opium was contraband under Chinese law. British fleets blockade to force import of opium into China. This was the Opium War.
9. The Treaty of Tianjin of 1858 for the right to a permanent embassy in Beijing.
10. The Boxer uprising in 1898 was a campaign of violent agitation against foreigners.
11. Nationalist troops retreated to Taiwan (Formosa) in 1949 after being defeated by the Communists.
12. Inventions by China- compass, paper making, block printing and movable type.
13. Mao to the Soviet request to set a base on China's Pacific ports: "Every country should keep its armed forces on its own territory and on no one else's. "
14. The end of the Vietnam War was signed in Paris in 1973.
15. China has always been worried by encirclement. Consider what has happened in the past with Russia, Korea, Vietnam and now the United States.

16. Vietnamese troops invaded Cambodia overthrowing the Khmer Rouge and installing a pro-Vietnamese government.
17. Tiananmen 1989 leading to the fall of the Berlin Wall and dissolution of the Soviet Union itself.
18. Chinese leaders see American policy as a design to keep China from reaching great power status.
19. Taiwan Strait Crises of the 1950's was the China's military exercises and missile tests of the Southeast China.
20. In 2008 China became the largest foreign holder of American debt.
21. U.S. did not support independence for Taiwan nor did it promote reunification.
22. China's problem with reduced exports if they were to raise the yuan's value- the big potential for Chinese companies going bankrupt with the major countries problems.
23. The United States is focused on overwhelming military power and that has a decisive psychological impact on China.

15. One Palestine, Complete   by Tom Segev

1. Britain ruled Palestine by virtue of a League of Nations Mandate and ruled the territory for about 30 years.
2. The first Balfour Declaration in 1903 was rejected by the Zionist Congress.
3. Hadassah was the women's Zionist organization that opened soup kitchens, aided orphanages and old age homes.
4. Most Jews in Jerusalem had always lived off the donations received from Jewish communities in Europe.
5. The Western Wall was in a Muslim religious trust that Weizmann was determined to purchase. He also stated that the minarets, bell towers, and domes were saying that Jerusalem is not a Jewish city.
6. Megiddo was the last cavalry victory in history in a campaign between the Jews and the Arabs.
7. Arabs believed that the Jews wished to expel them for the country.
8. The Zionist wanted land that included southern Lebanon, the Golan Heights, and a large area east of the Jordan River.

9. The British initially neglected Arab education because they did not want to finance it and feared its political effect.

10. During the war in 1940 the British army had a huge supply depot in Palestine that give support to the area with manufacturing plants and employment. The Italians bombed Tel Aviv in September of 1940.

11. The British proposed dividing the country but both the Zionist and the Arabs rejected it. At this time, the balance of power shifted from London to Washington.

12. On August 15, 1947 India declared its independence.

13. On November 29 1947, the United Nations voted to divide Palestine into two states, one for the Jews and one for the Arabs. Jerusalem was to remain under international control. The UN assigned almost twice as much territory for the Jewish state as in the original British partition plan ten years earlier. The Zionist had a strong and effective lobby to get what they wanted.

16. Sapiens by Yural Hrari

1. Three revolutions that shaped the course of history- Cognitive about 70,000 years ago, Agricultural Revolution about 12,000 years ago, and the Scientific Revolution about 500 years ago.

2. Organisms are labeled in Latin names with genes followed by species. As species sapiens are of the genus Homo, man.

3. Between 70,000 and 30,000 years ago- invention of boats, oil lamps, bows and arrows, and needles for sewing. This was the Cognitive Revolution.

4. Large number of people can cooperate together if they believe in a common myth.

5. Difference between humans and chimps is the glue that binds together large numbers of individuals, families and groups.

6. Agricultural Revolution-an iron law of history is that luxuries tend to become necessities and to spawn new obligations.

7. The life span of a chicken is 7-12 years and of cattle 20-25 years, Majority of domesticated chickens and cattle are slaughtered between the age of a few weeks and a few months- it cost more to feed them to maturity. However, if for eggs or milk they are allowed to live longer.

8. Earth surface is about 200 million sq. miles of which 60 million is land.

9. Affluent lawyers that bought famished peasants land spearheaded the French Revolution. The Roman Republic reached height of power in first century BC when its treasure fleets in the Mediterranean were at their peak. At that point, the Roman political order was collapsing into a series of civil wars.

10. Code of Hammurabi in 1776BC was a cooperation manual of ancient Babylonians. American Declaration of Independence of 1776 AD was a cooperation manual of America.

11. Africans over the years developed partial genetic immunity to local malaria and yellow fever. Not so as Africans were transported to other parts of the world and people died in droves of these disease as in early Virginia, Haiti, and Brazil.

12. In 1865 the US Constitution's 13th amendment outlawed slavery and the 14th amendment gave equal protection of races.

13. Unjust discrimination got worse- money comes to more money, poverty goes to more poverty, education goes to the educated, and ignorance-to-ignorance.

14. Alpha woman- Cleopatra of Egypt, Empress Wu Zetian of China in 700AD, and Elizabeth I of England. These are exceptions. Under Elizabeth's 45 year reign all government individuals were men- parliament, military, judges, and lawyers.

15. Large cultures normally break up into smaller groups, as did the Mongol Empire that expanded to dominate Asia and parts of Europe only to shatter into fragments.

16. Tomatoes, chili peppers, and cocoa are all Mexican in origin.

17. Cotes and his Spanish Conquistadors invaded Mexico in 1519. The Aztecs noticed the alien's interest in the yellow metal. The metal was then mined and returned to Spain for its growing wealth.

18. Total of money in the World is about $60 trillion yet the sum of currency is less than $6 trillion. $50 trillion appears in accounts on only computer servers.

19. Silver shekel appeared in about 3000 BC in Mesopotamia where the silver shekel was 0.3 ounces of silver. However, the first coin was struck about 640 BC by King Alyattes of Lydia in Anatolia.

20. Roman empire fell to invading Germanic tribes in 476 AD.

21. Kublai Khan's army invaded Japan in 1281.

22. Central figure of Buddhism is not a god but a human being- Siddhartha Gautama, an heir to a small Himalayan kingdom about 500 BC.

23. Arms races bankrupt all those who take part in them without really changing the military balance of power.

24. Microorganism first seen by Anton van Leeuwenhoek with a home-made microscope when he saw creatures in a drop of water.

25. Pres. D. Eisenhower in 1961 warned of the growing power of the military industrial complex.

26. Early Modern era was the golden age for the Ottoman Empire in the Mediterranean, the Safavid Empire in Persia, the Mughal Empire in India, and the Chinese Ming and Qing dynasties in China.

27. First Railroad in China was in 1876 and destroyed in 1877.

28. Prince Henry the Navigator and Vasco da Gama explored the coasts of Africa and seized control of islands and harbors. Christopher Columbus discovered America and claimed the land for Spain.

29. In 1831 the Royal Navy sent the Ship HMS Beagle to map the coasts of South America, Falklands, and Galapagos Islands. They needed a geologist and no one wanted the job but a 22 year old, Charles Darwin a Cambridge graduate.

30. On 20 July 1969 Neil Armstrong and Buzz Aldrin landed on the moon.

31. Juan Bermejo from the mast of the ship Pinta spotted land- now the Bahamas. Amerigo Vespucci, an Italian sailor, took expeditions to America in 1499-1504.

33. China's Admiral Zheng He of the Ming dynasty traveled the oceans from 1405 and 1433, and said to have landed on one trip on the now California coast.

34. As in the Vietnam conflict, guerrilla forces showed that even superpowers could be defeated if a local struggle became a global cause.

35. In 1776 Adam Smith published "the Wealth of Nations" an important manifesto.

36. Capitalism is when profits of production are reinvested in increasing production.

37. In 1717 the Mississippi Company from France colonized the lower Mississippi now the city of New Orleans.
38. The First Opium War between Britain and China in 1840-1842 was due to the British East India Company who made fortunes exporting drugs through Hong Kong. About 10% of the China population became addicted.
39. From the 16 to the 19 centuries about 10 million African slaves imported to America. Most worked on sugar plantations.
40. In 1825 British engineer connected a steam engine to a coal train.
41. Commandment of the rich is to invest for of the rest of us to buy.
42. In 1880 British time was determined from Greenwich.
43. Early revolutions- 1789 France, 1848 Libya, and 1917 Russian.
44. In 2000, wars and violent crimes killed 820,000 (1.5% of all those who died). At the same time 1.26 million killed in auto accidents, and 810,000 committed suicide.
45. In 1945 Britain ruled 25% of the globe now they only rule just a few small islands.
46. A new gene in pigs converts bad omega 6 to good omega 3.

17. Sea of Glory   by Nathaniel Philbrick

1. In late 1400's Chinese emperor Yung-lo sent a large flotilla that ventured to the east coast of Africa and the western seaboard of the America's.
2. Hudson's Bay Company dominated the Oregon territory. They surveyed the west coast of the Americas down to Mexico.
3. About 1838, Charles Wilkes undertook the expedition to discover the west coast and discovered Antarctica.
4. Ferdinand Magellan first to circumnavigate the world. He called and gave the name to the Pacific Ocean that was, however, earlier founded by Balboa. In 1830 the Vincennes became the first U.S. naval vessel to circumnavigate the world.
5. On Wilkes voyage all officers were instructed to keep a daily journal. At the journeys end they would become the property of the U.S. Government.

6. Cape Horn in South America was named after the town of Hoorn in the Netherlands.

7. Hawaii, the youngest of the islands about 1 billion years old, is made up of five distinct volcanoes. Mauna Loa is the largest.

8. Hawaiian Islands were settled between 300-800 AD. New Zealand was discovered around 1000-1200AD.

9. An Englishman James Smithson left ½ million dollars in gold coins for the establishment for the increase and diffusion of knowledge, which is now the Smithsonian in Washington, D. C.

10. Herman Melville uses data from the US. Exploring Expedition in his masterpiece Moby Dick.

11. In June 1846, the boundary between the U.S. and British Canada were established at the forty-ninth parallel with the signing of the Buchanan-Pakenham treaty.

12. Gold was discovered in California in 1848.

13. Mexican War started in 1846.

18. The American Revolution of 1800   by Dan Sisson

1.In 1913 due to the buying of Senators the 17th Amendment was made law.

2. Written in 1795, "For it is the nature and intention of a constitution to prevent governing by party".

3. Jefferson argued that we ought to have a revolution every century and a half to keep the Constitution intact.

4. Hamilton was for a hereditary King with a House of Lords and Commons corrupted to his will standing between him and the people. All as in Great Briton.

5. Per T. Paine "The fall of the Bastille included the idea of the downfall of despotism".

6. Fall of Athens- spirit of discord prevailed and liberty was destroyed. As the republic of Rome through ambitious Caesar blinded the vigilance of his country's friends seized it and triumphed. Party is a monster who devours the common good.

7. By 1798 factions blurred the separation of powers.

8. Adams expressed his contempt for those who would corrupt the election process in the pursuit of power. Political factions are the

key to the next stage of America's development- the politics of revolution.

8. The Virginia Resolutions of 1799-1800 were an attempt to expose the Federalists and their efforts to corrupt both elections and their values.

9. Hamilton's interest- industrial mercantile based on power influence and empire. Jefferson's interest more on the people- agricultural interest and the Constitution of separate branches of power.

10. In the election of 1800 Jefferson and Burr were tied with 73 electoral votes each. Delegate balloting repeated up to 28 times before Jefferson won enough votes with Delaware and S. Carolina abstaining thus preventing a pending civil war. This was the first time a change in power of government from one part to another without a cost in violence and bloodshed.

11. Jefferson thought that periodic revolution if kept in check was good for the country- oppression- rebellion and reformation over and over.

12. Reagan revolution had two dominant ideas- private sector can do things better than the government and government interference in private-sector would gum up the works leading to inefficiency. This led to deregulation.

13. Media regulation was reduced in 1982 by Pres. Reagan stopping enforcement of the Sherman Antitrust Act- led to large corporations. He also stopped the Fairness Doctrine. In 1996 the Republican Congress deregulated the media with the Telecommunications Act. 2012 under Pres. Obama Fairness Doctrine deleted from FCC regulations.

14. Reaganomics caused an imbalance of wealth inequalities.

15. After 50 years of the New Deal, Pres. Reagan placed the U. S. among the least socially mobile nations in the developed world suggesting a revolution could be brewing.

16. In 1976 Supreme Court case Buckley v. Valeo- a protection for money and its use even in politics.

17. In 1978, First National Bank v. Bellotti gave equal protection rights to corporations.

18. The Supreme Court brought the above two cases together in 2010 in the Citizens United v. Federal Election Commission ruling. Corporations are now persons.

19. The Day OF Battle   by Rick Atkinson

1. This book is on the war in Sicily and Italy, 1943-1944.
2. The constant mix-up of generals in war is due to their high egos and wanting to get all the glory and nothing else. This included almost all the 4 and 5 star generals.
3. Some generals, as Gen. Dawley, were incompetent and were released back to the states to a desk job. Gen. Dawley was demoted. However, due to his keeping silent, he was upgraded to a 4 star general and upon retirement to a 5 star General. Such is the military helping their own no matter what. He would not attack off of the beach in Salerno. General Marshall relieved him and pushed the Germans back.
4. Coordination with the ground troops and the air support was a big problem as they bombed the wrong areas and even killed ally solders- Polish, French, British, and Americans.
5. Coordination between all the allied armies and air power was difficult as the American Generals always wanted the glory with no concern for anything else.
6. The war in this theater started in Sicily then on to the foot of Italy. The main goal was Rome that the U.S. generals wanted to be there first to get the glory.

20. The Price of Civilization by Jeffrey Sacks

1. Single minded pursuit to wealth and consumption leads to addictions and compulsions rather than to happiness and life well lived.
2. Majority 71% describes the federal government as a special interest group looking out for its own interests.
3. The public distrusts banks, large corporations, news media, unions and entertainment industry.

4. Under President Bush by 2007 8.6 million jobs were shed from the peak employment and the worst since WWII. Fall in housing prices began in 2006.

5. Under President Clinton- a squeeze on spending – domestic and military combined with higher taxes collected from 1995-2002 brought the budget deficit under control.

6. China saving rate was 54% and used to build buildings, roads, subway lines and rail.

7. In world rankings in 2009 the US ranked- 15 reading, 23 science, 31 mathematics.

8. In the 1970's the top 100 earned 40 times average worker's pay. By 2000 it reached 1000. Median income for middle class has remained at about $45,000 since 1973.

9. The top 1% has higher net worth than bottom 90% and pretax income greater than the bottom 50%. This also occurred on the eve of the Great Depression.

10. US abandoned its monetary links with gold on August 15, 1971

11. Foreign born in US fell to 15% in 1924 to less than 5% in 1970 due to the immigration laws.

12. 1978 Revenue Act began the process of cutting capital gains tax and extended during Reagan years.

13. Pres. Carter tried to reform the energy sector but was blocked by the power of the oil and gas sector.

14. Four elements of the Reagan Revolution: Tax cuts, reduced fed spending, deregulation, and outsourcing of core government services. All are still in place today.

15. Top marginal tax rate 77% in 1918 when Hoover and Coolidge brought it back to 25%. The New Deal rate of then 63% and during WWII rose to 94% by 1945. Johnson lowered the tax rate to 70% and Reagan to 28% by 1988.

16. Reagan's thinking on tax reductions- improves incentive for innovation and entrepreneurship, increase government revenue, and lead to smaller government. Infrastructure was curtailed falling from 2% to 1% of GDP. Reagan dismantled research and development programs for alternative energy, started by President Carter, deregulated the S& L industry.

17. 83% of Americans agree that we need stricter environmental laws and regulations.

18. Paradox on anti-tax revolt: mostly red states are anti-tax states and receive the largest net income from federal spending.

19. Reason why we change- Technological revolution of computers, Internet, and mobile telephony via digital electronic age.

20. Large mega lobbyists exist for-U.S. military establishment after WWII (military industrial complex), and big corporations financing America's elections. Eisenhower warned in his farewell address in Jan. 1961- beware of the Military Industrial Complex.

21. Lobbyists hire family members of politicians, hire government and military brass after they leave their office. Half of the senators, 42% of Congressmen, and their aids become lobbyists after leaving office. That's 310 of former President Bush appointees and 283 of President Clintons. Corporate financing and lobbying are the key elements that keep the system intact and in their control of laws that they want.

22. Wealth begets power, and power begets wealth.

23. Wall Street key individuals in government office have steered our financial demise to their benefit in the companies they once worked for.

24. Big oil teamed up with the automobile industry to steer America away from mass transit and toward gas guzzling autos.

25. Businesses spend about $300 billion in advertising to manipulate demands

26. Of the 100 largest public traded corporations 83 reported operating in tax havens to reduce their taxes. Over $10 billion lost each year in taxes

27. America has become a media saturated society the first in history with TV, DVD, video games, internet, cell phones, etc.

28. Two of the greatest ethicists were Buddha in the east and Aristotle in the West. Happiness exists with a balanced life and moderation of all things was the key to eudemonia or human fulfillment.

29. One in five children grows up in poverty.

30. Four biggest challenges of America- national security, energy security, environmental, and industrial competitiveness.

31 U.S. Power source- 50 % coal, 20% each nuclear and natural gas, and the rest is mostly hydro.

21. The Revenge of Geography: What the Map tells us by R. Kaplan

1. General Scipio defeated Hannibal in 202 BC outside Tunis.
2. Eastern Europe denotes the half of Europe that was communist and controlled from Moscow.
3. In 1996, Anthony Lake codified an exit strategy doctrine before we send our troops into a foreign country.
4. Thucydides pointed out human nature as – motivated by fear, self-interest, and honor.
5. History repeats itself with the arrival of new conquerors, emperors and presidents.
6. Luxurious living strengthens the state initially but with succeeding generations leads to decadence and collapse signaled by the rise of powerful leaders.
7. Between 1921 and 1958 Iraq had a well-functioning parliamentary system.
8. Largely through the Mongols that the Silk Route flourished in the 13 and 14 centuries.
9. Landscapes in large measure control geography.
10. The fall of the Berlin Wall 1989. Globalization is erasing borders, regions, and cultural distinctions.
11. Mecca in Hejaz was the most important trading center in western and central Arabia as it was close to the Red Sea and intersection of two major routes.
12. Phidippides, a professional runner, was sent from Athens to Sparta to plead for help to fight the Persians.
13. Strategy, as defined by Napoleon, is the art of using time and space in a military and diplomatic manner.
14. The Turks in the 10 & 11 centuries overran the Middle East and with the ill treatment of the Christian pilgrims at Jerusalem that led to the Crusades.
15. The Boer War 1899-1902 was led by the imperialists of Britain.
16. St Petersburg in Russia was named for Peter the Great and was made the capital of Russia for two centuries.

17. Kremlin's whole empire fell apart by getting entrapped by guerrillas in Afghanistan.

18. According to Haushofer only nations in decline seek stable borders and only decadent ones seek to protect their borders with permanent fortifications.

19. Book to read:" American's Strategy in World Politics: the United States and the Balance of Power by Mackinder.

20. G. Washington attributed America's victory in its war for independence to France's control of the seas.

21. About 75% of Greek's businesses are family owned and rely on family labor- minimum wages laws do not apply.

22. In Europe those over 60 years old will reach 47% of the population by 2050 and they will lose 24 % of its prime working age population.

23. Russia supplies 25% of Europe's gas requirements, 40 % of Germany's, and 100% of Finland's and the Baltic states.

24. Russia's first great empire was in the 9th century in Kiev.

25. Cossacks referred to freelance Tatar warriors in Russia, Poland and Lithuanians.

26. Crimean Wars 1853-1856. The result of the Russo-Japanese War, 1904-1905, was that Russia lost the southern half of Sakhalin Island and parts of Southern Manchuria.

27. Bolsheviks moved the capital of Russia back eastward to Moscow from St. Petersburg in the Baltic's. Russia consisted of three Union Republics- Russia, Ukraine, Belarus, and 11 autonomous Republics and sub-regions.

28. Russia boasts the world's largest natural gas reserves, second largest coal reserves, and the 8th largest oil reserves- most lie in western Siberia.

29. Taiwan was acquired by China in 1683.

30. China-has about 25% of the world's metal and is a leading consumer of most metals of which Mongolia has an abundance. By 2030 they will fall short of water demand by 25%. They are mining for copper in Afghanistan and building roads, energy pipelines, and rail infrastructure.

31. The Great Wall of China was built in the 3rd century B.C. to keep out the Turkish invaders. But it was the Mongol invasion from the north that led to the end of the Ming forays in the Indian Ocean.

32. South China Sea- 1/3 of all sea borne commercial goods worldwide and 1/2 of all energy pass through here.

33. India has the 3rd largest Muslim population- 154 million. They have contributed to the building of Afghanistan's and Pakistan's road network along with Iran and Saudi Arabia.

34. In 1959 the Tibet uprising sent the Dalai Lama into exile in India.

35. India's air force is the fourth largest in the world. China has been helping to build sea ports around India. China adds more highways per year than India has in total.

36. The Middle Eastern population under 30 is about 65% and future problem.

37. Saudi Arabia- 40% are under 15 years and 40% of young adults are unemployed.

38. Iran- the World's first superpower- Persian Empire. Greater Iran began in 700BC with the Medes. They are the most tech advanced in the Middle East.

39. Turkey- 2/3's of urban working class prayed daily. They voted against U.S. troops on their land sent to stage their invasion of Iraq.

40. Most of Texas, New Mexico, Arizona, California, Nevada, and Utah were part of Mexico until the Texan and the Mexican American war in 1835- 1848. Prediction that by 2080 the southwestern states of U.S. and the northern states of Mexico will band together to form a new country.

41. Lewis and Clark Expedition 1804-06.

22. The State of Jones by Sally Jenkins

1. On Oct. 11 1862 the Confederate Legislation Passed "The Twenty Negro Law". This exempted the richest men from military service- one white man was exempt for every 20 slaves.

2. New law during the war where officials can walk off with 10% of the provisions on a farm.

3. After Pres. Lincoln was elected Miss. Gov. J. Pettus called for a secession ordinance. After which Lincoln states, " A house divided against itself cannot stand", paraphrasing The Bible and Aesop's Fables.

4. Emancipation Proclamation was signed Sept .1862.
5. Major crop of the South was cotton.
6. April 9, 1865 Lee surrendered to Grant at Appomattox.
7. Andrew Johnson became President when Lincoln was shot on April 15, 1865.
8. December 6, 1895 was when Mississippi ratified the 13th Amendment ending the institution of slavery.

23. The Worst Hard Time by Timothy Egan

1. Medicine Lodge Treaty of 1867 ratified by Congress of U.S. that promised Indian tribes hunting rights of the Great American Desert, the area south of the Arkansas River.
2. Bison can live in temperatures of over 110 to 30 below degrees while cattle are more fragile. Cattle were nearly wiped out in the winter of 1885-1886.
3. Crop threshold for growing without irrigation required about 20 inches of rain a year.
4. The buffalo grass of the plains supported the American bison herd of about 30 million before the white migration homesteading of the land of the Panhandle.
5. Five flags had flown over No Man's Land in the central land mass in the now U.S. Spain was the first to claim it but two expeditions and reports from traders reinforced the view that it should be left to the animals and the Indians. Spain gave the territory to Napoleon. The French flag flew for all of 20 days until it was sold to the U. S. as part of the Louisiana Purchase.
6. Texas was admitted to the Union in 1845.
7. Oklahoma is a combination of two Choctaw words: Okla- people and Homma-red.
8. The First Homestead Act was in 1862 and the Enlarged Homestead Act was in 1909. John Fremont said "Free soil, Free Men, Fremont".
9. In 1929 nearly 25% of the jobs were on farms. Now there are less than 1% of farm jobs.
10. In the 1930's the Nebraska people were burning grain and surplus corn for heat.
11. In 1930 the price of oil wet from $1:30 to $ 0.20.

12. Senator Morris Sheppard of Texas had a whiskey still and was the author of the 18th amendment,

13. In 1931 the Bank of the United States collapsed, 20 million people were without jobs and that was 25% of the work force.

14. Major cause of the Dust Bowl was the removal of the prairie grass where 33 million acres were stripped which had been held by the Indians and migrating animals for hundreds of years. The hearty grassland held down the earth. The homesteaders tilled most of the soil for other crops and the wind and little rain did the rest.

15. Oklahoma became the 46th state under President Theodore Roosevelt.

16. Pres. Hoover believed the cure for the Depression was to prime the pump at the producer end helping factories and business owners while President Roosevelt said that it made no sense to gin up the machines of production if he people could not afford to buy what came out of the factory doors.

17. Volstead Act amended to permit sale of 3.2% beer and later prohibition was gone.

18. Pyrheliometer measures sunlight.

19. In 1934 the government offered contracts to wheat farmers to not plant acreage in an attempt to regulate prices. This was the start of the subsidy system that still exists.

20. Hugh Bennett and President Roosevelt started the land conservation with replanting hardy African grass and trees in the Panhandle.

21. In 1935 President Roosevelt signed the Social Security Act, started the Works Progress Administration and backed the National Labor Relations Act.

22. Timber Culture Act- allowed people to claim a significantly large homestead if they agreed to plant and maintain trees on a portion of the land.

23. Tree rings and their width tells the amount of the rain in any one year. Wet years were thick and dry thin. There were 20 droughts in the past 748 years.

24. The government purchased 11 million acres of land to return it to grass land.

25. The Ogallala Aquifer in the Panhandle is the largest in the U.S. The water in that aquifer came from the melting of glaciers 15,000 years ago. This aquifer provides 30% of the irrigation water in the U.S. It will dry up in about 100 years at its current use. Some even say it will dry up much sooner.

24. World Order by Henry Kissinger

1. 30 year war, 1618-48, in Central Europe, population reduction by 25%.
2. Westphalia peace treaty-four centuries ago in Germany without involvement of most other continents.
3. 7th century Islam, three continents religious wave, unified the Arab world to govern Middle East, North Africa, and parts of Asia and Europe.
4. American vision of peace is the spread of democratic principles.
5. To be sustainable peace must be just for leaders and its citizens.
6. Fall of the Roman Empire -476 AD
7. Chinese Navigator Zheng He, died in 1433. That put an end to overseas adventures. The Emperor had all vessels over three sails destroyed.
8. Moveable type for printing – mid 15th century.
9. Protestant Reformation destroyed world order when Christianity split the papacy.
10. Conclusions from Richelieu- a. foreign policy is a long term strategy, b. statesman must use the vision to a purposeful direction, c. act through experience and aspirations.
11. 1682 France's North American territories were named "Louisiana" the year King Louis court moved to Versailles.
12. Russia- Peter the Great moved the capitol from Kiev to St. Petersburg.
13. Crimean War- 1853-6 broke up the unity of the states- Austria, Prussia and Russia.
14. In 1862-70 Bismarck placed Prussia at the head of a united Germany.
15. Islamism- Muhammad born in Mecca in 570 and at 40 wrote the Quran. He died in 632 when the council of elders selected this father in-law, Abu Bakr, as successor or caliph.

16. 1917 Balfour Declaration letter by British Foreign Secretary to Lord Rothschild to establish a home for the Jews in Palestine. The document included that nothing was to prejudice the civil and religious rights of existing non-Jews.

17. 1950's & 1960's monarchical governments in Egypt, Iraq, Syria, Yemen and Libya were overthrown by their military leaders to establish secular governments.

18. In 1928 al-Banna founded the Muslim Brotherhood to combat degrading effects of foreign influence and secular ways of life.

19. The kingdom of Saudi Arabia is a traditional Arab-Islamic realm with both a tribal monarchy and Islamic theocracy.

20. 1590 warrior, Toyotomi Hideyoshi, unified Japan ending the century of civil conflict.

21. Treaty of Portsmouth of 1905 mediated war between Russia and Japan.

22. The Great Wall of China extended over 4,500 miles with branches for a total of about 14,000 miles.

23. People who conquered China- the Mongol's in the 13 century and the Manchus in the 17th century.

24. Louisiana Purchased in 1803. Jefferson was also interested in Cuba.

25. Monroe Doctrine of 1823 made territories off limits for any foreign colonization.

26. After the Spanish-American war of 1898, the U.S. in 1 1/2 years reduced the military of about one million to 65,000.

27. Korean War was the first was that America renounced victory as an objective.

28. North Vietnamese was defeated by South Vietnamese without U.S. help. Cease fire followed.

29. For most of history Afghan tribes and sects have been at war with each other and united to resist invasion from outsiders.

BOOKS IN A NUT SHELL
FINANCE AND ECONOMICS

INDEX   PAGE

1. Change the Story, Change the Future
by David C. Korten

1. A continuation of current trends both in social and ecological terms will inevitably led to the collapse of civilization.

2. Sacred Money and Markets: This story is about money humanity's defining value, while unregulated global markets serve as its moral compass and destroying life to make money count as wealth creation.

3. Our lack of concern for our planet and of money concentration means "the last one to leave shut off the lights."

4. Revolutions in the past have been mostly a response to the frustrations of poverty and lack of money to buy necessities.

5. Policies have been shifting from people and nations, to global corporations and financial markets delinked from moral sensibility and public accountability.

6. We call development as a process of alienating people from lands and waters from which they make their living to where people become dependent on money for their needs.

7. Corporate power aligns with the interests of money while the expanding of the people power movement aligns with the interests of life.

8. Proposal to avoid further collapse and treating the symptoms of a system failure: a new regulation, a tax on bad behavior, subsidy incentive for good behavior.

9. Connection to nature and community is essential to our physical and mental health to benefit all. Revert from social dysfunction, ruthless competition, greed, and individualistic violence.

10. U.S. Congress established the U.S. Bureau of Reclamation in 1902 to build great dams to bend nature. Now they are removing dams to reclaim rivers for nature.

11. Social Darwinist suggests we either dominate nature and other humans or become victims of their domination over us.

12. Team decision making is more creative and effective in dealing with complex problems than an individual decision maker

13. From 3000BC, with the rise of imperial civilizations to the most recent four hundred years of modern science, we began to manipulate and suppress the Earth.

76

14. Early rulers established a monopoly on the use of armed force to control means of living (land and water), money and debt, all increasing their power.

15. In the 1500's the kings of Europe rather than warring against one another fulfilled their imperial ambitions by colonizing distant territories in Asia, Africa and the Americas and outsourcing the dirty work to commissioned privateers.

16. By the 1600's European monarchs issued charters to private investors for limited-liability stockholders-owned corporations. This gave monopoly-trading rights for particular goods and regions reaping substantial fees and dividends for the monarchs. The British East Indian Company was an early model.

17. Corporate power in the late twentieth century saw a rapid growth in size and global reach. They absorbed or displaced their competitors, extended their reach to other states and countries. This evolved into global corporations.

18. GDP (Gross domestic product) of corporations counts for everything even if it results in the destruction of fisheries and forests, and poisons rivers and aquifers. Financial-sector income, for the most part, produces no real value from generating short-term profits for the financial sector.

19. Paradox- in a free market as successful corporations grow the bigger they get, the greater their monopoly power to be controlled by bigger government. Reduce corporate size can result in reduce government size.

20. There is a need for schools for decision makers in skilled areas managing society of goals, money and markets to reconnect us with one another and nature.

21. Society has changed through the : collapse of British rule in India, race and gender relations, the fall of the Berlin Wall, disintegration of the Soviet Union, the end of apartheid in South Africa, and the ouster of the Marcos dictatorship in the Philippines. All was seen as impossible until it happened.

22. The Living Earth narrative acknowledges our dependence on and responsibility to contribute to the Earth's community and its life.

23. Life is not a destination but a journey of exploration and discovery where we are born to contribute to that journey. Just

think in the past 200,000 years we have developed speech, created complex languages, and mastered the use of fire, produced tools, art, cultivated our own food and created systems of knowledge to create a great civilization. Now it is up to us to continue it by keeping it for future generations.

2. Dealing with CHINA by Henry Paulson, jr.

1. China produces and uses nearly half of the worlds cement, iron ore, steel, and 40% of copper and aluminum.
2. China needs to shift their $10 trillion economy from export to domestic consumption.
3. An outside country must build strong relationships to enter their markets. They have a strong sense of honor and stick to their word.
4. China has products manufactured in Hong Kong with no corporate taxes marked up when shipped overseas.
5. The first China stock exchange opened in 1987.
6. The government created China Telecom. They are ruled by men and not laws
7. In 1949 Mao Zedong was in power and helped them break from dominance on imports. By 1970 they were the 9th largest producer of and exporter of oil mostly to Japan. By 1980 they would need to import oil due to their increase in manufacturing.
8. Premier Zhu proposed cutting the Army of 8 million in half and ministries from 40 to 29.
9. In 1998 BP would merge with Aramco, and Exxon and Mobil would merge.
10. Oil prices in 1998 were $10 a barrel and reached $27 by 2000.
11. Guangdong the first China economic zone grew at 14% in the early 1990's and became a China's factory zone.
12. Bankruptcy laws in place by 1986.
13. Universities were closed in 1966.
14. 90% of Chinese people belong to the Han ethnic group. There are 55 others along with the Mandarin group in densely populated coastal and central regions.
15. No single entity could own more than 20% of a Chinese bank with total foreign ownership limited to 25%. Other developing

countries as Brazil, Russia, and India allowed foreigners to own 100%.

20. Estimated in 2007 that pollution cost China 5.8% GDP and home to 16 of the world's 20 most polluted cities.

21. U.S. Naval Academy founded in 1845.

22. Foreign investment in the US increased jobs by 5 million and 30% in higher wages.

23. 60% of the wealthy individuals in China with investment assets of at least $41.6 million were looking to leave or have left China, or invested abroad.

24. After double-digit growth in the past 30 years, growth fell to 7.4% in 2014.

25. In 1978 80% of China's people tilled the land at the start of Deng Xiaoping's Reforms.

26. Since 2006, China built 7,000 miles of high-speed rail. Over 2 million people per day use this rail system. By 2020 they are targeting for subways in 40 cities from 21 today. U.S. has 15 cities with subways.

27. China has 31 provinces. But the government owns all the land.

28. In 2013, Chongqing produced 25% of the global production of laptops.

29. Beijing has 6 roads ringing the city and working on another.

30. Due to pollution, China must move away from coal-powered plants. Coal now powers 70% of their generation plants.

31. In the next 15 years China expects to add the equivalent of the power generated in United Kingdom each year.

32. Private enterprise accounts for 90% of new jobs. They have 73 of the largest companies listed in the Fortune 500

33. China tried to buy Unocal in 2005 for $18.5 billion- rejected by U.S. Congress.

34. Total debt to GDP in China in 2014 was 206 compared to 102 in the U.S..

35. Their banks are well capitalized and have $4 trillion in foreign exchange reserves and own $1.3 trillion of U.S. debt.

36. Partners can own from 33 to 49% of a company.

37. Second largest number of billionaires after the U.S.

3. Red Ink: Inside the High-Stakes Politics of the Federal Budget by David Wessel

1. Nearly two-third of annual federal spending is on autopilot and doesn't require an annual vote by Congress.
2. The US defense budget is greater than the combined defense budgets of the next seventeen largest spenders.
3. Twenty cents of every dollar of defense spending in 2011 was spent on Iraq and Afghanistan.
4. Of the 4.4 million government workers 35% are military and 29% are civilians working for departments of Defense, VA and Homeland Security.
5. About half of all spending on health comes from federal, state and local governments. Nearly all the growth in the federal budget over the next ten years will come from spending on health care and interest payments unless changes are made.
6. Today's deficits mostly came from revenues lost, taxes cut and spending increased because of the recession.
7. About 46% of households did not pay taxes in 2011. Tax breaks add up to $1.1 trillion in 2011 while income was $1.3 trillion.
8. Gov. at all levels took in taxes at 25% of the income of the economy in 2010. Compare this with 27% Japan, 31% Canada and 35% in Germany and United Kingdom.
9. In 2011 for every $1 spent 36 cents was mostly borrowed from China.
10. Pres. Johnson created the Federal Medicare Health Insurance program for the aged and Medicaid for the poor.
11. Due to Medicare Americans spend 13% fewer days sick.
12. In 1974 was the first time spending on interest, SS, Medicare and other benefits exceeded defense and domestic spending.
13. Pres. Reagan promised to - cut taxes, rebuild the defenses, and balance the budget. 1980 broke the pattern where the Gov. ran big deficits only in wartime. In Pres. Reagan's 8 years in office his debt averaged 4.25% of GDP.
14. Under Pres. Clinton from 1998-2001 the Fed Gov. ran a surplus.
15. Pres. Bush's first tax cut exceeded that of Reagan's and the first expansion of Medicare in 40 years.

16. Medicare and Medicaid account for about 21% of all Federal spending.

17. By past laws the pharmaceutical companies had to charge the "best price" they charged anyone for drugs but that was changed in 2003 under the Bush administration. That best price would have save the Fed Gov. about $155 billion over 10 years.

18. The government reverted the farm insurance program to private insurers and pays about 60% of the premium cost costing the taxpayers $10 billion a year and growing.

19. The number of taxpaying workers for every SS beneficiary was 5.1 in 1960 and projected to fall to 2.1 by 2029.

20. The U.S. navy is larger than the next 13 combined countries. The bulk of the Pentagon's budget goes for: personnel, operation and maintenance, and buying weapons.

21. The navy estimates each aircraft carrier costs in excess of $1 billion per year and is more than Medicare spends annually on knee, hip, and shoulder joint replacements. Congress by law requires the navy to maintain 11 carriers.

22. About 15% of enlisted men and women and 50% of officers stay in the military 20 years to retire to qualify for health insurance often retiring in their 40's.

23. 65% of dams in the US are privately owned. There are about 84,000 dams in the U.S..

24. In 2011, the US collected $2.3 trillion in taxes, fees and other revenues and borrowed $1.1 trillion.

25. Payroll tax, levied on wages but not capital gains, interest or dividends, was imposed in 1937 to finance Social Security and expanded in 1983 to shore up SS.

26. In the 1950's more than 30% of federal revenues came from corporate income tax. Now the figure is about 10%.

27. There are about 13,000 registered as lobbyists in Washington all trying to influence government.

28. Affordable Care Act, imposes an additional 0.9% Medicare payroll tax on wages over $200,000 on individuals and $250,000 on couples.

29. Nearly 60% of gross income of the very rich in 2008 came from capital gains, taxed at 15%. Only8% of their income came from wages taxed at 35%.

81

30. In 1955 less than 5% of U.S. federal debt was held by foreigners. Today, federal governments and private investors hold nearly half of US debt with the major holders being China, Japan, and Saudi Arabia.

31. The U.S. debt to GDP exceeded 100% during WWII but came down drastically after the war. History shows a high debt to GDP is a danger zone for the country.

4. The Ascent of Money by Niall Ferguson

1. Earliest coins 600 BC at Ephesus in Turkey. Rome used three metals- gold, silver, and bronze coins. China in 221 BC standardized on bronze coins. Our dollar bill came from the German work thaler.

2. Cash in American hands is titled M2. Credit comes from Latin Credo meaning "I believe". Hammurabi Law prescribed debt forgiveness every three years. This did not deter private nor public lenders.

3. Fibonacci numbers are the addition of the two previous numbers as 1 + 2= 3, 3+2=5, etc.

4. Early centuries, under Christianity's money, lending at interest was a sin. So they went to the Jewish ghetto where interest could be charged. The Jews read the book of Deuteronomy to say they could lend to a stranger but not to their brother at usury interest. Jews expelled from Spain in 1492 or forced to adopt Christianity by a decree of 1497.

5. In 1500's Jews granted Venetian status but could not engage in retail trade hence restricting them to financial services.

6. Bank deposit was introduced in 1933. In 1976 Maine was the first state to legalize interstate banking. Gold standard removed on 15 August 1971 when Nixon closed the gold window.

7. June 1815 Battle of Waterloo occurred not far from Brussels,Belgium.. Napoleon Bonaparte fought against the British, Dutch and German troops. Napoleon when captured was exiled to the island of Elba.

8. The fall of New Orleans in April 1862 was said to be the real turning point of the Civil War due to the command of the Mississippi River entrance.

9. In 1826-9 South American countries as Peru, Columbia, Chile, Argentina defaulted on loans issued in London.
10. Inflation cannot occur without political malfunction per Milton Friedman.
11 Argentina in 1913 was one of the richest countries in the world due to its silver mines. In 2001 announced a moratorium on its foreign debt including its bonds. This was the biggest default in history.
12. Without easy credit a financial bubble cannot occur. VOV, the East Indian Company, was the first big corporation. They had a monopoly on some spices like clove and nutmeg.
13. Lloyd's insurance was formed in 1774.
14. Insurance loss of Katrina about $45 billion- same as 9/11 attack.
15. Original hedging was agricultural for future contract pricing. In 1874 the future exchange was created. 1982 was the start of future contracts on the stock market.
16. Call options- right to buy, put option the right to sell, -swap, -default swap were put in place as protection against companies defaulting on bonds.
17. Roosevelt's New Deal initiated many new agencies including the Public Works that spent 15% of its budget on housing and slum clearance. Also had a Home Owners Loan Corporation to refinance mortgages on a longer term to 15 years. He also introduced the FDIC and FEMA. In 1977, the Community Reinvestment Act under Pres. Carter followed this.
18. As of 1913 interest on mortgage payments was tax deductible.
19. Opium in China- the Emperor of China prohibited in 1729 the selling of opium due to the high social cost. Opium was coming from the British East India Company. China tried to stop it but Britain had control of the ports in Hong Kong. In 1841 Hong Kong became a British possession. US was looking for exports to China and developed and encouraged opium growth in Turkey to replace the current crop to compete with the British.
20. China declared bankruptcy in 1923 and defaulted on their external debt.
21. 1993 Mr. Black of Goldman Sachs and Mr. Scholes of Stanford Univ. developed theory of option trading and formed Long Term

Capital Management. Compensation was 2% of assets and 25% profits. Eventually they took over the entire company, over-extended and went into bankruptcy. It was said due to globalization and not understanding the action of globalization. They tried to get Buffet and Soros to help but both said no. Reason their model did not work was that they only went back 5 years and did not cover the 1987 stock market crash.

22. IMF estimated US losses worldwide at $2.2 trillion. About half was written off the other half has yet to be written off. Capital to Asset (C/A) ratio is about 4% now as compared to 25% in early 1900's. B of A C/A was 1.4% in 2008 not including off balance-sheet commitments.

23. In October 2002, President Bush said, "We want everybody in America to own their own home. He challenged lenders to create 5.5 million new minority homeowners by the end the decade. Bush signed the "American Dream Down Payment Act in 2003, designed to subsidize first-time house purchases to lower income groups. Lenders were encouraged by the administration not to press subprime borrowers for full documentation- Fannie Mae and Freddie Mac came under additional pressure from HUD to support subprime market.

5. The Big Short by Michael Lewis

1. A mortgage bond was a claim on the cash flows from a pool of thousands of individual home mortgages.
2. Bond investors initially were reluctant to invest in home mortgage loans because the borrowers had the right to pay off the loan any time. That was the problem in the 1980's.
3. Accountants that audited giant Wall Street firms could not figure out whether or not they were making or losing money, too complicated for anybody.
4. The decline in lending standards started in early 2004.
5. Look at incentives to predict how people would behave.
6. ISDA- international Swaps and Derivatives Association had the task of formalizing the terms of new securities.
7. Allen Greenspan assured us that home prices are not prone to bubbles or major deflations on any national scale.

8. In 1930's roughly half of all mortgage debt was in default and 80% collapsed nationwide.

9. Bond salesmen could say and do anything without fear that they'd be reported to some authority.

10. It was Mike Burry's idea of betting against U.S. home loans by buying credit default swaps on 3B subprime mortgage bonds.

11. Rating agencies Moody's and S & P approved and gave 3A ratings on subprime bonds that eventually went bad. The 3A bonds were combined with B rated bonds to fool the buyer and did not bother to down grade these bonds as they are paid by the finance companies that the bonds were coming from. The finance company lobbyist made sure that no other firms could be admitted as rating agencies.

12. Most individuals on the bond trading desks of the stock market companies had gone to Ivy League schools.

13. The less transparent the market and the more complicated the securities, the more money for the trading desks at big Wall Street firms.

14. Financial options were systematically mispriced.

15. CDO- Collateralized Debt Obligation. Hardly anyone could understand a subprime mortgage backed CDO.

16. People were going long but were not allowed to go short.

17. Wall Street firms continued to publish favorable bond market research reports.

18. Rating firms could not get information on the bonds to analyze the CDO they were rating.

19. Complicated financial stuff was being dreamed up for the sole purpose of lending money to people who could never repay it.

20. During the period that the index of subprime mortgage bonds collapsed, the market insuring them hadn't budged. Slowing the control the finance companies had in hiding the real problem.

21. Subprime mortgage credit default swap (CDS) conceived in 2003 between Morgan Stanley and other banks or insurance companies outside of the gaze of the wider market.

22. Mr. Hubler at Morgan Stanley created the largest loss of any single trader in Wall Street history at $9 billion and when he left he was given a $10 million severance package.

23. IMF put the US originated subprime related assets loss at a trillion dollars.

24. In Oct. 2008 the US government stepped in to absorb all the losses in the financial system to prevent the big Wall Street firms from failing.

25. The first mortgage derivative was at Salomon Brothers in 1986.

26. Cause of failure was greed from investors and bankers.

27. John Paulson and Ben Bernanke both initially advised that no problem existed. Paulson had a stake in one of the financial companies.

28. One could gain by turning an investment bank into a public corporation and leveraging its balance sheet with exotic risks that they could not do in a financial corporation. This transferred the risk from the corporation to the shareholders.

6. The Billionaire's Vinegar by Benjamin Wallace

1. Thomas Jefferson hosted parties in 1789 with wine he ordered. He was the Washington wine expert and ordered for other presidents of the United States.

2. At one time in 1784, Jefferson ordered 124 bottles of Haut-Brion that never arrived and some that was ordered were short one box in 1789.

3. In May 1967 in London, Christie held the first "Finest and Rarest Wines" sale. It included 1830 Tokay, 1911 Sandeman Coronation Vintage Port, and strange, flat Champagne called Sillery.

4. Michael Broadbent was the founding director of Christie's wine department. He went around mostly Europe collecting wines in old cellars for sale. He found one of a Chateau Lafite -1787 which was the oldest red wine ever to come up for auction. Christie's engraved and sold Jefferson bottles with the initials "THJ". The bottle was supplied by Hardy Rodenstock who gave stories how he found it but no specific details of where or from whom they came.

5. Rodenstock purchased all wines from sellers for cash and did not report any for tax purposes. Some claimed that they were from a Nazi cellar.

6. Bottle sizes: Magnum- two bottles, Marie-Jeanne- three bottles, double magnum – two magnums, Jeroboam- six bottles, Imperial- eight bottles. The Nebuchadnezzar is the largest size at 20 - 750ml bottles.

7. Chateau d'Yquem and the king of sweet white wines. - due to low yield of 70 gallons an acre compared to about 400 for the leading red wines. A single vine can produce an entire bottle of dry red wine while it only produces just one glass of Yquem.

8. The Montrachet is the most famous white Burgundy wine.

9. Prices paid for the Jefferson 1787 bottle of wine was upward to $200,000.

10. As the story goes, nobody could find out where the wines were collected from and suspicion evolved around Broadbent to investigate. They found that there were more bottles sold that could possibly have been produced for Jefferson. Rodenstock was respected and few doubted the bottles. He had deceived the public and wine buyers. He sold an illusion.

7. The Day after the Dollar Crashes by Damon Vickers

1. U.S. imports about $800 billion of oil. Only real gauge is what we export.

2. Options- go to war to get more resources, cut benefits, adopt one child policy when there are too many people for food and jobs.

3. M3 tracks money supply but now unreliable due to U.S. printing money for the economy.

4. About 70% of all antibiotics used in the US are fed to healthy farm animals.

5. With deforestation and fossil fuels, carbon dioxide has increased by 35% in the atmosphere. The CO_2 mixes with water in the oceans to make it acidic and eventually if too much is absorbed the fish die off.

6. Unemployment Compensation- 1991 was 13 weeks, Feb 1992 changed to 33 weeks, 2002 revised to 39 weeks, July 2008 to 52 weeks, and finally in early 2010 it went to 99 weeks.

7. About 45% of aquifers have been impacted or are at risk from depletion or contamination.

8. Health Care bill will only decline when we find and do something about the cause of sickness like cancer. We only treat the symptoms not the cause and claim we are attempting to cure the cause.

9. First bankruptcy laws appeared in 1592 in England and designed to benefit creditors to seize the company's assets.

10. Sovereign debt is government debt or national debt.

11. The length and duration of every bear market is in direct proportion to the bull market that preceded it. The bull market in bonds has been going on now since 1982 and probably near the top.

12. The oceans provide about 30-40% of the world's food. We are losing ocean food due to overfishing and higher acid count.

13. There are about 619 oil rigs.

14. Biphenol A or BPA in plastic bottles are banned in Europe but not in the US.

15. We have cut down over 90% of all trees in the US in the past 100 years.

16. Hydrofracking has put 45% of our drinking water in the US in jeopardy.

8. The Death of Money by James Rickards

1. Solution to systemic risk- break up large banks and ban most derivatives.

2. Future international monetary system will not be based on dollars. Possibilities are gold, SDR, or a network of regional reserve currencies.

3. China has over $3 trillion of U.S. investments. Every 10% devaluation in the dollar represents $300 million wealth transfer from China to the US.

4. China's GDP rose from $260 billion in 1979 to over $7.2 trillion in 2011.

5. Main drivers of labor force expansion are demographics and education while the main drivers of productivity are capital and technology.

6. Shadow banking in China consists of – local government obligations, trust products, and wealth management products.

7. Share of Chinese GDP attributable to wages has fallen from over 50 to 40%. The U. S. has remained steady at 55%. Higher earners in China have a lower propensity to spend.

8. In China bad investments and wage suppression will affect the twin crises of bad debt and income inequality igniting a financial panic leading to social unrest even revolution.

9. Charlemagne (called by Popes the Father of Europe) was the first emperor in the West following the fall of the Western Roman Empire in A.D. 476. The empire extended to present day Spain, France, and even England.

10. Prior to Charlemagne's European monetary standard was a gold sou, a Byzantine roman coin introduced by Constantine I in AD 312. This was switched to silver due to gold's shortage when trade was shut off do to Islam's rise.

11. The First Reich under Otto I in 962 lasted until it was dissolved by Napoleon in 1806.

12. The Berlin Consensus emerged from the ashes of the 2008 global financial crisis consisted of seven pillars- promote exports, low corporate taxes, low inflation, investment in infrastructure, competitive unit labor costs, etc..

13.The EU building a high speed rail, the Gotthard Base Tunnel , to open in 2017 and run through the Swiss Alps and will be the longest in the world.

14. In 2010 fraud uncovered in Greece's accounting enabled off the books swaps provided by Goldman Sachs and other Wall Street banks.

15. In 2010 the U.S. initiated a cheap-dollar policy intended to import inflation from abroad in the form of higher import prices on most products.

16. Over the next 10 years the EU is destined to possibly evolve into the world's economic superpower.

17. BRICS taking new position away from the existing Bretton Woods and San Francisco agreements of IMF, World Bank, and the United Nations. Meaning the US losing its first place economic power.

18. Since 1945, the US has guaranteed Saudi Arabia' security in exchange for energy exports, support of the dollar through exports

exchanged in dollars and purchasing of weapons, and infrastructure from the US.

19. After WW II the debt to GDP in the U.S. was 100% about where it is today and was reduced by taxing, infrastructure projects, and reducing the military.

20. Low borrowing costs and higher inflation are the two ways the Fed can improve deficit sustainability.

21. The IMF seeks to control finance, to contain risk, and to condition economic development on a global basis.

22. Larry Summers promoted the two most financially destructive legislative changes in the past century: the Glass-Steagall repeal in 1999- allowing banks to operate like hedge funds, and, derivative regulation repeal in 2000.

23. The first Central Bank in the U.S. was the Bank of the United States from 1791-1811, followed by the Second Bank of the U.S. 1817- 1836. There was no central bank from 1836 to 1913. A central bank has three primary roles- makes loans, creates money, and employs leverage. Now routed through the IMF that is mostly a rich nations club that lends to support their economic interest.

24. Gold is said to be the true risk-free asset.

25. In 1971 Pres. Nixon ended the US dollar convertibility into gold by foreign central banks.

26. Major countries are storing gold. Russia is the world's fourth largest gold producer.

27. Student loans are the new subprime mortgage bubble and today it is over $1 trillion.

28. The U.S. appears to be the Japan of yesterday with its high taxes, low interest rates, too big to fail banks and labor market rigidities.

29. Gold swap- two central banks exchange gold for currencies and agree to reverse in the future. Lease arrangement- one central bank leases gold, for a fee to a private bank that sells it on a forward basis.

30. Rising home prices are held up by investor pools purchasing large tracts of homes with leverage, restructuring homeowner debt or converting to rentals.

31. Over time the dollar's weight in the SDR basket will be reduced in favor of the Chinese yuan.

32. Once the dollar is devalued against the SDR the US economy will face severe structural adjustments in the form of savings, insurance policies, annuities and retirements benefits will be largely wiped out. Gold could go to $9,000 per ounce.

33. President FDR under the Enemy Act confiscated gold from American citizens in 1933.

34. A sign of a problem is the bank lobbyists' defeat of efforts by US regulators and Congress to limit the size of big banks, reduce bank asset concentration.

35. Another sign of a global problem is the financial disintegration in China.

36. Investments of protection- gold, financial stocks, utilities, emerging markets, sovereign debt.

9. The End of Prosperity by Arthur Laffer

1. Top 1% earners- 40% tax collection, top 5% earners- 60% tax collection.

2. Killers of prosperity- trade protection, tax increases, government spending, regulations and government interventions. Comment: At times regulations are needed to prevent corruption. Trade protection must be equal with other countries, and tax increases to a level that is acceptable.

3. Supply side tax reduction is OK up to a point. However, must be balanced with a reduction in government spending and used in the right areas, as infrastructure, otherwise massive debt will ensue as we have seen with the Reagan and Bush administrations.

4. Laffer curve- a bell shape of Tax to Revenues. Comment: The breaking point, the top rate at which revenue is reduced or increased, appears to be about 70% for top earners on a sliding scale.

5. U.S. income tax is in the16[th] amendment of 1913- Presidents who reduced tax rate- Harding, Coolidge, Kennedy and G.W. Bush.

6. In the 1920's with tax rate reduced from 70% to 25% revenue increased about 40%

7. Gerald Ford in August 1974 became the first unelected president to sit in the White House. First fuel efficiency standards

for autos, unemployment at 7% and windfall profit tax on oil companies.

8. President Carter- budget deficit from $40 billion to $74 billion – 1979-80. Oil went from $50 to $100. President Reagan deregulated the oil companies and oil dropped to $35.

9. 1970 tax rate- 70% on dividends & investments. Under the Kemp-Roth amendment tax rate went from 50% to 28% in 1986. The Steiger bill cut Capital gains tax from 49% to 28% and Reagan cut capital gain tax from 28 to 20 and later to 15% for lower tax brackets.

10. National debt tripled under Reagan's two terms. 1981-89 doubled defense budget.

11. President Reagan deregulated- railroads, airlines, phone companies and financial services. At first, prices fell in these industries from 1978-95 all good for the stock market in these industries.

12. President Clinton- 1993 budget no tax cuts, high income tax increases, gasoline tax, energy tax and a stimulus package.

13. Flat tax- Hong Kong-15%. Sweden eliminated estate tax.

14. One in four new jobs due to international trade. Foreign companies in the U.S. employ 5.4 million and 34% of the manufacturing jobs. Manufacturing jobs have been in steady decline since 1979 even with growth in our economy. Comment: Tells us that the economy was increasing not due to us but to foreigners and a negative effect will transpire in the future.

10. The Great Deformation -The Corruption of Capitalism in America by David Stockman

1. 8 years of GW Bush spending spree- prescription drug, education spending, Homeland Security Dept., farm subsidies and Defense budget doubled.

2. Goldman Sachs given $10 billion to save itself. They generated $29 billion surplus and distributed $16 billion in salaries and bonuses.

3. Massive debt burden fueled by 30 years of mortgaging the nation's future.

4. Prior to 1980 total public and private debt rarely exceeded 1.6 times GDP

5. Every recipient had the balance sheet to absorb AIG's hit so the bailout was protecting short-term earnings, executive's and trader's salaries and bonus. All the recipients including Goldman could have absorbed the losses without taxpayers help. Goldman's part was less than 8 months of profit and bonus.

6. The $20 billion bailout of Wall Street banks during the 1994 Mexican peso crisis were unnecessary.

7. Merrill Lynch and B of A failed due to the inadequate capital to shield losses.

8. 1930-3 bank runs fueled by wartime and postwar debt booms and not by Fed's mistake after 1929.

9. In the housing booms between 2003-6 mortgages were originating up to 75% of high-risk mortgage business in Wall Street not banks.

10. 2008 commercial banks had assets of $11.6 trillion and only 1.7% ($200 billion) was a toxic asset.

11. Banks were permitted to "Gain on Sale" accounting. Book lifetime profits on consumer loans when loans were issued.

12. Bernanke had Paul O'Neill removed for Sec. of Treasury for suggesting tax cuts and unfinanced wars were a recipe for disaster.

13. Pres. Nixon caused U.S. to default on its Bretton Woods obligations to redeem unwanted dollars in gold. Stated, "Deficits don't matter."

14. Pres. Reagan's federal outlays averaged 21.7% of GDP. Higher than Carter years of 21.1% of GDP and 19.3% under Lyndon Johnson's 4 years.

15. Fed should have increased interest rates to encourage saving and reduce household debt, not accumulate more borrowings.

16. Under Pres. Reagan from Nuclear threat we added 100 navy ships, 13,000 tanks and Bradley fighting vehicles, and 18,000 aircraft etc. all useless and unwanted.

17. Soviet had no defense against these land and sea based forces and no prospect of developing one. Eisenhower rejected all these as marginal value against a nuclear adversary.

18. Standard aircraft carriers are accompanied by 80 aircraft and 12 escort ships.

19. U.S. had 150 surface ships and submarines to launch cruise missiles – inventory 5,000 tomahawks with a range of 700 miles.

20. Under Reagan purchase of 9,000 planes when only 3,000 were purchased in previous 8 years.

21. Eisenhower reduced the military and built a smaller and leaner defense budget   He believed in strong civil economy and national security and left office with a Dept. of Defense 1/3 smaller than Harry Truman's years. He said the military Industrial Complexes would extract unwarranted and excess defense spending through fear and pork barrel dynamics.

22. Pres. Ford- called for spending cuts (1975) to keep budget under $300 billion and 5% surtax on income of corporations and affluent households. Congress ignored suggestion.

23. In the U.S. during WWI there was an export boom between 1914–1929. After that a deep depression existed due to the collapse of the export markets causing banks to collapse from loans to the agriculture and export markets.

24. Under Hoover, after the war, 50% of industrial production collapsed and the recovery had begun.

25. In 1935 35 million people lived on 7 million farms and consisted of 25% of our national output. Today less than 2 million Americans live on famers with output of 4% of GDP.

26. July 1944 U.S. held 80% of the world's gold.

27. August 1971 Nixon announced the U.S. dollar was no longer convertible to gold at $35 per ounce.

28. Between 1955 and 1980 household savings was between 7.5 – 10 of disposable personal income. In 2001 it reached a low of 2.5% and rebounded to 3.5 % by 2012.

29. By 2002 the value of household investments in stocks and mutual finds declined by 4%.

30. The five major brokerage dealers became hedge funds and not investment bankers and the five-mega banks were in equity trading options and future trading.

31. There is no economies of scale in Banking above $50 billion.

32. 1999 repeal of Glass-Stegall by a Republican controlled Congress of both houses.

33. Bank lenders were the main source of mortgage funds until the 1980's when mortgage brokers went into commercial RE and junk bonds they knew nothing about.

34. G. H.W. Bush signed the Housing and Community Development act of 1992.

35. ACORN was wholly owned by Fannie Mae foundation.

36. Prior to August 1971, home mortgage finance was through local savings and loan banks.

37. Under G.W. Bush mortgage debt rose from $5 to 11 trillion, housing prices rose by 50% 2000-2003 and wages only rose by 6%.

38. Subprime loans accounted for nearly 25% of total mortgage lending. These loans grew from $60 billion to $400 billion in 2006. Second mortgages grew from $130 to 430 billion, from 2001 to 2006. 82% of these loans were bundled and sold off to capital markets and not retained on the original lenders.

39. Tax Reform Act of 1986 top income tax rate lowered to 28%.

40. 1997 capital gains rate raised to 20% while the ordinary tax rate was raised to 39%. Republicans with the K street lobbyists in 2001 lowered the capital gains tax to 15%. You want to get elected change the law.

41. Key Leverage Buyout firms- KKR, Blackstone, Apollo, and Bain Capital issued new debt to companies and none of the funds went to company operations or debt payment. A lot of these firms eventually filed for bankruptcy.

42. With the reduction of interest rates there was a $435 billion decline in personal interest income and business loans declined by 18%.

43. Following the great depression- agri, mining and manufacturing accounted for 70% of GDP. By 2008 it was reduced to 17% of GDP. Brazil, China and Australia became the world's new mining and mfg. economy that was the U.S. of the 1930's.

44. GM-had 47 plants and needed only 16 to produce its key brands of Chevy, Cadillac and GMAC trucks. They were losing money in their finance division. JP Morgan would have lost their $6 billion loan if GM declared bankruptcy. 40% of auto loans went to those who could not afford them and would default. GM's Delphi was a dumping ground for GM's debt.

45. 2000-2007 GDP grew by 40% through a total debt of $20 trillion not by rising productivity and earned income.
46. Debt to income was 105% in 1981 and 205% in 2007.
48. Sarbanes-Oxley accounting rules- criminal penalties for misrepresentation or willful negligence.

11. The Great Equalizer by David M. Smick

1. Central Banks slashed interest rates and flooded the economy with liquidity. The economy has still underperformed with greater debt mostly on the middle class and more profits for the big and corporate companies.
2. The Great Equalizer will be the mass of small business startups and innovations.
3. Women start firms at twice the rate of men based on a 2014 study.
4. China and emerging markets are bogged down with massive amounts of excess supply. With this prices fall and trade slows.
5. Total World debt as of 2015 was a staggering $180 trillion and rising.
6. Banks borrowed at window prices at next to nothing. They then purchased long-term higher-yielding debt on the open market making a guaranteed profit. At the same time, corporations with the low rates are taking on more debt.
7. The richest 1% in America received almost 60% of the growth in wealth between 2009 and 2014.
8. A January 2016 national survey showed that a third of young adults aged 20-39 are saddled with student loans.
9. At least 75% of large multinational corporation new jobs take place overseas.
10. President Reagan lowered the top individual tax rate from 70% to 28%. President Clinton raised the top rate on the affluent to 39.6% but cut the capital gains rate.
11. In 1983 Pres. Reagan and Democratic House Speaker Tip O'Neill compromised and saved the Social Security system.
12. On August 3, 1981 Pres. Reagan fired 11,345 members of the Air Traffic Controllers Organization (PATCO) when they tried to shut down the nation's airports with an illegal strike.

13. Stephen Hawking quote, "The greatest enemy of knowledge is not ignorance, and it is the illusion of knowledge".

14. 69% of owners of McDonald's franchises once flipped burgers in their youth.

15. The decline of IPO's is partly due to the legal and regulatory costs evolved in the wake of the Enron scandal with the 2002 Sarbanes-Oxley Act.

16. The bulk of new jobs is created by small businesses less than five years old that become publicly financed.

17. The U.S. financial sector is limited to total leverage of about 12 to 1. At the time of the financial collapse in 2007, Wall Street firm Bear Stearns was leveraged at 36 to 1 and Lehman Brothers was at 31 to 1.

18. 80% of today's IPO's are unprofitable. The only other time this occurred was in 1999 just before the dot-com stock market crash.

19. During President Obama's second term the unemployment rate was halved and the total non-farm payrolls jumped by 8.8 million.

20. A century ago half of Americans worked on farms. That figure now is about 1.4% employed in agricultural jobs due to technological advances. Could this happen to other sectors of industries as technology in the future?

21. In 2010, Google's Eric Schmidt estimated that "every two days we create as much information as we did (throughout history) up to 2003".

22. Larry Summers said, "It is difficult if not impossible to remain the world's greatest power while also the world's greatest borrower."

23. "What country today is the number-one per-capita consumer of YouTube on the planet Earth?" Saudi Arabia's women!!

24. Estimates suggest a loss of 7 million U.S. jobs in the next five years alone as a result of biotech, AL, robotics and other technology changes with the creation of only 2 million new jobs. Although maybe radical, in two decades from now, nearly half of the U.S. workforce could be replaced by machines.

25. Loss of jobs and increasing productivity could make it possible to see a 15-hour workweek envisaged by Keynes nearly a century ago.

26. Manipulation of patent law with legal maneuvers and lobbying pressure to extend patent's termination dates involve a cost to Americans of $360 billion a year. Corporate capitalists use government connections to produce monopolies.

27. The Twin Towers in New York City took three years to build starting in 1968. After 15 years, the World Trade Center in New York is still yet to be completed.

28. Since the 2008 financial crisis the U. S. banking system is now controlled by only a dozen giant zombie banks that control 80% of the investment capital. Before the crisis these banks controlled only 45-50% of such capital.

29. JPMorgan Chase, Bank of America, Citibank, and Wells Fargo control nearly 60% of all U.S. bank assets. All four have been fined for illegal banking practices.

30. The question is "how much government regulatory control of the private sector is enough and how much is counterproductive".

31. Projected U.S. public debt has grown to more than $19 trillion exceeding 100%. Only one other time in U.S. history that has occurred- during World War II. At that point and after the war, taxes were raised, military was reduced, and major infrastructure programs were initiated.

32. Major problem for the U.S. is the projection of unfunded liabilities for entitlements including Social Security, Medicare, and Medicaid.

33. In 1970 U.S. entitlement spending was 29% of federal budget outlays and in 2016 it was over 64%.

34. Corporate monopolies maintain high healthcare costs in medical insurance, hospitalization, and pharmaceuticals.

35. In 1950 the average female gave birth to five children. Today that number is 2.5. This birth rate reduction is leading to a growing population of older individuals.

36. Before the 2008 crisis the household debt to GDP was at 100%. By the end of 2013 it was about 80%.

37. In China the total debt has reached 237% of GDP. In 2007 the total debt was less than 150% of GDP. New debt is being used in large part to make payments on old debt. In 2009 their cost of debt service was 13% of GDP.

38. If the current trend of debt continues, the world's young people will have no future.

39. America needs to resume its global leadership role not as the world's police officer but as its symbol of values that provides stability under a new global economic and financial architecture.

40. The steel capacity in China exceeds by 5 fold that of the U. S. and Japan combined.

41. A stronger currency leads to: 1. Export decline due to lack of price competitiveness, 2. Domestic corporations move plants offshore- cheaper currency and lower labor costs.

42. Putin conducting a campaign to challenge the status of the dollar. He is getting reception from the Europeans and Chinese in the world economy as debt grows, growth slows.

43. Civilizations change along a boom-bust cycle of about 200-250 years. This is about the time span the United States has formally existed.

44. Americans with a college education have an unemployment rate half that of those with only a high school diploma. High-tech companies have thousands of high-paying unfilled jobs. In 2016 it was estimated that 48% of nearly half of small enterprises in America have job openings but no qualified applicants.

45. When the marginal income tax rate on individuals was 91%. That actually paid by the top tenth of 1% of income earners was between 26.9 and 29.5. This compares to the same group during the Reagan years that paid between 23.7 and 29.5%.

46. In the 19 century Britain was the world's dominant economic power. That changed after WWII with the U. S. taking their place as the world's economic power.

47. In 1340 England defaulted on its war debt, causing an enormous financial crisis. Then, beginning in the 1770, financial panics came at least once a decade.

48. America dependents on exports are around 12% of GDP. Other major countries are more dependent on exports to the extent of from 26% to 44% of their GDP. When the global trade collapsed after the 2008 financial crisis these economies took the largest hit.

49. Since the financial crisis foreigners have been buyers of everything American. Since 2008 foreigners have accumulated

roughly $23 trillion of U.S. financial assets. In the prior 20 years to 2008 they accumulated less than $14 trillion.

50. Shrinking labor force due to lower birth rate will make it difficult to support the older population and difficult to service the country's high debt. Some of this can be assisted by immigration of youth and a labor force. However, education must be increased as the technical world advances.

12. The New Confessions of an Economic Hit Man by John Perkins

1. My job was "to encourage world leaders to become part of a cast network that promotes US commercial interests" all this when leaders become ensnared in a web of debt that ensures their loyalty.

2. Corporatocracy- network of corporations, banks, colluding governments, and the rich and powerful people tied to them.

3. Don't play the game and you get overthrown or assassinated- Mossedegh of Iran, Arbenz of Guatemala, Allende of Chile, Lumumba of the Congo, and Diem of Vietnam.

4. IMF and World Bank loaned money to countries for projects on condition of using US engineering firms. Money loan to countries was returned to US companies to buy airplanes, medicines, tractors, computers, etc. The country was in debt with interest they could not pay.

5. The coordinating company was MAIN. They would make the deal with the country to borrow funds from IMF and World Bank, and the money would go to large US engineering companies as Bechtel, Halliburton, & Brown & Root. All this making sure the country went into bankruptcy and become beholden to their creditors for favors as with military bases, UN votes, oil, etc.

6. Downfall of Mossadegh in Iran: Kermit Roosevelt through payoffs and threats organized street riots and violent demonstrations, and pro-American Mohammad Reza Pahlavi a dictator replaced Mossadegh.

7. Empires of the past as Persia, Greece, Rome, the Christian Crusades, etc. all fell due to the wealthiest cultures. The countries

were plagued with highest rates of suicide, drug abuse, violence, and they tried to controls others with their power.

8. Panama was part of Colombia when in 1881 the French undertook to build the Panama Canal. This ended in disaster in 1889. In 1903 U.S. seized and they killed the militia commander and then declared Panama an independent nation. A treaty was signed with the French and no Panamanian sign the document.

9. Guatemala under the head Arbenz promised to help the poor. United Fruit did not like the arrangements and lobbied the US to depose him. In 1954 the CIA did just that and was replaced by Colonel Armas a right-wing dictator. Land reform was reversed, eliminated secret ballot, and abolished taxes on interest and dividend of foreign investors.

10. Who owns United Fruit? - Zapata Oil, George Bush's company and our UN ambassador.

11. After the Oct. 6, 1973, the Yom Kippur war, attack by Egypt and Syria on Israel, Israel tried to sink the US Liberty while they were monitoring Israel military communication during the war. The US air force stopped this attack which killed 30 US sailors on board the ship. Pres. Reagan did nothing to reprimand Israel. The oil Cartel then announced a 70% increase in posted price of oil due to U.S. involvement. The cartel cut back oil by 10%.

12. In 1819 Simon Bolivar was victorious over Spanish royalists and made Colombia independent.

13. The Public Utility Regulatory Policy Act was passed by Congress in 1978. Encouraged alternative fuels, all under President Carter's desire to reduce US dependence on oil.

14. The US launched an invasion of Panama in 1986 to get rid of Noriega.

15. Iraq controls much of the water resources in the area as the Euphrates rivers flow through Iraq. Who controls water controls all.

16. George Washington took his oath of office as the first president of the US at Federal Hall, 26 Wall Street on April 30 1789.

17. CIA supported coups-: Chile- put Gen Pinochet in power -1973-1990, Peru supported to depose Pres. Fujimori, then Guatemala-CIA mounted a coup overthrowing the democratically elected

governor in 1954, and Venezuela where the Bush Administration did everything to overthrow Chavez mostly due to oil.

18. Companies, for leverage, locate their production plants in one country, tax-sheltered banking is a second, phone call center is a third, and headquarters in a fourth.

19. Bosporus the waterway that allows transportation between the Mediterranean and the Black Sea also separates Asia from Europe, and was a key avenue of commerce for ancient Greece, Persia and Rome. Trade and heavy debt bound the countries.

20. Arms industry lobbies forced production of the F-35 fighter bomber, the most expensive weapon system in US history at a cost of $1.5 trillion and doesn't work.

21. Subsidies- fossil fuels industry received $550 billion and four times as much as given to renewable energy companies. Most large corporations receive subsidies including Ford Motor, GE, JP Morgan Chase, Lockheed Martin, etc. to the extent of $60 million or more each. Walmart workers are subsidized to about $6 billion a year in public nutrition, healthcare and housing assistance programs due to their pay scale.

22. Mercenary forces in 2012 by the US of about 110,000 in Afghanistan alone compared with 68,000 US military personnel. In comparison in Vietnam there were 70,000 mercenaries and 359,000 military forces. The number one mercenary firm is G4S that employs more than 620,000 people and earned more than $12 billion in 2012. Blackwater was renamed Academi due to the killing of Iraqi civilians.

23. A system based on fear and debt, history has shown that these empires never last. That was the demise of Soviet Union as the corporate barons maximized profits, manipulated legal systems, and corrupted politicians.

24. How do the World Bank, IMF, US, and China operate their debt? They do this by forcing countries voting in the UN, trading only in dollars, allowing military bases occupied by foreign troops, and free trade agreements all to control the countries and their resources.

25. Four pillars of modern empire: fear, debt, insufficiency, and divide and conquer mind set. Everything is justified- coups, assassinations, drone strikes, NSA eavesdropping.

26. Per the Dalai Lama- "You can pray for peace but if that is all you do it's a waste of time. You must act, every day."

27. You must follow your passions and use your talents in the most efficient, satisfying, and enjoyable way you can.- Join nonprofit, nongovernmental organizations, and consumer movements aimed at boycotting specific corporations.

13. Too Big To Fail by Andrew Sorkin

1. Galileo said: "All truths are easy to understand once they are discovered: the point is to discover them".

2. Bear Stearns was the weakest and most highly leveraged of the Big Five financial institutions and was the first to fall.

3. JP Morgan agreed to absorb Bear Stearns in March 17, 2008.

4. H. Paulson was CEO of Goldman Sachs.

5. New IRS rules allowed executives to enter Government and sell their investments without penalty. Paulson saved over $100 mil in taxes.

6. Roy Zuckerberg in 1998 retired from Goldman's executive committee.

7. Jamie Dimon of Goldman Sachs is a third generation banker.

8. Glass-Steagall Act of 1933 removed by a bill of Phil Gramm and Jim Leach.

9. Anna Schwartz wrote -A Monetary History of the United States, 1867-1960.

10. Under Herbert Hoover the Fed tightened the money supply and choked off the economy.

11. Illiquid investments for banks were valued at cost. Under FAS 157 it changed to mark to market. Up or down.

12. Merrill Lynch's balance sheet accounts were loaded with subprime loans and unable to get rid of about $ 27 billion.

13. CDO- Collateralized Debt Obligation- debt of various credit ratings and yields.

14. The CEO of AIG was fired and given a $1 million monthly consulting contract.

15. Newt Gingrich and Ralph Reed worked as consultants for Fannie or Freddie.

16. Bank holding companies have access to the Fed's discount window. The Federal Reserve regulates these companies.
17. John Paulson was the most successful hedge fund investor having shorted subprime's and making $15 billion and took home $3.7 billion.
18. Merrill Lynch's employees were paid an incentive compensation of $5.8 billion the year after their bailout/buyout by Bank of America.
19. 1989 the RTC created by Congress, loaned $400 billion to the failed 747 banks as part of the S & L Crisis.
20. Sept. 2008, TARP was announced.
21. About half of GE profits came from GE Capital.
22. Michele Davis was Paulson's communications chief.
23. Original vote for TARP in the Congress was rejected 228-205 with more than 2/3 Republican's voting against it as well as a large number of Democrats.
24. Pres. Bush signed TARP in 2008 with $700 billion.
25. Deregulation of banks in late 1990 was to push for increase home ownership with low interest rates that gave Wall Street compensation for short-term risk taking- the entire perfect storm.

14. What Should We Be Worried About?
by John Brockman

1. Increases in productivity waned, debt driven consumption became the tool of general in economic growth.
2. In 2008 we needed $4-5 dollars of debt for $1 of growth. China now needs $6-8 of credit to generate $1 of growth. Debt allows society to borrow from the future and it accelerates consumption.
3. 1972 had the highest number of youth on the planet. Ever since the average age on Earth has been increasing each year.
4. The super collider, the CERN, has turned up nothing after 30 years and $9 billion.
5. In 2007 MRSA deaths in the U.S. surpassed HIV deaths.
6. Some suggest that marriage reduces the likely incarceration of men by 50%. Unmarried men lower per-capita GDP. The problem is getting worse in China with the lack of females.

7. Cost of all autistic people in the US is $35 billion (one in 80 children has autism spectrum disorder), Schizophrenia -1% of the population with an annual cost of $33 billion. In relation, Annual cost of the Afghanistan war is about $100 Billion.
8. Firemen get calls to a fire only about 20% of the time. Other calls are for traffic accidents, medical emergencies, cats in trees, etc..

15. When Money Talks by Derek Cressman

1. 7 of 27 constitution amendments were overturned by previous Supreme Court rulings. That included women's and 18 year olds right to vote (26 amendment in 1971).
2. The Supreme Court regulates who is allowed to speak before their Court. Conditions are: Must be a lawyer, a member of the bar of the Supreme Court, and approved by the court. Regular citizens are forbidden to speak at a hearing.
3. A Brief in the Litigation from the 2010 oil spill in the Gulf of Mexico was submitted in the 35-page limit. However it was noticed that the spacing was reduced to get in more pages and had to be revised and if that was tried again the brief would be disallowed. If we can limit the voice of the corporation why can't we limit its spending?
4. In 1976, the Supreme Court took up Vermont's mandatory spending limits in elections and it rejected those limits.
5. 2007 the Court in FEC v. Wisconsin Right to Life in a 5-4 Roberts Court said that a no- profit Corporation could fund political attack ads as long as they could show it was not an effort to defeat that candidate.
6. The Citizens United Court overruled its previous ruling of McCain-Feingold and Austin v. Michigan Chamber of Commerce on money limits for elections and corporate treasury funds for political campaigns.
7. 1886 Santa Clara County v. Southern Pacific Railroad ruled that the 14th amendment protected the corporation as persons in so many words.
8. 1935 Supreme Court opposed enforcing any rules in the market place for child labor policies.

9. The 1935 Supreme Court struck down Pres. Roosevelt's National Industrial Recovery Act even though it passed through Congress. Pres. Roosevelt then packed the court by increasing the number of justices on the court noting that Congress has the authority to do this. The court then changed its decision on this case and it became known as "switch in time that saved nine."

10. Congress can remove a justice through impeachment. In 1969 Abe Fortas resigned to prevent being impeached as he received a speaking fee from American Univ. from sources that had business before the Supreme Court.

11. Clarence Thomas did not recuse himself from the Citizens United case even though his wife was involved and accepted money from organizations involved. These gifts and travel from a Dallas developer was not reported and Clarence Thomas even lied on a federal form that he signed under oath.

12. Article III, Section 2 of the Constitution says " the Supreme Court shall have appellate jurisdiction with such exceptions and under such regulations as the Congress shall make" Congress could then pass a law limiting money in politics with a provision excluding the Supreme Court jurisdiction to review it.

13. Article V of the Constitution provides that state legislatures may pass an amendment without relying on Congress if 2/3's of the states approved at a convention and Congress refuses to draft the amendment. Then ¾ of the states would need to ratify any proposed amendment.

14. Lord Acton's famous aphorism "All political money corrupts; unlimited political money corrupts absolutely".

15. It takes 67 votes in the US Senate to propose an amendment compared to only 60 votes to break a filibuster and pass legislation.

16. The 1976 Supreme Court ruling in Buckley v. Valeo was the first to equate money with speech and made worse in the 2010 decision in Citizens United ruling.

17. Citizens United overruled McCain-Feingold and Austin v. Michigan Chamber of Commerce that banned using corporate treasury funds for political campaigns. In 1886 Santa Clara County v. Southern Pacific Railroad ruled that corporations were a person under the 14 Amendment.

18. Citizens United did not create super PACs which started from Speech-Now Org v. FEC in 1974.
19. 1924 Supreme Court ruled restrictions of child labor
20. James Madison wrote the Bill of Rights as the first 10 amendments to the Constitution.
21. Hollings-Specter amendment- to give Congress power to set limits on contributions given to nominate a candidate.
22. In 1909 the Oregon legislature controlled by Republicans sent a Democrat to the US Senate as he received the most popular votes. The first law passed to have voters elect US Senators was in 1891 in California.
23. Roberts Court struck a blow to Voting Rights Act in Shelby County v. Holder in 2013 and in 2014 ruled for Hobby Lobby case that corporations could use a claim of religious freedom to evade the Affordable Care Act.

16. Why Economies Rise or Fall   by P. Rodriguez

1. Medium growth rate of the 150 developed countries is about 2%. We can then say that growth rate above 3% is fast and below is very slow.
2. Before the Industrial Revolution of the 17th-18th centuries almost 90% of the population was agriculture related.
3. The U.S. has been the largest economy since about 1870 beginning after the Civil War. In 1913-14 the government created a central bank, regulations, and national income tax to promote stability in the financial system.
4. 1913 to 1928 was one of the fastest growth periods and ended with the Great Depression in 1929 when 25% of the population was out of work.
5. Between 1950-73 Japan grew at the rate of 10% per year. The government subsidized the auto industry and structured favorable export policies. The people had a very high saving rate enabling investment in education and infrastructure while keeping the value of the yen low.
6. The Asian Tiger secret to economic growth is increasing average worker productivity, low wages, and political stability.

7. Lesson for a strong economy is competition through innovation, openness of trade, investment in education, research and development.

8. Gray market is prevalent in lower income economies and almost completely absent in rich or developed economies. However, they give up legal protection.

9. Per Adam Smith: Absolute advantage- over another in production of a product with the same resources. Specialization allows both to benefit from production of the same commodity.

10. Two factors that characterize successful economic growth- efficiency and productivity.

11. About 70% of all financial assets are held in the U. S. dollars.

BOOKS IN A NUT SHELL

KEY ISSUES

INDEX   PAGE

1. Al Gore the Future- Six Drivers of Global Change
By Al Gore

1. High frequency trading represents more than 60% of all trades.
2. Oil derivatives traded is 14 times the value of the barrel of oil traded.
3. Chinese Admiral Zheng: He pre date the discovery of America by Columbus- 1430-46.
4. Coal production increased by 133% as jobs decreased by 33%. 166 proposed coal power plants were cancelled.
5. Ipad has more power than the Cray 2 super computer of 30 years ago.
6. Average Congressmen spends 80% of their campaign money on 30- second advertising.
7, Utah has a $2 Billion NSA building.
8. Brittany woods- NATO/NATO/9.
9. Robber Baron era: 1889-1890's when price of votes was haggled over.
10. Supreme Court designated corporation as persons under the 14th amendment- Santa Clara County v. Southern Pacific RR.
11. Roosevelt prohibited the use of corporate funds directly or indirectly for political purposes.
12. U.S. population is about 26% Hispanics and 22% African Americans.
13. The elite can use money, power and mass persuasion to control policies of the United States per Lippmann's words "America is no longer a democracy.
14. China is consuming- half of the world's cement, iron ore, coal, pigs, steel, lead, and 40% of aluminum and copper.
15. Ground water aquifers are being depleted in China, India and Western U.S.
16. Most military weapons sold to countries around the world originate in the United States.
17. Estimated that the U.S. has spent $5.5 trillion on its nuclear war capability more than all programs except SS.
18. Inequity in the U.S. is larger than any time since 1929.

19. According to the UN the U.S. has the highest poverty rate, highest infant mortality rate, biggest prison population and highest homicide rate.

20. About 50% of retired Congressional personal become lobbyist. Expenditures by lobbyist increased from $100 million in 1975 to $43.5 billion in 2010.

21. U.S. produces 40% of world's corn and soybeans but 19% of the world's phosphorus.

22. Salt water comprises 97.5% of all water on earth.

23. China gets 70% of its energy from coal. Australia is the largest coal exporter in the world. About 1200 new coal power plants planned in 59 countries. 166 proposed plants have been cancelled in the US.

24. In 2011 the U.S. had over 8 disasters over $1billion.

25. Chinese individuals age 11 to 60 are required to plant 3 trees a year- now over 100 million trees have been planted.

2. Anti-Intellectualism in American Life
by Richard Hofstadter

1. The Eisenhower administration was the era of McCarthy rage.

2. 1957 Soviets launched Sputnik.

3. Scientists were saying that obsession with security was demoralizing to research due to the slackness of American education.

4. Regard for intellectuals in the U. S. is subject to cyclical fluctuations.

5. In elementary schools too much stress is directed to mere knowledges opposed to development of physical and emotional life and this threatens to produce social decadence.

6. Intelligence seeks to grasp, manipulate, re-order, and adjust while intellect examines, ponders, wonders theorizes, criticizes and imagines.

7. Presbyterians established the College of New Jersey, later the name was changed to Princeton in 1746.

8. Religious conquest of America was mainly from Methodists, Baptists, and the Presbyterians.

9. The Alien and Sedition Acts was passed by Congress in 1798 in preparation for an anticipated war with France.

10. 1824- 1828 contest between Andrew Jackson and John Q. Adams were of contrasting ideas. Jackson was against Intellectual men and Adams was for intellectual temperament for political leadership.

11. Some asserted that college background was of no use in practical politics.

12. President Wilson was elected in 1912 and was supported by intellectuals.

13. FDR chose college professors for his administration, away from Wall Street individuals.

14. At the end of 18th century 9 out of 10 were farmers, in 1820- 7 out of 10 were, and in 1880 it was 5 out of 10.

15. The 1887 Hatch Act created the system of federal experiment stations working in co-operation with agricultural colleges.

16. Grade schools were developed in the 1820's and prevalent by 1860.

17. Until 1830 most teachers were men with women dealing mainly with very small children and summer classes.

18. Women were paid about ½ of what men were paid. This led to using more woman than men. By 1870 woman constituted almost 60% of the teachers, by 1900 -70%, and now well over 80% in most schools and a higher percentage in elementary schools.

19. U.S. is the only country in the Westernized world that put elementary education almost exclusively in the hands of women.

3. Billions and Billions by Carl Sagan

1. The sun is 93 million miles from earth. Earth's age is 4.6 billion years.

2. U.S. defense budget about $700 billion.

3. Fan is a short for fanatic.

4. Music- middle C is 263 sound waves reaching us every second or 263 hertz. At sea level sound travels at 700 miles per hour. Octave above doubles the hertz value.

5. Different frequencies of sound perceived by us, as different musical tones and different frequencies of light, are perceived as

different colors. Every color has a frequency. On an object all colors are absorbed except what is reflected and that is the color we see as the object.

6. An astronomical unit is the distance of the earth from the Sun or 93 million miles. Jupiter is 5 astronomical units from the Sun.

7. Coal, oil, and gas are called fossil fuels because they are mostly made of the fossil remains of beings from long ago.

8. About 30% of U.S. oil imports come from Persian Gulf. Oil constitutes more than half of all US balance of payments deficits.

9. U.S. has 5% of world population and uses about 25% of the world's energy. Auto's responsible for 1/3 of the CO_2 production in the atmosphere.

10. President Carter put solar on the roof of the White House and President Reagan ripped it down. There was also a tax credit for solar power, which Reagan Administration eliminated.

11. American Civil War was about freedom extending the benefits of the American Revolution to make valid "Liberty and justice for all,"

12. In 1901 life expectancy in the US and West Europe was 45 years. Today it is approaching 80 years.

4. Fracking: The Outrageous Inside Story
by G. Zuskerman

1. U.S. Government in 1991 helped develop fracking and horizontal drilling techniques in the Barnett field in Texas.

2. A fracking mixture of water, sand, and chemicals is used by all companies.

3. Petroleum is derived from two Latin words- petra-rock and oleum-oil.

4. Currently in use are 3 dimensional seismic machines to locate oil.

5. In 2010 Range Resources discovered Marcellus Shale. Shared names of chemicals used in their fracking. Marcellus field goes from Pa. to NY.

6. Names in the early stage of fracking- Geo. Mitchell- Barnett Shale, Steinsberger, McClendon, Tom Ward, H. Hamm of Continental Resources and Chesapeake Inc.

7. At one time, Souki 's Cheniere Company built an LNG plant for imports but price of liquid gas (N2) went from $14 to $7 and now to $4. At this low price it appeared practical to only export LNG.

8. Bakken field in North Dakota took years to find the right method to frack and use horizontal drilling.

9. In July 2008 U.S. gas production was at 1.86 t cu. ft. highest since 1974. In July price was at $13.58.

10. Current oil import into the U.S. is about 40% and was 60%. Middle East supplies 8%, but most are from the Americas.

11. George Mitchell is considered the father of fracking shale. He had 3000 wells in 1974.

12. France and Bulgaria outlawed fracking.

13. Shale formations trap 10% of world's crude and 32% of the world's gas.

14. About 26% of US crude and natural gas are trapped in U.S. shale.

17. Interstate oil and gas commission granted FracFocus to share chemical data on fracking. Not all companies participated.

18. Monterey-Santos shale in Southern California holds 64% of U.S. total shale resources.

19. In the U.S. fracking counts for 45% (3.5 mil barrels per day) oil and 55% of natural gas.

20. Some countries and locations in the U.S. have been outlawed due to: water, noise, air, and seismic hazards. Fracking is banned in Santa Cruz County, Calif.

5. Outliers   by Malcom Gladwell

1. Outlier- noun- away from or classed differently from the main, observation different from the others in a sample.

2. Of best players, 40% are born between Jan and March, 30 % between April and June, 20% between July and Sept, and 10% between Oct and Dec.

3. Canadian eligibility for hockey players at 10 years olds starts on Jan 1. This is a big advantage from those born later in the New Year.

4. People at the very top work much, more than others.

5. The magic number seems to be 10,000 hours in a max of 10 years to be great at anything. Mozart didn't reach his greatness until he reached this 10,000th hour of practice. Practice isn't the thing you do once you're good. It's the thing you do that makes you good.

6. Being born in a particular decade is an advantage as opportunities are greater; jobs are more available, etc. The lower the birth rate in a given decade gives those individuals a greater opportunity to find work after college. The birth rate was lowest in the 1930's and after college there were numerous jobs.

7. To get a job students should be long on family connections, on ability, on personality or a combination of these.

8. Three things most people agree are the qualities one has to have for the work to be satisfying- autonomy, complexity and connection between effort and reward.

9. Laws were passed prohibiting miscegenation (marriage between different races), the last of which were not struck down by the US Supreme Court until 1967.

10. Sugar is an agro industrial complex. You have to have the factory right at the sugar plantation because sugar starts losing sucrose within hours of being picked.

6. Playing by the Edge by Mich Hayden

1. Espionage remains our first line of defense.

2. Harry Truman created NSA in secret in 1952.

3. Counterterrorist chiefs at NSA had three tasks: follow the money, follow the arms, and follow the people.

4. CIA had no pressure for a case for war with the White House's VP Cheney.

5. August 2, 1964, Gulf of Tonkin Resolution that launched a major U.S. escalation in Southeast Asia was flawed via false data about the attack on the U.S. destroyer Maddox in international water. The Maddox was supporting raids on the North Vietnamese coast.

6. Cyberspace, a man-made domain, is critical to all military operations. A Stuxnet attack was the American-Israeli cyber-attack on the Iranian nuclear facility at Natanz. This legitimized the Iranian response against Aramco and American banks.

7. In the U.S. spying is controlled by Title 50 of the U.S. Code and overseen by Congress while warfare falls under Title 10 of the Armed Services Committees.

8. NSA is limited to defending American information and stealing other peoples.

9. CIA, NSA, NRO, FBI, NGA, and DIA are government organizations for intelligence.

10. 2002 was the first time waterboarding was used.

11. In 2006 only about 5% of information came from detainees.

12. In 1950 the CIA was responsible for overthrowing the Mossadegh Regime in Iran.

13. We fight a ten year war while the middle easterners are prepared to battle for a hundred year's war.

14. Article 3 of the Constitution is vague in treatment of prisoners like prohibiting of humiliating and degrading treatment.

15. Thomas Edison once said, "Many of life's failures are people who did not realize how close they were to success when they gave up."

16, Pres. Bush launched the current metadata program in 2006 and PRISM effort in 2008.

17. You cannot have 100% security, and then have 100% privacy and zero inconvenience.

7. Sleeping with the Devil by Robert Baer

1. King Ibn Sa'ud (Aziz) united Saudi Arabia into a single kingdom in 1932.

2. Victor Bout, a former Russian military officer, supplied contraband to Osama bin Laden through Dubai where most of the funds for the 9/11 attacks came from.

3. The 15 Saudi hijackers of the 9/11 disaster were supplied with funds from al-Rajhi Banking & Investment Corporation. The visas of All 15 should have been turned down.

4. Between 1997-9 Qatar dumped $23 million to Washington lobbyist and law firms close to the White House.

5. In 1996 Saudi government declined Sudan's offer to turn over Bin Laden, as he was too popular in Saudi Arabia.

6. In Saudi Arabia most woman are kept in their home, 5% work and women cannot drive. When going out women have to be escorted by a make relative.

7. Past activities of Saudi individuals:
   a. Blew up a National Guard facility in 1995.
   b. Blew up the Khabar barracks in 1996.
   c. Behind the attack of the U.S. Cole ship.
   d. Hijacked a plane to Baghdad in 2000.

8. Saudi used off the books foreign aid via free oil in lieu of cash to the Taliban and Afghanistan.

9. Saudi Arabia keeps about $1 trillion on deposit in US banks in an agreement to offset the US deficit. They have another trillion in US stocks.

10. Most Saudi Princes, as Prince Bandar the ambassador to the US in 1983, got Congress to give his country AWAC radar systems over Israel's objection. He also gave money for the Iran Contra affair, the Bush Library, and to the University of Arkansas.

11. The Muslim Brotherhood was founded in 1928 by Hassan al-Bamma, an Egyptian, to purify Islam and rid Egypt of foreign influences.

12. In 1980 President Carter matched dollar for dollar with Saudi Arabia for the Afghan resistance of the soviet occupation.

13. U.S. military officers of all ranks felt that the US exaggerated the threat of Saddam Hussein but as an excuse to keep troops in Saudi Arabia and in other areas of the region.

14. Abdallah called the 1993 Oslo accords a lie. They were told that the Palestinians would get some sort of workable state in the West Bank and Gaza per Resolution 242. The Jewish settlers in the Jordan Valley consumed 75% of the water and Jewish settler population in the West Bank rose from 250,000 to 380,000.

15. In 1973 an Afghanistan military coup ended centuries of foreign and tribal rule. In 1978 Soviet leftists seized control of the government.

8. The Botany of Desire by Michael Pollan

This book is based on some history and facts of four plants, for their sweetness, beauty, intoxication or control. These plants are the apple, tulip, marijuana and potato.

Apples- fruit

1. Johnny Appleseed (John Chapman) planted apple orchards from western Penn. Through central Ohio and into Indiana.
2. Edible apple plants had to be grafted otherwise the apples were sour. Cider was the fate of most apples up until Prohibition.
3. The apple industry came up with the slogan "An apple a day keeps the doctor away." This was to keep the government from demanding that apple trees be cut down during Prohibition.
4. Seed facts: seeds contain cyanide, and each is genetically different from one another called heterogosithy.
5. Each apple has about 5 seeds.
6. They are said to have come from Kazakhstan.
7. Eating apples were the invention of grafting by the Chinese about 2000 BC.
8. Apples are the second most popular fruit after the banana.
9. Hard cider from apples is from their fermentation that converts the glucose to ethyl alcohol and carbon dioxide. Corn liquor was popular before the sweeter hard cider.
10 There about 2500 varieties of apples.

Tulips- flower

1. Honeybees favor radial symmetry to daisies and clover while bumblebees prefer the bilateral symmetry of orchids, peas and foxgloves.
2. The more perfect the symmetry of the flower the healthier and sweeter the flower.
3. Ogier Ghislain de Busgecq of Austria claimed to have introduced the tulip to Europe by sending a consignment of bulbs from Constantinople in 1554.
4. The word tulip comes from the Turkish word for "turban."
5. It takes 7 years for a tulip from a seed to flower and show its color.

6. The black tulip is called "Queen of the Night."
7. Each tulip has six petals in two tiers. The three inner petals are smaller and have a cleft top while the outer ones form uninterrupted ovals.
8. The tulip crash came in the winter of 1637.
9. Flora, the Roman goddess of flowers, was a prostitute famous for bankrupting her lovers.

Marijuana -drug
1. Compounds called flavonoids change the taste of plants on the tongues of certain animals.
2. Coffee was discovered by Abyssian herders in the 10th century observing that animals became frisky after nibbling on the shrub' berries.
3. Peruvian legend discovered quinine by observing sick cats were restored to health after eating the bark of the cinchona tree. Catnip contains a chemical called. "Nepetalactone."
4. Most marijuana smoked in the U.S. was grown in Mexico until the mid-1970's when the Mexican government at the request of the U.S. to spray the crop with the herbicide paraquat to help eliminate the crop. The product could easily be identified because it grew to 15 feet tall with purplish green leaves.
5. Search for a type that grew shorter was found in Afghanistan that rarely grew taller than 4-5 feet.
6. The earliest known religion was the cult of Samoa who ate the intoxicant of the Amanita Muscaria, a mushroom sometimes called "fly agaric".
7. Marijuana is known to alter parts of the brain as the cerebral cortex (inner thought), hippocampus (memory), basal ganglia (movement) and amygdale (emotions).
8. Nietzsche said "they are the power of forgetting" consist in a kind of radical editing or blocking out of consciousness everything that doesn't serve the present purpose.

Potato-vegetable
1. The New Leaf potato was genetically engineered by Monsanto Corp. It produces its own insecticide.

2. The Colorado potato beetle was the scourge of the plant and ages the leaves overnight.

3. Ireland in 1588 almost everything grew poorly. The potato seemed to be the best to grow and with milk was a complete nutritious diet because it provided protein, and vitamins B, C, & A.

4. In 1845 from America to Europe arrived spores of a potato fungus.

5. The potato famine was the worst catastrophe to befall Europe since the Black Death of 1348.

6. Ireland depended on only one kind of potato, the Lumper that was not resistant to a potato blight. When the blight started it destroyed all the potatoes in Ireland.

7. The Incas and other societies in South America grew multi crosses of potatoes so that no one blight could destroy the entire crop.

9. THE DIVIDE: American Injustice in the age of Wealth gap   by Matt Taibbi

1. 1947 UN designated ½ Palestine to Israel and the other to the Palestinian people.

2. Between 2000-2008- high fines with limited or no admission of responsibility and no criminal charges for large corporations, banks and financial institutions.

3. A Federal Crisis Inquiry Committee was formed in 2010 with $10 million budget. At the same time funding for social crimes as street crimes was increased to $15 Billion.

4. Small crimes treated differently than big crimes. Big companies as Wells Fargo, Goldman Sacks, Chase, UBS etc. pay fines for fraud from corporate funds and individual are not charged. Small crimes by individuals or small corporations doing the same on a much smaller scale pay fines and go to jail.

5. Lower regulations make this all possible. Dodd Frank bill attempted to close these loop holes. High money lobbies stop much of the regulation.

6. It was thought that the money paid from corporations was settlement without much work or satisfaction. Otherwise all

would be tied up in court for years fighting numerous high priced lawyers by appeals.

10. The Emperor of Scent by Chandler Burr

1. The book is the story of perfume. Luca Turin invented a way to image scent or smell through vibrations. His claim was that all smells had a range of vibrations that the smell could be determined. Efforts to probe this method was thwarted by all the large firms.
2. Smell is unlimited.
3. 1% of genes are devoted to olfactory receptors or sensors in the nose.
4. All molecules pulse with vibrations just like musical instruments and can be identified through a spectroscope.
5. There are 112 known types of atoms but only five are molecules of common smell ability- carbon, hydrogen, oxygen, nitrogen and sulfur.
6. Virtually all perfumes are manufactured by five companies- International Flavors & Fragrances, Givaudan Roure, Quest International, Firmenich Haarmann & Reiner, and Dragoco and Takasago.
7. Types of smells- Sweet, sour, salt, bitter, Umami (richness) and astringent. They are said to respond to 10 thousand smell molecules.
8. We cannot smell molecules over 10 angstroms wide.
9. Decay enhances smells and flavors. Beer smells like burp gases from the stomach, again a product of fermentation that is decay.
10. Chanel #5 was created in 1921 by Ernest Beaus. He used a molecule called an aldehyde that is carbon atoms- CE, C5, C6 doubled bonded to an oxygen atom.
11. Chocolate releases opiates (a sedative) in the brain.

11. The Right Path: from Ike to Reagan
by Joe Scarborough

1. Book outlines the rise and fall of the Republican Party.
2. Reagan won 49 states in 1984 then raised taxes and exploded federal deficit.
3. Archduke Franz Ferdinand assassinated in Sarajevo and ignited WWI.
4. August 6, 1965 voting Rights Act was passed into law.
5. Pres. Lyndon Johnson passed Medicare, Medicaid, Head Start, and the Civil rights Act of 1964.
6. Civil war ended in 1865. Democrats protected segregation.
7. Pres. Nixon created EPA & OSHA.
8. Under Pres. Reagan Kemp-Roth tax rate reduction bill of 1981 passed and reduced marginal income tax rates. Pres. Clinton raised tax rates and paid for it in later elections.
9. Pres. Reagan proposed a ban on assault weapons- they are 1% of guns but 10% were used in crimes.
10. Clinton's major accomplishments- balanced budget and welfare reform.
11. Pres. G. Bush increased domestic and military spending at record levels while passing a $7 trillion Medicare entitlement. Dick Chaney advised that "Deficits don't Matter."
12. Nancy Pelosi became the first female speaker of the House.

12. The Sixth Extinction   by Elizabeth Kolbert

1. There have been five great mass extinctions during the history of life on this planet. Most recent is the Cretaceous period when it wiped out the dinosaurs.
2. In the Anthropocene period everything alive today descended from an organism from the meteorite impact.
3. The Ordovician extinction was caused by glaciation.
4. Fuel combustion and deforestation causing 40% rise in CO_2 in the air over the last two centuries and methane has more than doubled.
5. Since the start of the Industrial Revolution we added 365 billion metric tons of CO_2 into the atmosphere, while deforestation

contributed another 180 billion tons and we add 9 billion tons each year or 6% annually. This will cause, by 2050, a temperature rise between 3.5 and 7 degrees.

6. The ocean covers about 70-75% of the earth's surface. Ocean acidification played a role in at least two of the five extinctions.

7. When CO2 dissolves in water it forms carbonic acid H2CO3.

8. Warming is occurring at 10 times greater than the end of all those glaciations.

9. Anthropods in the tropics is home to 30 million species. There are about 10,000 species of birds in the world and 55 hundred species of mammals.

10. Humans arrived in Europe about 40,000 years ago.

11. Animal population reduction has been caused by poaching, disease and habitat. Chimpanzees and gorillas population has dropped by half.

12. Neanderthal bones found in La Ferrassie, France.

13. The Unmooring of American Military Power
by Rachel Maddow

1. Government information facilities fill 22 U.S. Capitol Buildings powered up 24 hours per day and one million professional spies with a budget of $30 billion. All this with 1270 government agencies and 1931 private companies under government contract collecting the data.

2. The founding fathers feared that maintaining military would drain resources. That happened in the 18th century fighting the British military burdening the colonies.

3. Thomas Jefferson in 1792 said that one should never keep an unnecessary soldier.

4. After WWI Congress completely dismantled the forces reducing the military from 4 million to less that 300,000. After WWII forces were reduced from 12 million to about 1 ½ million, that is about an 88% reduction.

5. Post WWII GI Bill gave the military one year of wages, paid college tuition and a living stipend.

6. War Powers Resolution of 1973 required the President to petition Congress for the authority to go to war within 30 days. If

Congress did not grant approval the operation would have to end in 60 days.

7. President Reagan's quote on the Panama Canal, "We bought it, we paid for it, we built it and we intend to keep it."

8. President Reagan's strategy was to double the defense budget in five years and include the largest tax cuts in American history. Military expenditures doubled from $150 to $300 billion until it represented 30% of annual budget or 6% of GDP.

9. In the 1980's The U.S. embarked on a trillion dollar defense buildup. As a result the country neglected schools, roads, bridges and health care. From here the U.S. went from the greatest creditor nation to the greatest debtor nation.

10. In 1983 the US invaded the Caribbean Island of Grenada.

11. On October 23, 1983 a suicide attack occurred on the U.S. marine barracks in Beirut, Lebanon. A question might be why we were there in the first place.

12. Boland amendment- a legislative move to block the President from doing what he wanted to do by cutting off funding.

13. Under President Reagan the U.S. sold weapons to Iran in exchange for releasing hostages. The weapons went through Israel. This violated the Arms Export Control Act. Eventually we sold directly to Iran through a private party by the name of Richard Secord. The missiles were returned by Iran. President Reagan kept Congress out of the loop.

14. Contra arms were in part supplied by money from Saudi Arabia.

15. In Iran-Contra report written by Wyoming Rep. Dick Cheney maintained that the President had the authority to wage war any tine he wanted and a right to defy Congress. However, later under the Dellums v. Bush suit the judge's decision was that Article 1, Section 8, Clause 11, of the U.S. Constitution grants Congress the power to declare War.

16. Cost of toddler's to the families of U.S. military personnel was $6,200 per year for 575,000 pre-school children. Two thirds of military personnel had wives that worked outside the home.

17. A 1996 Task Force Defense Board recommended outsourcing and privatizing some military activities. The activities for-profit companies were for food service, garage collection and other

activities to military bases overseas. These companies included Boeing, GE, Westinghouse, Bear Stearns, Halliburton, and Military Personnel Resources Inc.

18. The largest contract went to Halliburton that VP Dick Cheney was a former CEO of. The contract stipulated that the Military couldn't oversee the company's operations.

19. The first Gulf War lasted 100 hours and all troops were home in 5 months or less.

20. The Military outsourced some info technology, data processing mapping, intelligence gathering, etc.

21. An outsourcing company, MPRI made up of retired military personnel was training ROTC programs in over 200 universities.

22. The number of military troops that legally could be employed was exceeded by private contractors. Our military budget was over half the military budgets of the combined budgets of all other major countries.

23. The U.S. military peacekeeping troops were in the Balkans for more than 8 years without the public being aware.

24. Private contractors accounted for about 25% of U.S. intelligence jobs.

25. Suicide rate among active duty servicemen doubled in the first five years of the Afghanistan war. We lost more soldiers to suicide than to enemy fire.

26. Famous words of Rumsfeld during the Bush Administration on the Iraq invasion war, "It could last six days, six weeks, I doubt six months."

27. In our counterterrorism efforts the U.S. in 2010 had over 3,000 government organizations and private companies in 10,000 separate locations.

28. In 2011 there were 45,000 U.S. troops and 65,000 private contractors in Iraq.

14. Unions for Beginners by David Cogswell

1. In 1955 union membership in public sector was 36.2%; in private sector it was 6.9%.

2. 2011 Republican congress tried to squash unions in public sector starting in Wisconsin- took away the right of public

employees to be represented by collective bargaining. Gov. Walker started to replace state workers with prison inmates.

3. Marginal tax rates- 1952-63 about 91%. 1964 lowered to 77, 1965-81 lowered to 70%, 1982-86 lowered to 50% and now at 35%. Long term capital gains went from 28% to 20% to 15%.

4. Unions helped via- wages, maternity leave, occupational health and safety regulations, Medicare, and the right to collective bargaining.

5. Unions created for the interest of group's relationship with wealthy industrialists. Conflict with corporation's mandates by law to maximize shareholders value via profit.

6. Karl Marx advised unregulated capitalism leads to overcapacity, under consumption and destructive financial crises fueled by credit bubbles.

7. Pres. Grover Cleveland said, "As we view achievements of aggregated capital, we discover trusts, monopolies while citizen's struggle."

8. Thomas Jefferson warned- banking and moneyed corporations would destroy freedoms won in the American Revolution.

9. Art of mass persuasion goes back as far as 500 B.C. in Greece where rulers maintained control of subjects by use of propaganda and has increased today via mass propaganda.

10. Edward Bernays founded the first PR firm in 1919 that led to the building of Route 66- his client Mack Trucks.

11. Emancipation Proclamation of 1863 under Abe Lincoln. Prior to that slavery was a part of American life.

12. First unions appeared in 1790's by craft journeymen and shoe makers in Philadelphia and printers in NYC.

13. In 1800, Jefferson initiated 24 years of Democratic-Republican rule when Federalists lost power in state and local governments which provided public education.

14. During the Civil War and by 1868, laws were passed to limit the workday to 8 hours. The success was via the new union development.

15. Europeon financial collapse of 1870's bled into the U.S.. Unemployment rose to 14% and salaries cut by 45 %- all known as the Panic of 1873.

16. Mother Jones in 1903 campaigned for child labor laws and co-founded Industrial Workers of the World in Chicago.

17. Debs founded American Railway Union that was the first industrial union in America.

18. Coal was discovered in the Colorado Rockies in the 1800's.

19. In 1932 Congress passed the Norris-LaGuardia act barring federal courts from issuing injunctions against nonviolent labor and recognized the rights of workers to join unions.

20. Reuther negotiated a merger of the CIO with the AFL under George Meany in 1955.

21. From 1969 to 1970 consumer and environmental organizations formed and got regulation on the National Environmental Protection Act and Clean Air Act banning cigarette commercials from radio and TV.

22. In 1971 there were 175 companies that registered lobbyists in Washington, in 1982 there were 2,500 and over 1200 PAC's.

23. Astroturfing- creating shell organizations that appear to be powered by grassroots support but only a front for corporate advocacy under false pretenses.

24. In 1907, Theo. Roosevelt called for campaign finance reform. Forty years later that labor unions were also banned from making political donations under the Taft Hartley Act of 1947. Unions developed the PAC to get around these restrictions.

25. In 1978 corporations, unions and wealthy individuals were given the right to donate money as long as it was not directly used to influence federal elections and became known as "soft money".

BOOKS IN A NUT SHELL

IMPORTANT TOPICS

INDEX

1. American Bitter Pill by Steven Brill

1. We spend $17 billion on artificial knees and hips
2. America's total healthcare bill for 2014 was $3 trillion. That is larger than the next ten biggest countries.
3. Advances have increased costs instead of lowering them
4. Healthcare employees are 1/6th of the work forces and the largest expense in the family.
5. Healthcare lobby spends 4 times the military.
6. 60% of the bankruptcies from medical bills.
7. Healthcare premiums for workers increased four times faster than wages.
8. US ranks 31st in life expectancy.
9. Blue Cross started in 1929 in Dallas Texas.
10. Healthcare costs about 20% was 6% in 1966.
11. T. Roosevelt in 1912 proposed national health insurance in his 3rd part ticket.
12. Government own insurance- single payer modeled after Europe.
13. Pres. Johnson established Medicare insurance for the over 65.
14. Pres. Nixon proposed to force employer to buy insurance for all workers. Include Subsidies for low income levels.
15. Lobbyists convinced Congress to prohibit Medicare from negotiating discounts with drug companies. This costs over $40 billion per year. All other countries as Canada enforce price controls on drugs.
16. U. S. doctors order 70 % more CTY scans than German doctors and the bill is 4 times as high. Estimate reform could save $70 billion per year.
17. No version of pending draft covered people here illegally.
18. Obamacare subsidies less generous than Romneycare plan
19. Baucus's Cadillac tax would yield over $30 billion per year.-tax on plastic surgery, high earners tax on capital gains and dividends.
20. Republicans in Congress defunded exchanges which helped to close some in the rural areas hospitals..
21. About 80% of those buying online in low to middle class families got ½ premiums paid for the Uncle Sam.

22. McKinsey & Company found drug prices in U. S. 50% higher than other developed countries.

23. In 2012 the U.S. spent about $280 billion on drugs.

24. Healthcare workers about 16% vs 10 % in France.

25. Drug companies in the US can advertise on TV but not in Canada or Europe. In 2013 Amgen spent $5 billion on advertising, $3 billion on new products and reported $6 billion income.

26. Hospital beds declined from 1 million to 800,000 and still are only 65% filled in 2014.

2. Antifragile Things that Gain from Disorder
by Nassim Nicholas Taleb

1. Steve Jobs- you have to work hard to get your thinking clean to make it simple

2. Antifragility more upside than downside.

3. T. E. Lawrence (Lawrence of Arabia) struck a deal with the Arab desert tribes to help the British against the Ottoman Empire. Britain and France later split the land among themselves breaking the agreement after the battle was won.

4. Brazil bankers are made liable for the extent of their own assets.

5. Do not ask what a person has but just ask what they have in their portfolio.

6. 80/20 principal by Vilfredo Pareto- 20% of the people owned 80% of the land.

7. Education and income- Korea had a lower literacy rate than Argentina and about 1/5 the income. Today Korea has three times as much. This also applies to Taiwan vs Philippines.

8. In 1863 only 20% of the people of France spoke French.

9. Fasting has a body healing power.

10. Medical errors are responsible for about 3 to 10 times the deaths of auto accidents.

11. The more one intervenes in other countries for the sake of stability, the more they become unstable.

12. Central spot of the Silk Road was Levant.

13. Half the sales and 90% of the profit goes to the top 0.1%.

14. Switzerland, perhaps the most successful country in history, has a very low level of university education compared to the rest of the rich nations. They have utilized apprenticeship models-vocational standards for employment.

15. Hydra Greek observed that small doses of poison stimulated the growth of yeast while larger doses killed.

3. Blind Descent   by James Tabor

1. Kitum, a deep cave in Uganda, is believed to be the birthplace of the ultra-germ Ebola virus.

2. First mechanical ascender to a major cave appeared in 1933.

3. In 1990 the Soviet Union broke up into 15 separate republics.

4. Kubera, near Sochi in past winter Olympics' Ukrainian, is the deepest known cave at 5,609 feet. This follows Krubera Cave in Abkhazia at 5,130 feet. Another deep cave is in Zagreb, Yugoslavia.

5. Some key Explorers- Perry at the North Pole, Amundsen at the South Pole, Hillary and Norgay on Mt. Everest, and Picard and Walsh in the space shuttle Challenger Deep.

6. A deep Mexican super cave is at Cheve and is about ½ mile deep and three miles from the entrance. In 1994 the Huautla cave expedition in Oaxaca, Mexico determined it was 4.300 feet deep and four miles from the cave entrance.

4. Consider the Fork: by Bee Wilson

1. The word technology comes from Greek – Techne means art or skill and logia means study something.

2. Soft food tends to make you gain fat. Fibrous food has to do more work and energy in the body.

3. What has lips, mouths, necks, shoulders, bellies and bottoms- POTS. Pots became common about 10,000 BC in S. America and N. Africa.

4. Earliest recipes came from Mesopotamia (Iraq, Iran, and Syria) on three stone tablets about 4000 years ago.

5. First non-stick pans in France by Tefal Company in 1956. M. Gregoire, a French Engineer, developed PTFE.
6. First fires- striking pyrite rock against flint.
7. Thomas Edison first created a successful light bulb in 1897.
8. In 1795 France decreed a law to use liters, grams, meter (metric system).
9. Only three countries have not adopted the metric system- the United States, Liberia and Myanmar.
10. Cuisinart was launched in the U.S. 1973.
11. Mayonnaise- egg, tablespoon of vinegar, two tsp of mustard, and salt and pepper. Put in bowl and whisk.
12. Why did Italy adopt the fork?- pasta.
13. Chopsticks- Japanese are shorter at 22cm vs. Chinese at 26cm and have pointed ends.
14. Clarence Birdseye created the modern frozen food industry in the 1920's.
15. In 1930 50% of women were in paid work. In1950 it dropped to 34% and in 2000 it was 60 %.
16. Ergonomics- study of equipment that fits the limitations and abilities of the human body.

5. Enough by John Bogle

1. To be strong in will, to strive, to seek, to find and not to yield, is what this whole life is about.
2. The great game of life is not about money; it is about doing your best to join the battle, to build our communities, our nation, our world and ourselves.
3. The U.S. with 4% of the world's population produce 21% of the worlds output, consume 5% of it and earn 26% of the world's income.
4. It is not money that determines our happiness but the presence of some combination of three attributes: autonomy, maintaining connections with other human beings, and exercising competence using our God given self-motivated talents, inspired, and striving to learn.

5. Albert Schweitzer got it exactly right "Success is not the key to happiness. Happiness is the key to success."
6. Rene Descartes reminded us four full centuries ago that "A man is incapable of comprehending any argument that interferes with his revenue."
7. Profit motive is hardly the only motive that lies behind the labors of American business leaders. Other motives include the love of power, prestige, altruism, pugnacity patriotism, and hope of being remembered through a product of institution.
8. Nothing in the world can take the place of persistence. Talent will not educate, education will not persist and determination alone is the omnipotent.

6. Everything a New Elementary School Teacher needs to know   by Otis Kriegel

1. Make sure you are able to view everyone from anywhere in the classroom.
2. Once desks are set pull out chairs and walk through the room.
3. Keep towels or newsprint to put on the floor to mop up anything that might occur in the room as water, etc.
4. Have well written lesson plan for a substitute teacher including activities.
5. Have a separate school e-mail for parents- never give them your personal phone number or personal e-mail.
6. Scaffolding- providing sequential support to facilitate a student's development- helps students build up a new skill.

7. FABRICATED- The New World of 3D Printing- by Lipson & Kurman

1. 3D printers make things by following instructions from a computer and stacking raw material into layers.
2. In 1986 Carl Deckard and Joe Beaman invented the first Selective Laser sintering printer.
3. The technical name for 3D printing is "additive manufacturing"

4. Voxels are 3D pixels

5. 3D printing shortens the time from design to the end product creating on the spot product prototypes quickly and cheaply.

6. Used in auto industry to save time from concept to design to sample.

7. 40% of the world's 3D printers are in the United States.

8. Half of U.S. firms employ fewer than 10 employees and 25% fewer than 5 employees.

9. 3D Systems is the largest and oldest company that sells 3D printers, the IBM of the 3D industry. They have purchased roughly 24 companies in the past 3 years.

10. Estimated 60% of the world population owns a cell phone.

11. Industry leading companies- 3D System, MakerBot and PP3DP. They are investing heavily to create consumer friendly platforms and products.

12. A major family of 3D printers uses selective binding process to fuse and bind raw material into layers.

13. The word bionic is derived from two Greek words- bios- living and onic from electronic.

14. There are apx. 210 cell types found in the human body. The first was identified in the 1980's.

15. The average human heart beats nearly 100,000 times per day.

16. Heart valves- mechanical or harvested from a cow or a pig are cleaned and cured liked a soft piece of leather.

17. Ultrasound- sound waves, MRI- magnetic protons in the bodies water molecules, and PET- position emission tomography all detects gamma rays from radioactive material in the body.

18. Printer color ink – cyan, magenta and yellow.

19. 80% of animal species walk on six legs

20. 3D manufacturing disruption- shape optimized, ready to print inventory files, and need to produces locally.

22. Trademark if not used in five years is considered abandoned. Objects that do things can't be protected by copyright. You must ask alleged infringer before filing a copyright lawsuit. Patent comes from the Latin work patere- to lay open

23. Biological life is composed of 22 building blocks- amino acids.

8. How Eskimos keep their babies warm
by Mei-ling Hopgood

1. Disposable diapers are a $27 billion dollar business as of 2012. Companies involved are P & G, Kimberly-Clark and J & J. Earliest versions emerged in the 1940's in Japan and Sweden. The waterproof diaper was invented in 1946 years later in 1970's the disposables sales took off.

2. The common American advise was that the child should be trained no earlier than eighteen months and more likely between two and four years of age or older.

3. The pygmy men of the African Aka Tribe, on the border of Congo and Central African Republic might be considered the Best Father in the World. While the women hunt, the men look after the babies and even let them suck their nipples (no pacifier's their).

4. Sweden was the first in 1993 to introduce paternal leave requiring 13 months (now at two months) of paid leave for the fathers,

5. Buddhists believes that everything in the universe is composed of five elements: earth, wind, fire, water, and space.

6. When the Dalai Lama was in exile the government resided in Dharamshala, India across the Himalayas from China.

7. The United States is ranked 47th in infant mortality rate at 6.06 per 1,000 births.

8. A good emotional and mental health can improve the conditions for conception pregnancy studies show.

9. In Sweden 99% of parents receive prenatal and postnatal care, all taxpayer-subsidized.

10. U.S. students on doing something bad said that the main reason not to do it was that they might get caught and punished. While Japanese students said the main reason not to do something bad was it would hurt other children or cause them to feel shame or guilt.

11. Marble toys date back to the Harappan civilization in western part of South Asia around 2500 BCE. They were made out of stone. In Ancient Greece and Rome children played games with round nuts.

12. Statistics show that Asians do better in school with an average SAT score for Asians in America in 2009 at 1623 while Caucasians

average was 1581. Asians make up 5% of the US population and constitute 15-20 % of graduates from Ivy League schools.

13. After testing ½ million fifteen-year old students in 2009 in 70 countries the US ranked 17th overall for reading, 23rd in science and 31st in mathematics. Graduation rate was third from the bottom just above Mexico and Turkey.

14. Tendency for aspirations in academics rubs off on immigrant families and declines in the third generation.

9. How I killed Pluto by Mike Brown

1. Kuiper belt was first seen in the summer 1992.
2. Pluto was located in Feb. 18, 1930's by Clyde Tombaugh by comparing pictures of the sky on various nights.
3. Greek meaning of the word "planet" is "wanderer" or something that moves in the sky.
4. Original seven planets named after the days of the week- Sun (day), Satur (day) and named after ancient Germanic and Roman, Norse gods.
5. Uranium named after the planet Uranus. Its moons are named after Shakespearean characters.
6. The term asteroid was named after the Greek word for star or "aster".
7. All planets except Pluto orbit the Sun in a flat disc. Pluto has a tilted disc of about 20 degrees.
8. The word comet comes from the Latin word coma meaning "hair" or fuzzy appearance in the sky with a tail.
9. Plutonium was named after the 9th planet Pluto.
10. One of the largest telescopes is in Hawaii on the summit of Mauna Kea volcano at 14,000 feet above sea level.
11. The 10th planet, Xena is in the constellation Cetus, the whale.
12. Continent is any island on its own continental plate. Greenland is on the North American plate. The Seven continents were assigned by tradition.

13. IAU decree- moons of Jupiter named after consorts of Zeus, craters on Mercury named after poets and artists, and features on Saturn are named after mythological places in literature.
14. IAU decided Pluto, Xena, Charon, and Ceres will be called dwarf planets.
15. Gravity pulls big space objects into the shape of a sphere.
16. Planets were named after major Greek and Roman gods and goddesses, etc.
17. Xena, the 10th dwarf planet was renamed "Eris" after the Greek goddess of discord and strife.

10. How Plants Work by Linda C-Scott

1. Tannins were named for early use in tanning leather. In wine or green bananas a dry mouth taste binds your salivary proteins.
2. Flower colors- birds see best in red, bees in blue and are signs of pollination guides.
3. Vitamin B1 stimulates new root development and reduces shock. However, plants make their own B1 so adding it does nothing.
4. Gibberellins regulate plant height and development.
5. To ripen green tomatoes put them in a bag with a ripe banana. The ethylene released from the banana will transform the rock hard tomatoes into a soft and juicy one.
6. Overwatered plants tend to turn the lower leaves yellow due to release of ethylene from stressed soaked roots.
7. The tree green cambium under the bark is the growth factor to elongate the tree.
8. Mycologists is the study of fungi. Endo means inside and ecto means outside when used with words. The roots of fungi limits disease and root pests.
9. Soil sulfur deficiency causes yellowing in plants. Phosphorus is needed for constructing membrane and is almost always in the soil.
10. Gypsum is calcium sulfate an inorganic fertilizer. Don't add nutrient to soil without knowing if it needs it as it could have a negative effect on plants.

11. Hydrangea colors of blue and pink is partially due to aluminum content.

12. Never add phosphate fertilizer to bulbs, groundcovers, perennials shrubs or trees unless testing shows it's needed.

13. Green chlorophylls and orange carotenoids trap photosynthesis. The color you see is the wavelength light that is not absorbed by the object.

14. Plants use the sun's energy to transform carbon dioxide and water into sugar and oxygen- That is photosynthesis. $6CO_2+6H_2O=C_6H_{12}O_6$ (SUGAR) $+6O_2$

15. Water moves to where water isn't. Red leaves have anthocyanins in cellular water and means less water than green leaves. Harder for water to evaporate from red tissues.

16. Browning on the tips and edges of leave is an indicator of drought stress.

17. Plants close due to phenomenon called nyctinasty from the Greek words for night and pressing close. Plants measure time to close at night and open during the day by the light and the color reflections.

18. Some plants as rhododendron leaves are thermonastic. When temperature falls to freezing thy droop and curl to save heat. They open when the temperature increases.

19. Tropic from the Greek word to turn. Plants and trees follow the sun.

20. Heliotropic means follow the sun as sunflowers whereas paraheliotropic avoid the sun by keep their leaves parallel to the incoming sunlight.

21. Ausins cause the shadiest side of plants to grow the fastest. This causes trees to bend away from the shade and most leaves will be found on the least shaded side of the plant.

11. INDELIBLE INK: Birth of America's Free Press

1. Pres. Roosevelt said "Essential human freedoms are speech, expression, worship, want and fear."

2. U. S. was the first nation to monumentalize liberty of speech and the press as a fundamental right of its people.

3. The first slander laws took effect in 1275 under the reign of Edward I.

4. Under James I to defame another's reputation would be punishable by fine, imprisonment or the amputation of the ears. Libeling robs a man of his good name.

5, Reporters Without borders rated U.S. 46th out of 180 nations for the erosion of press freedom. This was due to the aggressive prosecution of whistleblowers with pressure on reporters to disclose courses of information in the public interest but embarrassing to government officials.

6. In the 16th century England secular and religious officials were fearful of the printed material as a goad to social unrest. Press control began in 1529 with Henry VIII's issuing a list of 100 banned books.

7. In 1610 Henry Hudson sailing under the Dutch flag named the new land New Netherlands (now New York). He traveled 150 miles north up this river (Now the Hudson River) to a tributary now the Mohawk River.

8. After the English Civil War of 1650 with the military dictatorship under the Stuart dynasty speech and writing was curbed.

9. The new Stuart dynasty in Britain moved in 1664 to displace the Dutch presence through a bloodless conquest. It was not a crown colony but a proprietorship named after the Charles II brother Janes the Duke of York, now New York. .It reverted to a royal holding in 1685

10. The Dutch recaptured New York but in 1664 the British naval forces recaptured the area and the territory was presented by King Charles to his brother James the duke of York.

11. Martin Luther's iconoclastic postings in 1517 lead to the Protestant Reformation.

12. In 1719 every governor was told that a license was needed to print matter as books, pamphlets, etc.

13. A local law imposed a 6% ceiling on loans to stamp out usury and doing business became easier in New York.

14. Progress was made via trade based revenues and not from higher taxes on big landowners.

15. The Indian Trade Act of 1720 law was easily circumvented by smugglers. This law set who could sell to the Indians and what they could sell to them.

16. Molasses Act- Would impose a duty on colonists for buying molasses and sugar imported from non- British territories as the French West Indies. Thus giving the British colonial planters a pricing advantage.

17. In 1722 Albany was the second largest settlement in the New York colony.

18. A commission in1725 was formed to relocate the boundary of New York and Connecticut agreeable to the then Governor Burnet.

19. Ever since Britain had established a colonial presence in America, the crown had assigned the power to grant land titles to either royal governors it appointed or to proprietors it gifted outright like William Penn.

20. Under question was "could a citizen be convicted to question or criticize in any way truthfully or falsely or by distortion the government's conduct."

21. The British Stamp Act in 1765 a revenue measure, had a serious impact on colonial America and a threat to printers' livelihoods.

22. In September 1776 the British troops seized New York City from George Washington who hastily retreated his little army.

23. From the court cases against Zenger and his Journal helped to implant in the Public mind that open protest against an imposed and arguable unjust government was both a social necessity and a civil right.

24. The first amendment to the Bill of Rights stated "Congress shall make no laws abridging the freedom of speech or of the press or the right to peaceably assemble."

25. Pres. John Adams tried to pass the Alien and Sedition Act of 1798 which held it a crime to publish "false, scandalous and malicious writing" against the government and its chief.

26. In the Branzburg v. Hayes the Supreme Court decision in 1972 denied reporters no more rights than any other citizen to withhold information sought by prosecutors. But it allowed the states and Congress to pass "shield" laws granting reporters the privilege of not having to disclose confidential sources. Only Wyoming did not pass the shield law.

12. Industries of the Future by Alex Ross

1. The world changes by technology, automation, and globalization.

2. Next change will challenge middle classes and possibly return many to poverty.

3. China's poverty was reduced from 84% to 13% in the last 20 years.

4. Key industries of the future- robotics, advanced life sciences, codification of money, cybersecurity, and big data.

5. We went from land-agriculture, to iron-industrial age, to the current data of the information age.

6. Japan allows only 50,000 work visas annually. They lead the world in robotics.

7. Americans drive apx.3 trillion miles per year and 30,000 die on the road.

8. Hajime restaurant in Bangkok uses robot waiters to take orders.

9. In 1950, 13% of China's population lived in cities. Today about ½ live in cities and they expect 70% to live in cities by 2025.

10. Vogelstein's liquid biopsy can detect tumors much smaller than MRI for finding cancer.

11. The body has: 78 organs, 206 bones, 640 muscles, and about 25,000 genes.

12. In 2002 only 3% Africans used mobile phones, today it is over 80%. About ½ of the $40 billion transferred in Africa is via mobile payments.

13. Bitcoin- Oct. 31, 2008 author identified as Satoshi Nakamoto.

14. Cost of cyber-attacks is over $400 billion a year over the GDP of about 160 of the 196 countries in the world.
15. N. Korea's internet connectivity is supplied by one Chinese company- China Unicom.
16. GDP of the world is about $100 trillion.
17. Cyber security market at $64 billion in 2011 and projected to be $120 billion in 2017.
18. By 2013 companies lobbying Congress on cybersecurity is 1500.
19. 90% of world's digital data has been generated in the last two years. Each year it grows by 50%.
20. Zettabytes is 1 trillion gigabytes.
21. 70% of freshwater is used towards agriculture.
22. Nitrogen from fertilizer has fouled water and creates dead zones in the water. These dead zones kill fish and crabs.
23. Every school in Estonia was online by 1998 just 4 years after the birth of the internet. They have the world's fastest internet speeds and universal medical health records that are not yet in the U.S..
24. India has 29 states.
25. By 1914 Argentina ranked among the 10 richest countries in the world ahead of Germany and France.
26. It is estimated that Saudi Arabia will not be able to export oil in 15 years.
27. Agriculture provides 85% of exports and employs 80% of the work force in Tanzania, East Africa
28. Multicultural fluency is becoming more important in the business world.

13. Ninety Percent of Everything by Rose George

1. There are 360 commercial ports in the U.S. that takes in international goods.
2. There are more than one hundred thousand ships at sea that carry all the solids, liquids and gases that we need to live.
3. Between 1972 and 1981 there were 223 oil spills.

4. There are fewer than 100 U.S. flagged ships. Only 1% of trade at US ports travels on an American flagged ship and the U.S. fleet has declined by 82% since 1951.

5. There are three words for going backward on a ship- stern, making sternway, and aft.

6. Malcom McLean invented the cargo containers and at least 20 million containers cross the world each day.

7. Before containers, transport costs ate up to 25% of the value of the item being shipped. Now it is in pennies.

8. Only 1-5 % of containers in Europe are inspected. U.S. ports receive 17 million containers and inspect about 5%.

9. More than two container ships are lost at sea each week.

10. In LA half of all smog from sulfur dioxide comes from ships.

11. Suez Canal takes 14 hours to transit. Pharaoh Senusert III chopped through a path in 1874 BC.

12. European Union calculates that 2,000 containers are lost at sea each year with 15% coming to land and 15% are floating at sea.

13. Whales have been devastated by shipping lanes due to sound which is in their spectrum.

14. The 1904 Military Cargo Preference Act requires that 100% of items owned procured or used by military or defense agencies to be carried on U.S. flagged vessels.

14. Prison Industrial Complex for Beginners
by James Peterson

1. The US incarcerates more people than any other nation in the world.

2. Incarceration rates- most developed nations have about 100 prisoners per 100,000 people but in the US it is 690 as of 2014, and comes to more than 2.2 million. This includes about 2200 serving less than one year and those in local jails.

3. The U.S. doesn't lead the world in quality of public education, access to health care, or life expectancy.

4. Poor men and women do not aspire to go to prison but they lack viable job opportunities and are assigned to underfunded and physically decrepit schools.

5. Blacks are 6X more likely to be incarcerated than whites and make up 13% of US population and 40% of the nation's prisoners.

6. Auburn prison model along with Sing Sing allowed congregation and did not isolate all prisoners.

7. The U.S. has remained a global leader in building of prisons for nearly 200 years.

8. Both the MIC (Military Industrial Complex) and the PIC creates economic opportunity for employment. In the 1990's PIC employed more than 500,000.

9. We spend over $100 billion each year on law enforcement, $80 billion on incarceration and $65 billion on private security.

10. U.S. accounts for 5% of the world's population and 25% of the world's prison population and as of 2006 the PIC incarcerated some 2.5 million people.

11."School-to-prison pipeline"- correlations between erosion of the nation's public education system and the growth of the PIC. Over 100 public schools closed in major cities impacting between 82 - 94% of low-income students.

12. It cost apx. $11,000 a year to educate a young person in the U.S. and about $90,000 to house one in the PIC. From 1990's to the mid-2010's PIC funding increased 530% more than education funding.

13. Anti-black racism in the U.S. is shown by the decisions of Brown v. Board of Education 1954, Civil Rights Act of 1964 and the Voting Rights Acts of 1965.

14. In 1968, 72% of Americans said the goal of the prison should be rehabilitation.

15. The ineffective war on Drugs has led to increased incarceration. Opium was popular during the Civil War era and by the late 19th century- cocaine and coca were popular.

16. Today over 90% of criminal cases in the US do not go to trial but are plea bargained for a shorter sentence.

17. Under Pres. Reagan's War on Drugs nonviolent law offenses increased from 50,000 in 1980 to 400,000 by 1997.

18. With the advent of the Asset Forfeiture laws financial incentive emerged for aggressive law enforcement. The take was about $15 billion to which they upgraded their operations and equipment.
19. President Obama became the first president to visit a prison in 2015 and stated the country could use this money of $80 billion for education.
20. The PIC is no longer invested in rehabilitation but Recidivism- rate at which released prisoners return to prison says a 2014 study conducted by the US Dept. of Justice – 2/3 released from US prisons in 2005 were rearrested within 3 years and ¾ within five years.
21. In 2008 Congress passed the Second Chance Act (SCA) to reduce recidivism and signed by President GFW Bush on April 2008.
22. The war on drugs is a war on poor people of mostly color protecting the wealthy and is an abject failure.

15. Spam Nation by Brian Kerbs

1. Email spam includes kidnapping, bribery, extortion, blackmail and corruption all are cybercrime.
2. Most spam includes pharma and porn. All big business.
3. 70% of transactions of rogue pharma websites of Spamit and Rx-Promotion are for drugs as Viagra and Cialis. Both offering cheap drugs.
4. Antis- underground derisive term for antispam vigilantes who act to take down large scale junk email operations.
5. The Russian Federal Security Service (FSB) is the conversion from the KGB
6. Most of the heavy spam was coming from Russia.

16. The 7 habits of Highly Effective People
by Stephen Covey

1. Goals- builds on a strong core of principles.
2. Leadership is communicating others worth and potential.
3. Apply what you learn- to learn and not to do is really not to learn- to know and not to do is really not to know.

146

4. We are what we repeatedly do. Excellence then is not an act but a habit.
5. Proactive people are driven by values- carefully thought about, selected, and internalized values. Reactive people are driven by feelings, circumstance, conditions and environment.
6. It is not what happens to us but our response to what happens to us that hurts us.
7. To make things happen use your R & I (resourcefulness and initiative).
8. Management is doing things right. Leadership is doing the right things.
9. Affirmation statement- personal, positive, present tense, visual and emotional.
10. Top performers are visualizers- experience before you do.
11. An effective goal focuses primarily on results rather than activity.

17. The Grand Design by S. Hawking

1. Crater Lake, Oregon- about 5600 BC Mount Mazama volcano erupted.
2. Homo sapiens originated B.C.
3. Height of early civilization about 500 BC according to Aristotle- 350 BC.
4. The number of vibrations per sec under fixed tension is inversely proportional to the length of the string.
5. In 250 BC Aristarchus was the first to argue that the earth is not the center of our planetary system but the much larger sun.
6. Catholic Church adopted Ptolemy's theory that the earth was the center of the universe in about 100 AD until 1543 when Copernicus proved otherwise.
7. Electron discovered in 1897 by British physicist J. Thomson.
8. Aristotle's theory that the world was made of four elements- earth, air, fire and water.
9. Quantum physics provides that nature operates on atomic and subatomic scales.

10. Earth's orbit has an eccentricity of about 2%. This causes our seasonal patterns along with the tilt of the earth. During the winter the North Pole is tilted away from the sun.

18. The little book of Talent by D. Coyle

1. SAP- each day pick one item to perfect.
2. Your brain works just like your muscles – "No pain, no gain."
3. Music educator Suzuki- practice on the days that you eat.
4. Practice in short segments or small parts of a composition.
5. Think like a gardener and work like a carpenter.

19. THE QUEST: Energy, Security by Daniel Yergin

1. Persian Gulf supplies 40 % of world oil market.
2. Developed world averages 14 barrels per person (bpp) per year and in the Developing world it is only 3 bpp.
3. Sept 1993, Arafat and Rabin signed the Oslo Accords.
4. Jan. 1, 1992, Russia was an independent state, traversing 11 time zones. In mid-1990" oil was 2/3 of their hard currency earnings.
5. 1917 Bolshevik Revolution closed off the Soviet Union with little oil flow. In the Caspian coastline, Baku was the most important city due to oil exports.
6. Ludwig Nobel was known as the Russian Rockefeller and his brother Alfred invented dynamite and the endower of the Nobel Prizes.
7. Constantinople in 1930 was renamed Istanbul.
8. Most famous antitrust case was the John D. Rockefeller's Standard Oil Trust.
9. Iraq- ¾ of its GDP was from oil before the war and 95% of revenues.
10. Cushing, Oklahoma is the gathering point for sweet crude oil known as West Texas Intermediate or WTI. In 1912 produced 20% of U.S. oil. In March 1983 futures started on WTI.
11. China imports about ½ its oil and is the second largest oil consumer. 75% of China's oil imports go through the Malacca Strait.

They depend on coal for 70% for its energy- 80% for electricity. Since they added more oil production and hydropower they are now about 80% self-sufficient.

12. The U.S. oil accounts for 40% of energy consumption. In China oil is only 20% while 22 % is from hydropower and 11 % from wind. Nat. Gas is about 2%

13. U.S. and China each import about ½ their oil requirements and account for about 35% of world consumption.

14. Oil industry was born in Titusville, Pa. discovered by Edwin Drake in 1859.

15. Today about 30% of oil is produced offshore. In 2010 was the first year in the U.S. that oil production increased since 1991. In 2011 the U.S. was 78% self- sufficient and imports declined by 50%

.16. Oil sands are primarily in Alberta, Canada. Composed of viscous bitumen embedded in sand and clay to form heavy oil.

17. European revolutions of 1848 were linked to frustrated and educated young people.

18. Off the shore of Qatar with independence from Britain in 1971 was North Dome the largest natural gas field in the world. Qatar has the highest per capita gross domestic products in the world and a main commercial hub in the Persian Gulf.

19. Fracturing or the original word fracking first used in the late 1940's. In 2000 it accounted for 1% of our oil, in 2011 it accounted for 25% and will eventually account for 50% if allowed to continue.

20. The Russian state was founded in Kiev that is now the capital of Ukraine, which was part of the Russian Empire from 1648.

21. Electricity was on display at the Chicago World's Fair of 1893.

22. Light water nuclear reactor is the basis for 90% of the 440 nuclear reactors in operation in the world. The Nautilus was the first controlled application of nuclear power for vehicle propulsion. In 1963 New Jersey utility ordered a commercial plant at Oyster Creek.

23. In 1978 Congress banned NG power plants due to the sharp increase in its prices. About 10% of capital investment is in power. Coal was about 55 and is now about 45%, NG is 23%, nuclear at 20% and hydro at 7%. In China coal is 80%, in India coal is 69% and in Brazil electricity is 80 % hydropower.

24. Under Pres. Reagan government reduced climate research. In 1970 President Nixon established the U.S. Environmental Protection Agency.

25. Mars has a thin atmosphere and is very cold while Venus has an atmosphere super rich in CO2 and very hot.

26. In 2007 utilities and industrial companies including GE and BP formed the U.S. Climate Action Partnership.

27. California Democratic House established the Bill 32 which required emissions levels back to the 1990 by 2020. Nancy Pelosi, the first woman speaker of the House, passed climate change legislation. Pres. Bush advised that CO2 is not a pollutant under the Clean Air Act. The Supreme Court however reversed that.

28. India produces 5% and China 23% of the worlds CO2.

29. The Republicans who won the house in 2010 denied funding for the EPA to run its CO2 programs.

30. In 2010 renewable energy accounted for 8% of U.S. energy supply and the same as in 1980. Under Pres. Reagan funding and incentives for renewable were slashed or eliminated.

31. In 1973 China introduced agri law that called for solar and wind energy. By 1988 in China wind power was hooked up to the grid. Also 70% of products of wind power must be made in China.

32. In the 1970's Solarex the first photovoltaic start-up was profitable. Needed money and later sold to Amoco then to BP where it sits in limbo.

33. In Brazil 60% of auto fuel is ethanol.

34. Jan 16, 1919 -18th Amendment to the Constitution – Prohibition of alcoholic. The 21st Amendment repealed it.

35. Dec. 25 1979 -Soviet Union invaded Afghanistan.

36. Carter slapped a tariff on Brazilian ethanol to prevent it from competing with U.S. ethanol. Corn is the largest agri crop in the U.S. by acres planted, however only 1% is eaten directly the rest goes to livestock and corn syrup and 41% goes to ethanol.

37. In the mid 1890's Daimler distributed cars through the piano maker William Steinway. The first gasoline powered car built in the U.S. in 1893 by Daimler. In 1908 Ford debuted his first Model T for $825. The oil crisis of 1973 started the need to regulate fuel

efficiency. Gas consumption increased by 50% from 1985 to 2003. By 2012 Pres. Obama provided $5 billion to research batteries.

38. Father of Smog- Profesor Arie Haagen-Smit. Transportation accounts for 17% of the CO2.

39. Natural gas vehicles make up only 1% of the light vehicles in the world.

20. THE TIPPING POINT by Malcolm Gladwell

1. The Stickiness Factor is a specific way of making a contagious message memorable by presentation and structure.

2. Three rules of Tipping Point- Law of the Few, Stickiness Factor, and Power of Context.

3. Six degree of separation will reach anyone you know or a relative.

4. Maxim in the advertising business is that an advertisement has to be seen at least 6 times before anyone will remember it.

5. If you can hold the attention of children you can educate them. It is not all verbal but must have some visual aspects.

6. Individuals between 18 and 24 perpetrate most all violence.

7. Broken window theory- fix it and the problem will go away.

8. Paradox- in order to create one outrageous movement you often have to create many small movements first.

9. Influence- we are powerfully influenced by our surroundings, our immediate context, and the personalities of those around us.

21. Unfinished Business- women, men, family
by Anne-Marie Slaughter

1. Mrs. Slaughter was on Policy Planning Staff of Sec. of State Hillary Clinton.

2. She wondered why success meant privileging career achievement above all else.

3. Money buys a safety net relieving stress and providing resilience against buffets of fate.

4. Success sometimes feels like sacrificing your loved ones wellbeing for your own aspirations.

5. Change society so expense and headache of childcare and eldercare don't sink women and their families. Change workplace so business persons do not have to be available 24/7.

6. The faster you become the boss the easier it is to fit in work and family.

7. As women become executives, spouses need to support moves and promotions, and take responsibility at home as male CEO's have always done.

8. Workers have fewer than eight hours a day of hard mental labor in them before they start making mistakes.

9. Men trade stocks on the trading floor on a rapid pace where as women prefer to take more time to analyze security and then make the trade.

10. Women hold 15% of executive officer positions in Fortune 500 companies and 62% of minimum wage jobs.

11. American single parents have the highest poverty rate and the weakest income support system.

12. Two great motivators of men and women- competition impulse to pursue our self-interest in the world and impulse to put others first.

13. Caring requires us to put others first in ways that allow them to flourish as independent people.

14. Caregiving items: knowledge, patience, adaptability, honesty, courage, trust, humility and hope.

15. Figure out what works moving between your own needs and the needs of another, and that between the needs of the moment and the needs over time.

16. Over half of American's stay at home dads either have a disability or could not find a job.

17. Pre 1967 interracial marriage was illegal in many states.

18. First woman Secretary of State was Madeleine Albright in 1997.

19. Cheryl Mills, Hillary Clinton's chief of staff, read all her email but did not respond for her unless a response was absolutely necessary and with that she put a K for OK on the email.

20. To solve today's global challenges what is necessary is collaboration, sharing credit, and patience not demand and go it alone.

21. By 2020 one in six Americans will be over 65 and more than one in three will likely have eldercare responsibilities. By 2030 retired to working age adults will double.
22. Canada has a higher % of foreign-born citizens than the US yet Canadians are twice as likely to move up the social and econ ladder as Americans.

22. What Remains to be Discovere by John Maddox

1. Copernican established that the Sun, not the Earth is at the center of the solar system.
2. A theory qualifies as an explanation only if it can be and has been tested by observation or experimented about.
3. Dr. Galen about 800AD discovered the functions of the heart, the arteries and the blood.
4. Spectrum is shifted to higher frequencies as the temperature is increased. By 1860 spectral lines had been recognized as a means of analyzing the chemical composition of stars.
5. In 1880 August Weissman recognized the structure in the cell nuclei that appears to be the transfer of inheritable characteristics from one generation of cells. These cells, called chromosomes, have two components: protein and the material called nucleic acid.
6. The brain consists of two halves which are almost mirror images of each other and which are linked together by a roust bundle of about a billion neurons forming a structure called the corpus callosum. The neurons from the sense organs are routed primarily to the opposite sides of the cerebral cortex. The left hand side of the brain is concerned with the production of human speech.
7. Greenhouse gasses- CO_2, methane (agriculture, waste dumps), refrigerants or CRC, nitrous oxide (vehicle exhausts) and water vapor.
8. Melting of ice from the last Ice Age took more than 1,000 years. Temperature of the Earth surface has increased by about 6 degrees during that period.
9. With no restraint on CO_2 the sea level is expected to be 50 centimeters higher by the end of the next century. All this due to the

melting of terrestrial glaciers and the expansion of warmed surface layers of the oceans.

10. If the West Antarctic ice shelf is dislodged due to melting it could increase the global sea level about 16 feet.

11. Rice production is the source of perhaps half the methane in the atmosphere. Some might consider switching to other available foods in the future.

BOOKS IN A NUT SHELL

HEALTH, FOOD, PLANTS

INDEX

1. An Introduction to Human Evolutionary Anatomy
by Chris Dean

1. Taxon- a group of organisms at any level of hierarchy.
2. Trabeculae or spongy regions of a bone is 25% renewed every year.
3. The mandible and the cranium together are known as the skull.
4. The temporal bones called because greying hair at the temples was the first sign of ageing.
5. Teeth- 32 in total and four muscles for moving the mouth. Most can open our mouths to about three-fingers between upper and lower teeth.
6. Bulk of all tooth tissue is formed of dentine and the crowns of teeth are covered with a layer of enamel which is the hardest biologically formed substance known.
7. All teeth pass through three phases: calcification, enamel formation and closure of the apical canal of the root
8. Four types of teeth- incisors, canines, premolars, and molars.
9. Interior of the cranial cavity is divided into three cranial fossae. The intracranial cavity is divided into compartments by tracts of fibrous dura mater and protect the brain.
10. Beneath and surrounded by the dura mater are the arachnoid and the pia mater all three known as the meninges of the brain.
11. The brain is regulated to about 37deg. C. or 98.6 F.
12. A neuron consists of a cell body and processes known as dendrites and convey information to the cell body.
13. Tissues of the central nervous system are composed of either grey matter or white matter. Gray matter contains cell bodies and white matter contains axons which appear white to the naked eye.
14. Motor nerve fibers are nerves that leave the brain via spinal cord that bring about movements. Sensory nerves refer to taste, vision, hearing or smell and enter the brain as cranial nerves.
15. Cerebral cortex is divided into – frontal, parietal, temporal and occipital loves.
16. Temporal loves are concerned with watching and hearing as music.

17. Hippocampus part of the limbic system and is associated with memory.

18. Patients with lesions of the cerebellum commonly experience slurring of their speech, and tremors.

19. Net weight of the human head is normally 5.4% of the body weight and is less in animals.

20. Larynx, a series of cartilages, is a valve like structure that guards the opening into the trachea or windpipe.

21. In humans there are 33 vertebras

22. Sternum, meaning solid or hard, are bones of the upper chest and divided into three sections.

23. In the hand there are 27 bones which 14 are bones of the fingers

24. Patella is the large bone of the knee in front of the femur muscle.

25. The foot is made up of 26 small bones including 7 ankle or tarsal bones.

26. Leg bones- femur (the largest), tibia, and the fibula.

27. The gluteus maximus is the extensor of the hip and the largest muscle of the rump or buttock.

2. Another Day in the Frontal Lobe by Katrina Firlik

1. The brain makes up about 80% of the intracranial contents. The other 20% is split between blood and cerebrospinal fluid.

2. Neurological organizations – AANS (American Assoc. of Neurological Surgeons) and CNS (Congress of Neurological Surgeons).

3. Dr.'s Watson and Crick discovered DNA in early 1950's.

4. Total human blood volume is about 5 liters (5.3 quarts- or 2.6 gallons or about 21.6# at 8.33 #/gal.

5. To work in the brain a hole the size of a nickel is drilled with a special tool, a perforator, that drills and stops when you are through the bone.

6. Benign tumors-meningiomas- arise from the outer covering of the brain and cause problems by indenting into the brain or pushing it aside. True tumors of the brain tissue, known as gliomas, are the most feared and known as primary brain tumors- metastases that originate from cancer outside the brain.

7. Cell death is called necrosis. Water on the brain is called hydrocephalus.
8. The cerebrospinal fluid surrounds the brain and fills four ventricles in the brain. It is produced and absorbed at the rate of about 450cc per day about ½ liter.

3. Brandwashed by Martin Lindstrom

1. By the age of 7 brand and product preferences are embedded in our minds.
2. Foods are primed in our minds by about 4 years old.
3. 53% of adults and 56% of teens use brands from their childhood.
4. Viruses are spread via tiny droplets in the air via sneezed or coughed by infected people.
5. Fear of failure rather than promise of success drives consumers. Promise of success tends to paralyze us.
6. Ads work because they induce fear and guilt
7. Averting gazes is associated with shame and social isolation while straight ahead gaze is a sign of confidence and connectedness.
8. Sales of domestic prescription drugs are about $236 billion.
9. How we get hooked on a brand: routine stage of daily use and emotional need.
10. Caffeine restricts the blood vessels in our brains.
11. Lip balms especially Carmex use phenol and salicylic acid that tears away at tissue like corns and calluses. Actually ends up drying the lips and require more use and stops the lips from excreting necessary oils.
12. In Europe more men wear fragrance than American females. When women choose a product 80% is emotional and 20% is rational.
13. A study showed that our brains are not fully matured until age of 24.
14. Less confidence or self-esteem one has the more they are dependent on brands.
15. Mentioning time in an ad is more likely to be successful.
16. Average person carries around 15 loyalty cards.
17. By the age of 2, 92% of American children have a digital footprint.

4. Doctors- Info from a DVD by DR. NULAND

1. Hippocrates 460 BC- father of medicine. Apollo was the father of healing. In this period doctors believed in the power of the snake. That is why there is a snake on a medical stick.
2. Golden age of Greece was the 3rd century BC. Observed if the individual was sick by viewing- blood, or phlegm- yellow or black. If the Individual had a fever they removed blood. Start of the ethical code in medicine.
3. Galen- 131AD-basic research and determined that acid dissolved food in the stomach. He started dissecting parts of the body and determined urine was made in the kidneys.
4. Versalius-1543- first book on anatomy. First school of medicine was in Selerno, Italy in the 6th century. In 1087 the University of Padua, Italy opened for the study of law, medicine and theology. Pope Sixtus IV's 1450 edict was that cadavers could be given to doctors and artists for study. Nothing is to be believed until verified.
5. Harvey 1578- Circulation of the blood, heart beats @ 72x per minute. Start of inductive reasoning. Systole is heart contracting. Diastole is heart at rest. Heart will hold 2 oz. of water. Determined that the heart pumps blood to the body. Malpighi 1621- heart pumps blood to body and capillaries return the blood to the heart.
6. Morgagni 1705- father of physical examination. – Age of enlightenment. He wrote a book on appendix.
7. Hunter 1750- First artificial insemination. The 7 year French & Indian war
8. Laennec- discovered the stethoscope, (a Greek word- stetho- chest and scope- to observe). In 1816 he first used a rolled up paper. Cirrhosis of the liver was studied and partially determined its cause
9. Morton- 1846 anesthesia. Used euphoric ether. Priestly used nitrous oxide in 1772.
10. Virchow1845- start of cell investigation to determine disease. Leukemia is the excess of white cells. Blood clot- thrombus, blood clot that kills is called embolis. There are 200 types of cells and 75 trillion cells.

11. Leister- germ theory -41% of amputees died of infection before antiseptic was discovered.

12. Halstead-1874- John Hopkins Hospital was started with the help of four women who helped raise $1 million on condition that women would be admitted and a college degree was required. This led to the admission standards.

13. Hernia is a hole in the abdominal wall. Development of rubber gloves in operating rooms was in the late 1800's.

14. Taussug 1923 development of cardiac transplantation.

15, Blue babies occur when a hole in right ventricle sends unoxygenated blood to the left ventricle. 1950 first heart machine. Discovery of a fungus, cyclosporine, helped to assist a heart transplant to accept a new heart.

5. FIGS, DATES, LAUREL, AND MYRRH
by Lynton John Mussenman

1. Trees are prominent in the Bible and biblical messages can be summed up by four trees: tree of life, tree of knowledge of good and evil, the tree that Jesus died on, and the tree of life in the last book of the Bible-Revelation

2. The leaves used on Palm Sunday are from the Date Palm

3. The Dead Sea is located at lowest spot on Earth below sea level- 1319 feet.

4. Banana is from banan the Arabic word for finger.

5. The English word for line is from the Latin word flax- linum. Words such as linear and lineage are derived from the same linguistic root.

6. Frankincense is a gum from specie of the boswellia tree or shrub. It is dried to a resin. The word means high quality incense.

7. Poison hemlock should not be confused with the common tree in English known as hemlock which is not toxic and is used to make the original root beer.

8. The laurel tree is mostly known for its leaves - bay leaves. The family of these trees is also known for cinnamon.

9. Mulberry bush is where the silk worms make their silk

10. Myrrh- is dried resin from the shrubs or small trees of the specie of Commiphora from the Hebrew word mor. There are two types-medicinal and fragrant.

11. Olive oil has five main uses- food, illumination, ointment, soap, and preservative. It can be stored up to six years. Fresh olives are bitter if eaten off of the tree. They turn black when ripe. They are soaked in brine to remove the bitter taste

12. Pine-seed for pine or pinyon nuts come from the stone or umbrella pine tree. Most now come from China. The pitch of pine trees were used for caulking on ships and sealing wine amphora.

13. Pistachio, cashews and mangos are in the same family as poison ivy. If allergic to poison ivy you may be allergic to these nuts.

14. Wheat is second most important plant after rice. All is used- straw for bedding, basketry, roofing, and bricks. Each grain consists of a minute embryo-germ, a large amount of starch-endosperm, and the fruit coat-bran. Four types of wheat are einkorn, emmer wheat, durum, and bread. Barley is the main ingredient in the production of beer although wheat was used to a lesser extent.

15. Wormwood is used to flavor alcoholic drinks and known as absinthe or bitters.

6. For All The Tea In China by Sarah Rose

1. Tea was first introduced into England in the 1880's.

2. Tea was grown in 1815 on the Himalaya's in the Assam Province in India.

3. Plants can survive for years kept in a sealed, well-lit environment without water.

4. The East India Company hired 'Robert Fortune a Biologist to go to China to discover their source of tea and bring it to India.

5 .Lilacs came for Persia, tulips from Turkey, citrus from Southeast Asia, camellias from China, cinchona from Peruvian to produce alkaloid quinine.

6. Mexico received independence from Spain in 1821

7. In China Fortune learned:

a. Green tea leaves were left exposed to the sun for one to two hours to dry. They were then put into a wok and cooked to break the cell walls down. Then put on tables and crushed by rolling with bamboo poles.

b. Green and black tea leaves come from the same plant. Black leaves are fermented while green tea is not. Leaves sit in the sun an entire day to oxidize. This treatment produces the tannins- bitter taste and dark color.

c. To the green tea the Chinese added two pigments- Prussian blue- Ferro cyanide and a yellow substance calcium sulfate dehydrate (gypsum). This was mixed with the green tea because the English wanted it to look green.

d. Black tea needs sugar, as it is bitter while green tea does not.

8. Leaves are picked from April to October from each bush every ten days. The best leaves are the small ones from the top of the bush. Each picker, mostly female, carries two bags each up to 60#'s.

9. Tea is easily cloned by cutting any branch, replanting it and left to sprout. It will develop a network of roots. This process is called gamogenesis

10 For centuries China had forbidden its people access to the ocean even to fish.

11. Slavery ended in Britain in 1833 and they could no longer find workers for its sugar colonies.

12. The first mass-produced mass marketed global commodities were sugar, coffee, tobacco and opium.

13. British defeated Napoleon in 1815 and they then did not need their extensive warships.

14. The Suez Canal was built and completed in 1869 by the French due to the heavy traffic from Far East trade in order to save sailing time around Africa.

15. Per pound black tea has more caffeine than coffee but contains half the caffeine as coffee by the cup because one pound of tea brews about 200 cups while a pound of coffee yields barely forty cups. Green tea has about 1/3 the caffeine as black tea

16. Caffeine is a chemical alkaloid, a base, and stimulates the nervous and cardiovascular systems.

17. Black tea takes sugar and green tea does not.
18. Plants can survive for years kept in a sealed well-lit environment without water.
19. Queen Elizabeth granted royal charter to the East India Company in 1600. They bought spices and fabrics from the Orient and sold them in London. They hired Fortune to investigate the tea of China. Once discovered he hid plants and returned to India to replant them.

7. Grain Brain by David Perlmutter

1. Your brain weighs about 3 pounds and has one hundred thousand miles of blood vessels.
2. Gluten is a "silent germ" and can inflect damage on our brain.
3. Pills focused on illness not wellness. This treatment of taking pills are often more dangerous.
4. A sugar level of 70-100 milligrams per deciliter is considered normal.
5. Brain disease for the most part starts with the diet. With too many carbs and too few healthy and unhealthy fats.
6. Insulin in our body escorts glucose into our cells. This promotes fat retention.
7. Type 2 diabetes is reversible through diet and lifestyle changes. There is no cure for Type 1 diabetes. Type 1 is known to be from genetic and environmental influences.
8. Diabetes jumped by 50% between 1995 and 2010, and 100% in 18 states.
9. High carb diet and gluten are the most prominent stimulators of inflammatory pathways that reach the brain for brain disorder
10. High cholesterol reduces your risk for brain disease and increases longevity. High levels of good fat is proven to be key to health and peak brain function.
11. High blood sugar greater risk of brain shrinkage.
12. LDL is not a cholesterol (lipoprotein) and nothing bad about it.
13. Celiac disease is when an allergic reaction to gluten causes damage specifically to the small intestine.

14. Neuropathy is nerve damage outside the brain and spinal cord. Causes numbness, weakness, or pain.

15. Following are gluten free: buckwheat, quinoa, soy, tapioca. Following contain gluten: beer, baked beans, blue cheese, bouillon, breaded foods, cereals, chocolate milk.

16. Framingham Heart Study- association between total cholesterol and cognitive performance.

17. Parkinson's disease strongly related to lower levels of cholesterol.

18. Heart attacks effects are at the same rate with either high or low cholesterol levels.

19. Consumption by individuals of highest amount of saturated fat had 19% lower coronary heart disease.

20. There has been no published study in the past 30 years to demonstrate that eating a "low-fat, low 'cholesterol diet" prevents or reduces heart attack or death rate.

21. Finding that it did not matter whether you ate large amount of fatty animal products or followed a vegetarian diet, the arterial plaque was the same in all parts of the world.

22. Gluten is found in high-carbohydrate foods -pasta, cookies, cakes, bagels or whole grain bread, potatoes, corn, and rice.

23. When the American Diabetes Association recommended Americans should consume 60-70 % of calories from carbohydrates the rate of diabetes exploded.

24. Carbohydrates not dietary fats are the primary cause of weight gain. Farmers fatten their animals with carbohydrates like corn and grain

25. Human brain consists of more than 70% fat.

26. Certain vitamins like A, D, E, & K require fat to get absorbed. That is why we need dietary fat in our diet.

27. Vitamin K good for brain and eye health and risk of age related dementia and macular degeneration.

28. Vitamin D is an anti-inflammatory helping the body to get rid of infectious agents.

29. Side effects of statins- fatigue, shortness of breath, problems with balance and muscular pain and loss of coQ10 in muscles- reduced energy production.

30. Aerobic exercise turns on genes linked to longevity and brain's growth hormone.

31. 20% of our oxygen is consumed by the brain.

32. Cumin main ingredient in the spice turmeric (member of the ginger family) and is good for the brain and good for detox along with green tea and coffee.

33. Coconut oil good for the brain and reduces inflammation.

34. Dark Chocolate with cacao above 70% is healthy.

35. U.S. is ranked #1 in the world in health-care spending and ranked 37th in overall health according to World Health organization.

8. Herbal Antibiotics by Stephen Buhner

1. Adverse drug reactions are the 4th leading cause of death in the U.S.

2. Per year over 60 million antibiotics are used in the U.S. in 2009 with nearly ½ used on animals.

3. Antibiotics promote exchange of plasmids which may contain resistances genes. Most water supplies in industrialized countries are contaminated with antibiotics.

4. Triclosan in toothpastes causes bacterial resistance.

5. Testing in 2011 found that 50% of store bought meat and poultry were contaminated with staph. To kill salmonella bacteria in eggs fry or boil for at least 9 minutes.

6. Flies found to be the main spread of resistant organisms in the general community.

7. The money's not in the cure it is in the medicine. Between 1983 and 2008 investment in antibiotic research development in the US fell by 75%.

8. Within 5 years MRSA will be completely untreatable by antibiotics and its over use. Green tea as well as pomegranate has properties that helps inhibit MRSA.

9. Over 70% of all pathogenic bacteria in hospitals are at least minimally resistant.

10. Herbs that can help infections- ginger, echinacea, juniper berry, licorice, oregano oil.

11. Some of the main herbs to treat MRSA are: sida, black pepper, usnea, juniper berry, licorice, ginger, honey.
12. Prior to 1977 no reports of resistance in cholera organisms but now common.
13. Top systemic herbal antibiotics: cryptolepis, sida, alchornea, bidens and Artemisia.
14. The herb cryptolepine is cytotoxic and kills cancer cells because it intercalates the DNA by inserting itself between the two DNA ladders.
15. Artemisinin is an antitumor and anti-cancer compound.
16. Top 4 non systemic herbal antibiotics: bebeerines, juniper, honey & usnea.
17. Honey- known to resist bacteria on infected skin and wounds. Good for treatment of colds and respiratory infections. Get organic and wildflower if available. Read labels as some include things other than honey as sugar. Good to be cloudy with pollen.
18. Licorice-moderately antibacterial and potently antiviral. The root and leaves are acceptable.
19. Ginger is a synergist which increases the actions of other herbs and boosting their effectiveness and increases circulation.
20. Reishi is a fairly potent anticancer acting herb. It helps reduce cancer cells.
21. Cold and flu drink: sage, cayenne, wildflower honey, lemon juice,
22. Nasal spray for sinus infections: five drops of each, cryptolipis, bidens, juniper berry and usnea

9. Incognito- "The Secret life of the Brain" by David Engieman.

1. The brain is built of cell: neurons and glia.
2. A neuron has about 10 thousand connections.
3. A brain weighs about 3 pounds.
4. Pitcher Nolan Ryan's fast ball at 100 mpr reaches the plate in about 4 tenths of a second.
5. Galileo Galilei on January 10, 1610 observed Jupiter and its moon and thought at first they were stars.

6. Ptolemy said the center of the universe is the earth. Copernicus said the sun was the center.

7. One third of the brain is devoted to vision.

8. Testosterone in boys produce prominent chin, a larger nose, fuller jaw, growth of muscles and broad shoulders. For females estrogen produces full lips, full buttocks and growth of breasts.

9. Front brain hemisphere is connected by fibers called corpus callosum. The left hemisphere of the brain is for language.

10. Parkinson's patients when given the drug pramilpexole turned them into gamblers. ParkinsonS is due to the loss of brain cells dopamine.

11. Roper v. Simmons stated that there was no death penalty for those under 18.

12. Ugly people receive longer sentences than attractive people.

13. Drug use as a teenager increases the development of psychosis as an adult.

10. Meatonomics by David Robinson Simon

1. Animal agriculture drives one of the largest causes of climate change through greenhouse gases and more than transportation and power plants.

2. Since 1983 milk consumption has climbed 12% to 620 pounds mostly through promotions.

3. Teenagers consume 78% more saturated fat and 48% more cholesterol than suggested by the government guidelines. One in three teenagers is obese or overweight.

4. Per "The China Study" cancer is related to animal protein. Study shows that animal based foods increased tumor development while nutrients from plant based foods decreased tumor development.

5. Animal cruelty is against the law.

6. It's unlawful to defame food in a quarter of the US states.

7. The 28 hour law where food or water must be served to animals do not apply to chickens or turkeys which account for 98% of all land animals killed for food in the US. This law does not apply to intrastate travel which is exempt.

8. The cows treated with rBST insulin is a carcinogen and is banned in Canada, Australia, NZ, Japan, and most Europe though not in the US. Industry has stopped this through bills.

9. Two thirds of Government farming support goes to the animal foods that the government suggest we limit. Less than 2% goes to the fruits and vegetables it recommends we eat more of.

10. The USDA spent $30.8 billion in 2013 supporting US farmers with loans, insurance, research, marketing, cheap water, etc.

11. Farm subsidies were $161 billion between 1995 and 2009. The large farmers – big corporations got 9/10 of the cash. Two thirds of the firms did not receive a cent.

12. U.S. subsidized products like corn and soybeans provide ½ the products consumed on Earth. Most goes to third world countries hurting their ability to produce their own produce.

13. Study shows that mothers who ate large amounts of hormone implanted beef during pregnancy decreased fertility among those children. It is banned in most countries except the US.

14. One third of the food we eat depends on honeybee pollination. Their colonies decreased by 50% since 1945 related to GMO and pesticides.

15. Due to sport fishing and depletion of smaller fish, the salmon family are now ½ the weight and length. Also effected are bears and eagles.

16. Fish susceptible to parasites and live only in salt water. In fish farms they are removed from their salt water and infested with chemicals.

17. 95% of farmed fish that Americans eat is imported from regions like China and S. America.

18. 90% of agriculture workers lack health insurance, 1/3 are undocumented, 1/4 live in conditions that the state agency called "extremely overcrowded. At the Smithfield plant there is 100% turnover each year when 5,000 workers quit.

11. Musicophilia   by Oliver Sacks

1. Imagining music stimulates the motor cortex and imagining the action of playing music stimulates the auditory cortex. Musical imagery is even intensified by deafness.
2. Musicians increase the prevalence of hearing loss with music overload in high pitch.
3. The corpus callosum in the brain of a professional musician is inherited and the plenum temporal enlargement indicates absolute pitch.
4. Young children respond to training by ear and imitation of the violin. Brief exposure to classical music can stimulate or enhance mathematical, verbal and visual abilities in children- so called the "Mozart Effect".
5. There are records of striking changes in the left hemisphere of children who have had only a single year of violin training.
6. Absolute pitch is highly dependent on early musical training.
7. Hindu music has 22 note scales.
8. Your inner ear, the cochlea, has 3,500 sterocilia or inner ear hair cells.
9. Impairments of melody usually go with right hemisphere lesions while rhythm involves the left hemisphere and other sub cortical systems including the cerebellum.
10. Amelodia means tune deafness.
11. The path of sound in the ear passes through the eardrum to the tiny bones, ossicles, on either side and on to the snail shaped cochlea with its 3,500 hair cells.
12. Inner ear hair cells although protected by the organ corti can be destroyed by very loud sound.
13. Cerebral right hemisphere is for perceptual skills and the left lobe the development of abstract and verbal powers. The cerebral left hemisphere takes longer to develop.
14. Early musical training, before 6 or 8, is crucial in the development of maintenance of absolute pitch.
15. Speech of words has inflections, intonations tempo, rhythm, and melody.

16. Loss of musical emotion is more common with damage to the right hemisphere of the brain.

12. Omnivore's Dilemma by Michael Pollan

1. Corn comes from a single specie known as zea mays- a tropical grass. Everything we eat comes from and uses corn. From cows, corn syrup, chicken.
2. 40% of Mexican diet comes from corn via tortillas- maize or "walking corn".
3. Corn has 4 carbon atoms- C-4. 97% of what corn is comes from air and three % from the ground. From the air it gets its carbon through its stomata or microscopic orifices in the leaves. A single corn seed yields more than 150-300 kernels. A wheat seed yields about 50 seeds.
4. Corn- eaten off the cob, ground into flour, brewed into beer or distilled into whiskey.
5. Maize is self-fertilized and wind pollinated. The tassel housed the male organs and yield about 14 million grains per plant.
6. The American Indians were the first to breed and develop corn for almost every environment. American corporate breeders figured out how to control the corn's reproduction so that the farmers had to buy new seeds each year.
7. Soybeans finds its way into 2/3 of all processed food via cattle, etc.
8. Corn in 1920 averaged about 20 bushels per acre about the same as the Indians.
9. Pesticides are based on poison gases developed for the war and now used by the chemical fertilizer industry.
10. Earth atmosphere is 78% nitrogen. More than half of the n2 is applied to corn. Corn now requires about 1/3 gal of oil to produce a bushel of fertilized corn today or 50 gal. per acre.
11. Corn has about 14% moisture.
12. Cargill and ADM buy about 1/3 of the corn in the U.S. and control the pesticide and fertilizer market, elevator, brokers, etc.

13. Cows normally eat grasses not corn. They have a separate digestive system called rumen to ferment the grass. Cows are now fast fed to grow in weight from 80 to 1,000 lbs. in about 14 months.
14. The modern coffee break began as a whiskey break called the elevenses.
15. Omega 6 is produced in the seeds of plants while omega 3 is in the leaves. Too high of 6 will contribute to heart disease because omega helps blood clot while omega 3 helps it flow. Hydrogenating oil eliminates omega 3.

13. Tale of the Dueling Neurosurgeons by Sam Kean

1. Frontal lobes of the brain help us plan, make decisions and set goals. Back or occipital lobes process vision; top of parietal lobes combine vision, hearing, touch and other sensations; side or temporal lobes help produce language.
2. Galen served as a doctor for Roman gladiators and was born in AD 129.
3. Nervous system contains two main types of cells- neurons and glia. Neurons process thoughts while gli, meaning glue, holds neurons in place and provides nutrients to the system.
4. Neurons have branches of dendrites and axons. The axon cables zip information from one gray matter node to another at speeds up to 250 miles per hour.
5. Brain's contain two distinct substances- gray and white matter. Gray matter has a high percentage of neurons and most reside on the brain's surface called the cortex.
6. In July 1900, Gaetano Bresci assassinated King Umberto I of Italy.
7. Nations first execution by electricity occurred in 1890 in Auburn, New York.
8. In 1938, Albert Hofmann in searching for a new drug developed LSD through fungi and tried it in April 1943.
9. Chinese surgeons performed the second face transplant in April 2006 with remarkable results. The first was performed in 2005 to unknown long term results.

10. Modern nursing began with Florence Nightingale in Crimea during the Franco-Prussian War.

11. Amino Acids are the building blocks of proteins.

12. Anosognosia- inability to recognize illness.

13. Right lobe of the brain controls the left side of the body and the left lobe controls the right side.

14. The brain needs thiamine to make myelin sheaths to build neurotransmitters. Our body needs B1 (thiamine via vegetables, beans or meat) to harvest energy for glucose the end result of digesting carbohydrates.

15. Alcohol prevents the intestines from absorbing thiamine and causes changes inside the brain especially to the glia cells. Without thiamine the glia cannot sop up glutamate and causes neurons to die or excitotoxicity.

16. Lying or continuously fibbing for no obvious reason is known as confabulation.

17. Hippocampus records and stores memories.

18. Largest structures in the brain are the left and right hemisphere lobes.

19. Back of the left hemisphere frontal lobe is known as Broca's area and controls speech production.

20. Parietal lobe handles basic arithmetic.

21. Reading disorder is known as alexia sine agraphia.

22. Darwin studied natural selection.

23. Corpus callosum is where seizures occur.

24, Right brain is for music.

25. Thalamus at the core of the brain receives information and relays it around the body.

14. Teaming with Nutrients by Jeff Lowenfels

1. 17th century Jean Helmont proved that plants actually didn't need fertilizers only water. Pulverizing soil particles makes them more edible to plant roots.

2. Plant cells size can be related to a period where five to fifty cells would fit into this area.

3. Polysaccharide fibers inside cell walls have a negative charge and attract positively charge particles known as cations.

4. Plasma is matter in a phase that can be in solid or liquid or gaseous state or all three.

5. Phospholipids are two-part molecules with its head a negatively charged phosphate ion that is water-soluble.

6. Cytoplasm is all the stuff inside the cell membrane except for the nucleus.

7. DNA- deoxyribonucleic acid and RNA- ribonucleic acids are the molecules replicating the genetic code used to build everything in a cell.

8. There are about 10,000 different kinds of proteins in each microscopic cell.

9. Nutrients form 3 types of bonds: covalent, ionic, and hydrogen.

10. Water can dissolve more elements than any other liquid. This is due to the hydrogen bonds, which is a great solvent.

11. Carbohydrates are carbon-based molecules- carbon, oxygen and hydrogen. It includes sugars, starches and cellulose.

12. Water moves in side roots by the xylem system that is three forces- transpiration, water cohesion and eater adhesion.

13. Stomata are leaf pores that open during the day to let in the carbon dioxide needed to make sugars.

14. All plants need a mere 17 of the 90 naturally occurring elements. There are 27 other elements but these are man-made and not required for plant survival.

15. Seaweed contains 60 natural elements.

16. Hydrogen, oxygen, and carbon make up 96% of the mass of a plant.

17. Earth's atmosphere consists of 78% nitrogen and 21% oxygen

18. Chlorophyll includes four nitrogen atoms and without these atoms there is no photosynthesis. Lawns yellow due to a lack of nitrogen for making chlorophyll green pigment.

19. Lack of calcium leads to malformed plants especially in new roots, shoots and young leaves.

20. Lack of magnesium in plants show that the leaves start to lose their green color in between the leaf veins.

21. Sulfur deficiency first appears in younger leaves when they start to yellow. This yellowing could also be a symptom of low iron
22. Silicon helps cucumbers and roses grow.
23. Maize plants transpire about 4 gallons of water per week.
24. Tree rings give a record of precipitation and temperature in the past. As rains dissipate and the temperatures go up this increases transpiration and thinner tubular rings are developed.
25. Guttation is when water is mixed with tree sap and accumulates in the xylem cells. They then expand pushing the xylem sap up the plant where there is less pressure.
26. If a plant loses leaves you do not want to give it much water because the roots need to adjust to the lower number of leaves they are feeding.
27. The pH of phloem saps is usually alkaline between 7.5 and 8.5. 90% of compounds in sap are sugars.
28. Soil pH can lock up nutrients making them unavailable to plants.
29. Temperatures effect on plants. The mycorrhizal fungi are most active between 41-95 degrees. They are responsible for much of the plant's phosphorus uptake.
30. Micronutrients become less available as pH increases and only sulfur is not affected by pH
31. Cation exchange capacity (CEC). These nutrients, if needed, should be added when they won't leach away from rains.
32. Chemical fertilizers have about 60% nitrogen content whereas organic fertilizers have about 12% nitrogen. Arthropods as mites and worms shun synthetic fertilizers. Mycorrhizal fungi are the largest single source of carbon in soils.
33. Pollution runoff from farms and gardeners from 32 states and two Canadian provinces enters the Mississippi River and flows to the Gulf of Mexico. In the spring the pollution causes huge algal blooms to form. When the algae dies they sink to the saltier water below, decompose and uses up the limited oxygen creating dead zones in the area where no fish can survive. Cooler weather in the winter disrupts this cycle for the time being.
34. Human hair- for every 7 pounds there is around 1 pound of nitrogen and is a good natural fertilizer.

35. Important to test your soil every 2-3 years to determine what nutrient it needs. Good nutrients can be supplied with cut grass, vegetables, annual flowers, etc.

15. The Cancer Chronicles; Unblocking Medicine's Deepest Mystery   by George Johnson

1. All mammals have precisely seven vertebrae in their necks. However, birds and amphibians are not bound by this rule as a swan can have 22 to 25.
2. Cancers are combated by antifolates. Sauté spinach with garlic.
3. Supplements sometimes increase the risk of a disease. As too much of something is a bad thing.
4. Little reason to believe that multi vitamins are helpful unless a person is severely malnourished.
5. Controlled trials have shown that a diet low in fat and high in fiber with fruits and vegetables had much effect or reduced colorectal polyps a precursor to colon cancer.
6. It matters mostly on how much you eat and not what you eat. Actually excess body fat reduces the chances of premenopausal women getting breast cancer.
7. A study has shown that for women every 4 inches over 5 feet increases the cancer risk by 16%.
8. Vitamin D lowers the odds for colorectal cancer but raises the risk for pancreas cancer.
9. PET stands for Positron Emission Tomography- recondite world of particle physics.
10. For tumors to expand it must find a way to reach into the circulatory system for blood.
11. In the 1920's Hermann Muller got the first hint that cancer is a disease and that X-rays and long exposure to the sun might be responsible for its ability to cause cancer.
12. X-rays by W. Rontgen in 1895 when used on mutated flies either killed them or sterilized them.
13. Paradox: cancer-killing rays could also produce cancers, transforming normal cells into malignant ones.

14. Ancient Rome mined uranium from a rock called pitch-blend for its yellow pigment for glass and ceramics. Not until 1896 was their exotic qualities known.

15. Coal tar applied to animals in lab experiments gave them tumors. When people smoke that was the same thing and shown to cause cancer.

16. Mitosis is the process of healthy cells dividing.

17. Scientists began in 1980's discovering anti-oncogenes.

18. P53 slows down the clock so that DNA repair can take place.

19. Hayflick- a normal cell can divide only 50-60 times.

20. Amphibians and planaria regenerate amputated body parts.

21. Human hedgehog gene involved in sprouting of hair from follicles- treatment for baldness.

22. Companies that produced the carcinogenic chemicals also make drugs used for the chemotherapeutic cures.

23. Cancer causes: tobacco 30%, obesity and inactivity 20%, diet about 20%, alcohol 4%, viruses 3%

24. In 1973 Ames showed that carcinogens caused cancer by inducing genetic mutations.

25. Black pepper contains safrole; mushrooms contain hydrazines that have caused cancer in mice. But it depends on the quantity taken.

26. Japan leads the world in stomach cancer due to salty fish eaten.

27. Cisplatin known as the penicillin of cancer has the effect of rapidly dividing cells but also has a sickening side effect.

28. Doxorubicin operated by interfering with the replication of DNA.

29. Cancer drug adriamycine pushes down your white blood cell count increasing vulnerability to infections. The name comes from the Adriatic Sea.

30. Paclitaxel or Taxol was originally isolated from the bark of the Pacific yew tree.

31. Striking a cancer with combination of different drugs increases the odds of killing it.

32. Mesothelioma is the cancer associated with exposure to asbestos.

33. There are approximately 25,000 genes in a human genome and at least 350 identified as possible cancer genes.

34. In 1928 in St. Mary's Hospital in London, Alexander Fleming discovered penicillin.
35. We didn't have the slightest idea of where as much as 50-60% of cancers comes from.
36. Sources of cancer: salt- stomach, red and processed meat-colon cancer, but smoking is the strongest for lung cancer.
37. Foods rich in cancer protective chemicals- onion family, cabbage family, vegetables as broccoli, cauliflower, kale, brussel sprouts, peas, tomatoes and deep yellow vegetables and fruits-raisins, prunes, blueberries.
38. Cortisol a stress hormone and melatonin regulate sleep.
39. The cerebellum is the center of muscular control and balance.
40. It is not clear whether screening via annual mammograms does any good and probably does more harm than good.

16. The China Study by Colin Campbell

1. Casein, which is 87% of cow's milk protein, promotes cancer. Least protein promoting cancer is from plants including wheat and soy.
2. People who eat the most animal food get the most disease.
3. One in 13 Americans has diabetes. We spend 1 of every 7 dollars on health. Other countries spend ½ what we spend and are healthier. U.S. is ranked 37 in the world on health
4. Proteins are a string of amino acids. They can all be derived from plant food.
5. Most all peanut butter is contaminated. With an AF (aflatoxin) factor of 300 times that judged acceptable by the US food.
6. Studies show nutrients from animal foods increase tumors while a decrease in tumor with plant food.
7. In US most of our calories of protein comes from animal food while in China a low % comes from animal food.
8. Coronary heart disease in very low in developing countries due to their high consumption of plant food.
9. People who eat the most animal protein have the most heart disease, cancer and diabetes.

10. The China study- people eating the most animal protein were taller and heavier and had higher total and bad cholesterol.
11. China's cholesterol levels were between 70 and 170. Safe level should be about 150.
12. Framingham Study shows that we treat disease not prevent it. Diet not considered. Fat has 9 calories per gram while carbohydrates and protein have 4 calories per grams.
13. Only 3% of breast cancer can be attributed to family history.
14. Cancer Research- exercise helps to prevent colon cancer. Men with highest dairy intake had double risk of prostate cancer.
15. Only 5-6% dietary protein required.
16. None of the top 25 medical institutes teach nutrition. Of the billion plus budget only 3.6% devoted to nutrition. These budgets are for the development of drugs and supplements.
17. Hippocrates advocated diet to prevent and treat disease.

17. The Drunken Botanist   by Amy Stewart

1. Agave is not a cactus but of the asparagus family. First drink made from the sap of this plant was pulque. The flowering stock is cut before it starts to form. Sap flows from this cutting. One plant can produce 250 gallons of sap. These plants only bloom once and then die.
2. Tequila, if standard, it is made up of 49% non-agave sugars. To be 100% agave it must be from Weber Blue with no sugar added and must be bottled by the producer in Mexico. Gold tequila is flavored, colored, and aged in oak barrels. It was named by Franz Weber in 1890's
3. Apples- contain more genes than humans. Cider is inhospitable to bacteria.
4. Yeast-eats sugar to form ethyl alcohol and carbon dioxide. At about 15% alcohol the yeast die.
5. Grains are packed with starch to make alcohol. The starch must first be changed to sugar. To do that you just add water.
6. Beer- Barley is one of the main ingredients. It originated in the Middle East then moved to Spain, China, and was brought to the

America's by Columbus on his second trip. It's what makes the foam in beer. There are two and six row barley's. The two row has the most starch and the best for a higher alcohol level.

7. Kentucky produces 90% of the world's bourbon supply. Must contain at least 51% corn. Straight bourbon is aged at least 2 years with nothing added. Blended bourbon must contain 51% straight bourbon and other items.

8. Vermouth is made from white wine and fortified with brandy to about 16% alcohol. Red vermouth is just made with red grapes.

9. Potato traces its ancestry to Peru. Vodka was first made in Russia and Poland, and made from grains. Vodka is made from sugar beets, grains, apples, grapes and acorns. Potato was made into vodka because of cheap source in Poland during the war. But all insist that the best vodka is made from rye or wheat.

10. Sweet potato is a vine related to the morning glory and not a potato at all. Native to South America.

11. Sugarcane originated in New Guinea. Used as building material in some cases or the early shoots were just picked and chewed. Columbus brought it to the Caribbean where it flourished. This gave us slavery in the 1500's because of the hard work to produce sugar. Today 25% of the world's sugar come from beets. In the United States this figure is 55%.

12. Aloe is related to agave plant and asparagus.

13. Artichoke- shown to protect the liver and lower cholesterol levels.

14. Clove is a tightly closed flower.

15. Gin is redistilled vodka with juniper and other items to add flavor.

16. Star Anise - 90% of the world's production is purchased by drug companies to make Tamiflu a drug to combat the flu.

17. Vanilla- native of Mexico. Difficult to cultivate, as its roots need to be exposed to air that is called epiphyte. Its vines climb trees. One flower per day, over 2 month period, awaits pollination by a single species of stingless bees.

18. The chamomile flowers-are used for anti-inflammatory drugs.

19. Hops in beer help to make the foam. Beer is mostly made from barley and other grains and flavored with hops. It also preserves it and adds the foam from its lupine resin that contains acids.

20. Beer bottles are brown because light makes the liquid taste skunky. Something in the hops breaks down to cause this.
21. Roses strengthen the stomach and the liver.
22. Saffron- it takes 4 thousand flowers to get an ounce of saffron.
23. Cinchona tree- source of quinine extract.
24. Cinnamon- it is from the bark of a tree native to Sri Lanka. The best comes from there but also comes from India and Brazil. Cassia cinnamon sticks are thick and form a double roll while true cinnamon look like a tightly rolled bunch of thinner bark. True cinnamon comes from Ceylon. It helps liver problems.
25. Eucalyptus tree's oil is good for mosquito repellant.
26. Jefferson encouraged replacing sugar grown from canes with slave labor with sugar from maple trees which required fewer slaves with less energy.
27. Grapefruit appears to be the hybrid of sweet orange and pomelo.
28. Meyer lemons- hybrid of a lemon and mandarin orange.
29. Lemon is a cross between lime, citron and a pomelo.

18. The Folly of Fools: the Logic of Deceit and Self-Deception in Human Life by Robert Trivers

1. The more ignorant the individual the more confident he or she maybe.
2. Bias begins early in life. By age three children prefer to play with certain group members.
3. Power tends to corrupt and absolute power corrupts absolutely.
4. About 1% of bird species is entirely dependent on other species to raise their young such as cuckoos.
5. Hippocampus part of the brain is where memories are stored.
6. The mind resists suppression and does the opposite.
7. White matter in the brain nourish the neurons via the glial cells. Liars have more white matter in the area of the brain involved in deception.
8. Right and left brains are connected by a corpus callosum. Left brain in the linguistic side.

9. Antidepressants accounts for about 25% of improvement and placebo effect accounts for the remaining 75%. Just believing you are getting something to help is over 1/ 2 the battle. Across the population- 1/3 very strong, 1/3 some, and 1/3 none on placebo effect.

10. Hypothalamus is involved in hunger and growth.

11. Every two weeks, roughly the maximum life span of white blood cells, the body produces a set of cells greater in volume that 2 grapefruits.

12. For every 1 Degree C increase in body temp we consume about 20% loss in total body protein or energy loss in sick humans.

13. The more sleep the higher the white blood cell count. Red cells are no part of the immune system.

14. The brain represents about 3% of the body weight but 20% of the energy consumption.

15. Light music mode helps the immune system and health of the body.

16. 100% of stocks change hands every Month and 5 billion are traded per day.

17. With spam 9 out of 10 e-mail messages are junk.

18. Lie detector tests- measure three variables- heart rate, breathing amplitude and galvanic skin response.

19. 45% of airplane accidents occur when a pilot or copilot is flying for the first time.

20 By law an elevator must be built 11 times stronger than required with full load and travel.

21. Harry Truman said "the only thing new under the sun is the history you do not know".

22. Due to the Spanish holocaust of the 1500's the population was reduced to 5% due also to diseases and genocide.

23. The U.S. invaded Nicaragua 13 times in the 20th century turning the contras loose on them in the 1980's.

24. Turkish Government committed genocide against the Armenians, Zionist conquerors ethnic cleansing of 700,000 of Palestinians. The early Americans of the U.S. did the same to the Indians of North America.

25 .In 1920 there were about 80,000 Jews and 700,000 Arabs in Palestine. Israel occupied southern Lebanon from 1982 to 2000 until Hezbollah drove them out.

26. Jewish state in 1947 via the UN mandate the size of Israel was 56% of Palestine and through a war expanded to 78%. 1994 Oslo accord was broken by increasing Jewish settlements.

27. Paul Wolfowitz of the Pentagon assured Congress that the war in Iraq would cost about a few billion .and would be paid for with their oil.

28. According to cognitive dissonance theory the greater the cost the greater self-deception.

29. The Black Plague wiped out 1/3 of the European population in the Middle Ages

30. Religious behavior have a positive correlation with health formulating rules of to avoid tobacco, alcohol, and gambling.

19. The Food Revolution by John Robbins

1. U.S. spends nearly double on health care per capita than other leading countries as Germany, Canada, and France. Every 30 seconds someone in the US files for bankruptcy for health problems.

2. Meat increases risk of diabetes and soy reduces the risk of hip fractures by 36%.

3. Livestock generates 65% of nitrous oxide gas and 18% of greenhouse gas emission higher than cars, shops and planes combined.

4. Blood pressure is lower among vegetarians.

5. Cancer Institute says being active can prevent most cancers, not smoking, and dietary items with plant based foods.

6. Food basis- to prevent lung cancer- green, orange and yellow veg's- 40% reduction. The best items are carrots, sweet potatoes, yams, apples, bananas, and grapes. To help prevent prostate cancer for men- eat tomatoes. Stay away from meat, dairy and eggs.

7. The National Cancer Institute spends only $1million/year on promoting fruits and vegetable.

8. Annual medical costs in the US from meat consumption- $100 billion and from smoking- $65 Billion

9. Best source of Calcium- Brussel sprouts, mustard greens, broccoli, kale and all are about double that of milk.

10. Chickens – about 50% are contaminated with salmonella.

11. Penicillin discovered by Sir Alexander Fleming. Do to over use, some bacteria is now resistant to this drug.

12. Nearly half the water consumed in the U.S. is for livestock.

13. The Ogallala aquifer under S. Dakota to Texas is the largest body of fresh water on earth.

14. #1 milk producing area in the US is Central California with only 4 water quality inspectors in Calif. Central Valley with 1600 dairies where the animals all contaminate the water supply.

15. About 2/3 of land in the central states from Montana to Arizona is used for livestock grazing.

16. Last 35 years the Arctic Ocean ice thinned by 40%. 23 of the last 25 hottest days occurred after 1975.

17. First genetically engineered food sold in the U.S. was the FlavrSavr tomato by Celgene Corp now a sub of Monsanto.

18. Monsanto Corp founded in 1901 to manufacture saccharin.

19. Soybeans now are about 80% genetic and yield 4-10% less. It was initially touted for a greater yield.

20. Organizations that regulate genetically engineered crops and foods in the US- FDA, USDA, and EPA.

21. Not required by law to advise the public that genetically engineered hormone is made from or included in a product as milk.

22. Global acreage planted to soybeans 54%, corn 28%, and canola 9%.

23. Monsanto has Roundup Ready for their genetic crops that the farmers must use by contract once they convert to their genetically modified products.

24. The only GMO potato is the Burbank Russet.

20. The Mind's Own Physician by Dalai Lama- Dialogue

1. Three fundamental elements: responsible behavior, mental collectedness, and development of insightful understanding.
2. There is strong evidence to show musical training can influence the brain. Learning new motor skills helps.
3. Our brain oscillates at the rate of about forty hertz.
4. Stress makes it difficult for the stomach to repair the beginnings of an ulcer.
5. Brain has two systems yin and yang responsible for positive and negative emotions.
6. Buddhist practice consists of three parts: ethics, mind training, and wisdom.
7. Destructive emotions such as anger and fear cause changes in the mind, body, and brain.
8. Three dimension pixels are known as voxels

21. "UNDERSTANDING THE BRAIN"
from Great Courses- DVD #29

1. Music is a sequence of tones and its relationships, and is the same for language.
2. Both language and music have rhythm, tempo, and anticipation.
3.   A. Musicians- powered by the left hemisphere
     B. Non-musicians –the right hemisphere is for rhythm and tempo, and left hemisphere is for anticipation.
4. Auditory is processed in the temporal lobe in the mid brain.
5, Amusia- music agnosia is the loss of the ability to appreciate music.
6, Music is a limbic system experience that increases dopamine and endorphins in the brain and all processed in the hippocampus. Some musicians can remember long sequences of music.
7. Music development- early childhood is important and the brain can develop this if exposed in this period.
8. "Music communicates emotional feelings that words cannot".

23. White Bread by Arron Strain

1. Companion- from Latin roots: com- work, and pan – bread.

2. Pharaonic Egypt workers received wages in bread and bread grains.

3. 13th century Britain workers on feudal manors ate 70 to 80% of daily calories in form of bread and cheese. Beer made up most of the rest.

4. By 1950 calories from bread went to 40-60 % of daily calories.

5. Cheap U.S. corn exported by multinational grain traders, subsidized by the US government, displaced a million or more small farmers in Mexico.

6. In 1830 Sylvester Graham named the graham cracker.

7. By 1890, 90% of bread was made at home by women. By 1930 90% was made by factories.

8. In July 1920 sliced bread was invented.

9. All wheat flour whitens naturally through oxidation as it ages for one to two months. Chemical bleaching is used to whiten the flour with chlorine or nitrogen peroxide gas, some bakers used chalk, boras and alum to whiten dark flour.

10. Court case to charge Lexington Mill and Elevator with selling poisonous ingredients in bread with their bleaching process. Supreme Court ruled that use of the word "may" in the 1906 Pure Food and Drug Act was enough for the Gov. to win the case. Flour then sold as unbleached flour. Previous all commercial flour was treated with chlorine gas or nitrogen.

11. Pro racers ate anti-inflammatory foods as raspberries, ginger and salmon to speed the recovery from injuries. Also ate gluten free foods and were mentally fresh, slept better and performed at a higher level.

12. Grains containing gluten as rye, barley, and sometimes oats. Gluten is added to some foods as ketchup and spices. With increased breeding in wheat it contains increased gluten levels.

13. Global cholera pandemic reached the US via Canada in 1832. Doctors recommended no meat or white bread and lots of pure water.

14. In 1915 a German battleship on a 255 day voyage with sailors on a diet of white flour, white potatoes, white sugar and red meat died of this diet.

15. Fasting was a weapon for the body to manage microbes from eating.

16. Due to lack of vitamins, the draft board doctors rejected 500,000 out of the 1 million for military service.

17. One half of the TV shows in the 1950's featured cowboys.

18. Pres. Truman mobilized the largest movement of wheat and flour for the war cause in 1946/7. In 1958, 96% of the staple in Greece was US flour or wheat and Turkey followed.

19. 1943 under the Rockefeller Foundation established the Office of Special Studies called Mexican Agriculture Program or MAP. Corn covered 65% of Mexican agriculture land and the main ingredient in their diet. They started using US pesticides, mechanized harvesting and synthetic fertilizer. By 1957 90% of their wheat seeds planted in Mexico were of the industrial varieties.

20. By 2009 whole wheat bread sales topped white.

21. In 1951 Congressional testimony of 17,000 pages on the question of bread "are we eating poisoned bread".

24. Wicked bugs by Amy Stewart

1. An aphid is a type of insect that we call a bug, an ant is not. Spiders, worms, centipedes, slugs and scorpions are not insects but are arachnids.

2. Columbus's second voyage to the New World was to the island of Hispaniola now Haiti and Dominican Republic.

3. Treatment for malaria is quinine extracted from the bark of the S. African cinchona tree.

4. Malaria is from the Italian word for "bad air".

PEOPLE

INDEX   PAGE

1. Alexander Hamilton by Ron Chernow

1. Birth place- Nevis in British West Indies and went to King's college in NYC but did not graduate due to the start of the American Revolution.
2. Established the US Coast Guard and Customs Service.
3. New York was a commercial venture of the Dutch West India Company in 1623 that had about 25,000 inhabitants.
4. Dec. 16, 1773, 200 people dressed as Mohawk Indians and dumped 342 kegs of tea in the water in Boston, known as the Boston Tea Party.
5. In June 1775 Washington was named head of the Continental Army.
6. Declaration of Independence was endorsed July 4th but not signed until August 2.
7. Hamilton created a national bank due to the depreciating currency.
8. November 25, 1783, Evacuation Day to end British rule and martial law in New York.
9. A major conflict was the question of Federal or State power- solved with equal representation in each state in the Senate, and proportionate with the state's population in the House.
10. England imposed a law banning export to America of any tools needed in the manufacturing of cotton, linen, wool, or silk.
11. Fear of Hamilton by Jefferson led Madison and his supporters to the Republican Party. Wealthy individuals led the Republican Party while commoners led the Federalist Party. Federalist later became the Democratic Party.
12. Thomas Jefferson resigned as Sec. of State on Dec. 31, 1893.
13. Whiskey Rebellion- was due to the whiskey tax to fund the military, mostly, and pay down foreign debt.
14. 1796 the first contested presidential race dominated by parties.
15. Under President John Adam's in 1798, the Alien and Sedition Act, and Naturalization Act was passed. The NA act stated that full voting rights could be established from 5 to 14 years. Alien act gave power to the President to deport without a hearing any foreign born resident deemed dangerous to the peace of the nation. Sedition act

rendered it a crime to speak or publish any false, or scandalous writings against the U.S. government or Congress.

16. Nine presidents owned slaves including Washington, Jefferson, Madison, and Monroe. Only Washington set all his slaves free.

17. On Feb. 11, 1801 the presidential ballot was tied between Jefferson and Burr with 73 each. The House of Rep. voted and Jefferson was elected after 36 rounds of voting when Delaware withdrew its Burr vote.

18. The standard for Libel cases was that you only had to prove defamatory not that they were false. Hamilton changed this with a new law that the question must be false, defamatory and malicious.

19. VP Burr of the U.S. killed Hamilton in a dual and was also found guilty of murder. However, the charges were dropped.

2. CAPITAL DAMES: The Civil War by Roberts Cokie

1. During the war 18 million women workers comprise 1/3 of US labor force. Woman entered the labor war force.

2. Today females make up ½ labor force and college graduates.

3. Equal pay act introduced in 1945 and passed 1964.

4. Emancipation was declared in Washington in 1862.

5. A Journalist Varina Davis, whose husband had been president of the Confederacy, became friends with Julia Grant wife of the commander of the Union Army.

6. Capitol building damaged by the British fire in 1814 during the war of 1812.

7. City of Washington depended on about 3,000 enslaved workers to build Offices.

8. Congress outlawed slave trade in 1807.

9. Compromise of 1820- admitted Missouri as a slave state, Maine as a Free State and outlawed slavery above latitude 36 deg.

10. Harriet Beecher Stowe's -Uncle Tom's Cabin – 1852.

11. Dred Scott-slave in Missouri when his owners moved to a non-slave state.

12. Spy Rose Greenhow for the Confederacy was eventually caught.

13. Mary Walker was the first female surgeon in America and only the second woman to have graduated from medical school. The first was Elizabeth Blackwell.

14. Clara Barton, angel of the battle field and later founded the American Red Cross, convinced the Congress to ratify the Geneva Convention.

15. Early on the law of Coverture forbade married women from owning property.

16. Homestead Act- settle in the west and get 160 acres of land free. Morill Act established land grant colleges to provide higher education in agriculture, mechanical skills and military training. Internal Revenue Act was established to levy taxes.

17. May Alcott- wrote Little Women- 1868.

18. First conscription law was to boost the number of soldiers as volunteers were all depleted. One could get out of the draft either by paying three hundred dollars or finding a substitute.

19. Women were introduced into the government.

20. Booth with John Surratt had a plan to kidnap Pres. Lincoln and hold him to get the release of prisoners.

21. Central government personnel grew from 5,000 to 15,000 during the war.

22. The 13th Amendment passed by 27 of 36 states, abolished slavery.

23. Alaska along with Nebraska was purchased in 1867 and both were admitted to the Union.

24. The Geneva Convention in 1864 established the principles of ambulance and sanitary personnel traveling under the symbol of a red cross the obverse of the Swiss flag.

3. Charles Darwin's series of books.

Voyage of the Beagle 1845

     1. Expedition was to complete the survey of Patagonia and Tierra del Fuego circa 1830, and the shores of Chile, Peru and Pacific Islands.

2. Falkland Island is about half the size of Ireland and contested by France, Spain and England. Buenos Aires sold it to a private individual as a penal settlement. Then England took it over. Horses there were introduced by the French in 1764.

3. Beagle Channel is about 120 miles long and two miles wide.

4. Palm trees grow in alt. 37° and are arbore scent grass very like a bamboo in alt. 40°.

5. Vesuvius and Etna in Italy, and Hecla in Iceland erupted on the same night as all are in the same mountain chain.

6. Galapagos Archipelago consists of ten principal islands and is situated near the Equator. All formed by volcanic rocks.

7. Near the Cape of Good Hope is the island of St. Helena with a huge black castle near where Napoleon's tomb is said to be.

On the Origin of Species 1859

8. National selection by plants in a given area leads to the stronger ones surviving.

9. Evolution has two dimensions- a. Modification of entire populations and b. Multiplication of species by splitting off and divergence of subpopulations.

10. Cattle determine the existence of the scotch fir but in parts of the world insects determine the existence of cattle.

11. The number of bumblebees in any area depends to the greatest degree on the number of field mice, which destroy their combs and nests.

12. Hermaphrodites- sex of both male and female- in plants having stamens and pistils.

13. The largest frogs/toads are the Marine frog of South America in the Amazon. The second largest are the Pixie toads in South Africa. A toad spends most of its time on land and the frog is both land and water oriented.

14. Egg shells are killed by sea water.

The Descent of Man 1871

15. All the bones of most mammals have the same bone skeleton as humans, monkeys, bats and seals. Muscles, nerves and blood vessels follow the same pattern.

16. With insects of all kinds the males are commonly smaller that the female's and can be detected in the larval state.

17. Male song-birds do not generally search for the female. The female chooses the best singer. Only small birds properly sing except for the Menura in Australia.

18. The Great Bower bird of Australia can fly forwards and backwards.

19. Some birds with plumage change the color of this during the breeding season to attract a mate and in the summer and winter as protection during.

20. Birds breed when food is abundance.

21. Weapons for battle: singing ornaments, colors have been generally acquired by the males through variation and sexual selection and laws of inheritance.

22. Development of beards and hairiness differ in men belonging to distinct races. Beards disappeared in the Chinese and the Japanese. Negroes have scanty or absent beards and they have no whiskers.

23. Females tend towards tenderness and less selfishness. Man is a rival of other men and delights in competition, and passes too easily into selfishness.

24. Hair on the face of American Indian is considered very vulgar. And every hair is carefully eradicated.

25. Butterflies have wings with a colorful top and a plain bottom as a defense and disguise. When on the ground they close their wings together to blend in with the ground.

The Expression of the Emotions 1872

26. Cats when terrified stand tall, arched back and spit or hiss.

27. Horses when savage draw their ears closely back and uncover their incisor teeth.

27. We cannot control or cause blushing as it is inherited. Blush does not commonly extend any lower down the body than the head. It is due to the relaxation of the muscular coats of the small arteries by which the capillaries become filled with blood.

193

4. Cicero by Anthony Everitt

1. Sicily was very important to Rome as it provided cereals, which ensured stability of its food supply and price. The oldest Roman province was won from Carthaginians in 241BC and required payment of 10% of their corn harvest.

2. Pompey had two main aims- first to ratify his eastern settlement and second arrange for a land distribution law granting farms to his veterans.

3. Caesar to increase population introduced a land bill to redistribute publicly owned land in Campania to Roman citizens with more than three children. It was currently rented out.

4. When Claudius took office as Tribune he distributed grain free to citizens in Rome to win support of the urban proletariat or poor people.

5. The first gladiatorial show in Rome was about 56 BC in a cattle market in the Consulship of Appius Claudius and Marcus Fulvius. It was done to honor their father's ashes at the funeral ceremony. Gladiators were hired slaves or condemned criminals.

6. The first public library about 46 BC was a project of Caesar when he hired Marcus Terentius Varro, a scholar.

7. The calendar was extended to 365 days in Jan 1, 45BC. It previously had 10 fewer days.

8. Caesar's death was on the Ides (15) of March 44BC. The Emperor Augustus named that day as the Day of Parricides and the Senate resolved never to meet on that date again.

9. Mark Antony was defeated in the sea battle of Actium in 31BC. He and Cleopatra committed suicide in Alexandria in 30 BC.

10. Julius Caesar believed that the constitution with its endless checks and balances prevented effective government. Cicero believed that government control with the checks and balances of the senate was more democratic.

11. Cicero (maybe about 80 BC) said "Victories in the field count for little if the right decisions are not taken at home".

5. Cleopatra BY Stacy Schiff

1. Cleopatra was a Ptolemy and a Macedonian Greek, and not an Egyptian. At 18 she and her brother assumed control of Egypt. They were very rich and descended from Egyptian pharaohs. Born in 69 BC she had three sisters and two brothers. She spoke nine languages including Hebrew.
2. In 48 BC Caesar defeated Pompey in central Greece. Pompey fled to Egypt and was decapitated there.
3. Caesar said "All men work more zealously against their enemies than they cooperate with their friends".
4. Caesar and Cleopatra struggled together to survive from individuals wanting to assassinate them. In the meantime Cleopatra became pregnant.
5. Alexander the Great was a Macedonian from the fourth century born from Olympias.
6. Cleopatra in Greek means "Glory of Her Fatherland".
7. Egyptian women had the right to make their own marriage. It is estimated that about 1/3 of Ptolemaic Egypt was in female hands.
8. In Egypt the Nile swelled in summer and subsided in the winter. The people kneaded dough with their feet and wrote from right to left. They also sowed seeds then plowed to cover the seeds in loose earth.
9. Discipline quotes: "The ears of a youth are on his back, he listens when he is beaten". "He who is not thrashed cannot be educated".
10. Cleopatra introduced coins of different denominations to Egypt and for the first time the markings on the coins determined the value. She was one of the richest individuals in the world at about $95 billion.
11. Cleopatra had children via Caesar and Mark Antony.
12. Actium was the battle that ended the rule of Cleopatra. Mark Anthony was then assassinated and Cleopatra took her life in the burial place of Anthony to the dismay of Octavian.

6. Creativity, Inc by Ed Catmull

1. Walt Disney Company acquired Pixar in 2006. John Lasseter and Ed Catmull were partners at the original Pixar.
2. The Art of Animation by Bob Thomas was a history of the Disney Studios.
3. A successful feedback system is built on empathy in a company and does not destroy it. All are in the job together.
4. People you choose must: A. make you think smarter, and B. put lots of solutions on the table in a short amount of time.
5. Failure is an opportunity for growth.
6. If the group is afraid to be critical try this technique- make a list of the top five things that they would do again and the top five things that they wouldn't do again. This balances positive with negative.
7. Projects sometimes take too long due to error prevention. Taking too long to be perfect and not necessarily right. Errors are Ok as they can be corrected.
8. Pixar was founded in the 1980's when Steve Jobs was working on NeXT computer. Jobs allowed IBM to use his software for $100 million but not future versions.
9. Steve Jobs liked individuals who would make suggestions, show possible problems without being afraid that they would get fired.
10. Failure isn't a necessary evil. In fact failure isn't evil at all but a necessary consequence of doing something new. Steve Jobs was strong willed but to prevent others from wilting from comments he shifted the emphasis away from the source of the idea and onto the idea itself.

7. Henry Knox by Mark Puls

1. Henry Knox put forth the idea of authorized military schools for theory in the art of war. This would eventually lead to West Point Military Academy 25 years later. He set up a military academy at his artillery headquarters in 1778 to train officers in strategy, tactics, logistics, and engineering.

2. Knox advised Adams that leading positions in the army should be given to Washington not state assemblies to appoint them.
3. Five states had pre ratified the Constitution- Delaware, Penn., New Jersey, Georgia and Connecticut.   Knox's home state of Mass. emerged as the critical swing state on Jan. 9, 1788.
4. George Washington was selected as the nation's first president (with 69 electoral votes) on Monday, April 6,1789, with John Adams as VP (with 34 votes). In the election whomever got the most electoral votes was elected as President and the second most votes was Vice President.
5. Henry Knox became the first United States Secretary of War on Sept. 12, Alexander Hamilton as Treasury Dept. head, and Thomas Jefferson as Secretary of State.
6. The American Revolution started in 1775. Knox gave the Continental Army cannons from Ticonderoga to liberate Boston in 1776. This allowed Washington to claim his first victory of the war.
7. Knox was charged with getting the patriot soldiers across the icy Delaware River on Christmas night 1776.
8. Knox's artillery corps devastated the British at Yorktown in 1781, thus providing the victory that ended the war.

8. Hero of the Empire by Candice Millard

1. November 1890 was the start of the Boer War. The British, attempted to displace the largely Dutch-speaking settlers who had been living in Southern Africa for centuries. The Boer capital was Pretoria in Southern Africa.
2. Winston Churchill graduated in 1894 from the royal Military College at Sandhurst.
3. The British Empire, at that time, covered more than a fifth of the world's land surface and a quarter of the human race of more than 450 million people. This was five times the size of the Roman Empire at its zenith.
4. The British army had been stretched impossibly thin as it struggled to keep the empire intact from Ireland to Egypt.

5. In 1895 Churchill went to Cuba as a military observer, joining a fighting column of the Spanish army during an uprising that was a prelude to the Spanish-American War.

6. The British had great difficulty to subdue India especially in the tribal lands of the Pashrun, an ethnic group renowned for their military skill.

7. The famous London Clock Tower, Big Ben, was built about 1859. It was famous for its 14-ton bell and named in honor of Ben Caunt a bare-knuckle boxer who had been the heavyweight champion of England in 1841.

8. British Empire colonized the southern tip of Africa round the Cape of Good Hope as a stop for supplies from travel in India to their homeport in England.

9. In 1867 a 15-year-old son of a South African farmer found what turned out to be the Eureka diamond, a 21.25-carat diamond, and the first diamond ever discovered in South Africa. This led to the formation of de Beer S. A., The largest diamond company in the world.

10. Two decades after the Eureka Diamond was discovered, the world's largest known gold reserve was found in the Witwatersrand mountain ridge. The area grew to become the largest and important city of Johannesburg.

11. In 1652 members of the Dutch East India Company established a shipping station at the Cape of Good Hope. The people were called Boers who could trace their ancestry back to Dutch. In 1806 the area became a British possession.

12. In 1833 the Boers moved inland hundreds of miles into Africa. After the discovery of diamonds the British annexed the Boer territory that led to the Transvaal War, later known as the First Boer War.

13. After the start of the war in South Africa Churchill, now a journalist was getting ready to leave Southampton, England for the war area. This port was the sailing point in 1620 for the Mayflower to the New World.

14. Churchill's first love was Pamela Plowden that he did not marry but kept in touch with all of his life. He met her in Bangalore, India. He later married Clementine Hozier.

15. Rudyard Kipling covered the Boer War for a newspaper in South Africa. He had published "The Jungle Book" five years earlier and later published his most famous poem "If".

16. Also during the Boer War a physician named Arthur Conan Doyle published his first Sherlock Holmes story, "A Study in Scarlet".

17. The word Boer means "farmer" in Dutch. The people eventually developed their own language.

9. It Worked for Me: In Life and Leadership
by Colin Powell

1. Jan. 20, George HW Bush took office from Pres. R. Reagan.

2. Loyalty is disagreeing strongly and executing faithfully.

3. After leaving the State Dept. a number of financial corporations offered Colin Powell a job. They wanted him only to give talks. He declined.

4. Under President Bush, the U.S. forged good relationships with China, India and Russia.

5. In 2004 it was well documented that the National Security team was dysfunctional.

6. Pres. Reagan's quote- "They say hard work never killed anyone, but why take a chance."

7. Officers retired after 20 years at half pay.

8. Only one out of 100 lieutenants would become a general.

9. What Powell looked for in a subordinate: competence, intelligence, character, oral and physical courage, ability to inspire, and loyalty.

10. Before joining the State Dept. Powell served for several years on the board of AOL.

11. His son was chairman of the Federal Communications Commission from 2001-2005.

12. There are more than 250 diplomatic and consular posts worldwide.

13. You cannot make good decisions unless you have good information and can separate facts from opinion and speculation.

14. His simple rules in a meeting: tell me what you know, tell me what you don't know, tell me what you think and distinguish which from which.

15. My speech to the UN on WMD in 2003 was not based on fact of what I thought it was.

16. An old adage- "bad news unlike wine doesn't get better with time".

17. His favorite maxim was that of Thucydides- "of all manifestations of power, restraint impresses men the most."

18. The president's plan was not followed. Instead Sec. Rumsfeld and Adm. Bremer elected to disband the Iraqi army and fire Baath party members.

19. V.P. Cheney convinced the president to have Libby, a lawyer, write the case as a lawyer's brief and not as an intelligence assessment.

20. Powell graduated from CCNY in the ROTC program and the first ROTC graduate, the first black and the youngest ever to become Chairman of the Joint Chiefs of Staff.

10. PLATO'S REPUBLIC by G.M.A. Grube

1. 447-438AD Parthenon was built under direction of Phidias. Plato was born 428AD at which time Athens was losing its empire and the war.

2. Whenever a man is a good guardian of something, he is also a good thief of it. This includes money.

3. Socrates gives no answer himself and only when someone else gives one then he takes up the argument and refutes it. The trick is always to take up the argument at the point where you can damage it most.

4. The man of great powers always gets the better deals.

5. No one can become an adequate player if he does not practice it from childhood and if he only considers it a sideline.

6. The ruler must be the best among the guardians and the highest of qualities from intelligences, able and caring. One cares most for that which one loves.

7. Per Socrates the guardians should be concerned with the happiness of the whole and not their individual happiness. When the city is good it will have four virtues: wisdom, courage, moderation, and justice. Aim is not to make any one group outstandingly happy but the whole happy.

8. Moderation is a certain orderliness of the mastery over certain pleasures and appetites indicating self-control.

9. Although men are stronger, the difference between the sexes is not relevant in politics. Woman should therefore share all the guardian duties even war and education.

10. Plato-education to be effective must start early.

11. Pythagoras discovered that musical consonances could best be expressed by mathematical ratios. He did this by varying the length of the string on a string instrument.

12. Rules- guardians that we must look for is a man with a good memory who is persistent and loves hard work in every way. Physical labor performed under duress does no harm but nothing learned under compulsion stays in the mind. Physical labor and sleep are the enemies of study.

13. Corruption of cities and characters: oligarchy with the love of money with wealth qualification for office and democracy with no control, and all equal where reason no longer rules and the army dominates. Excessive love of money destroys oligarchy where excessive love of liberty destroys democracy and leads to dictatorship where there is no freedom.

14. Guardian when dealt with outside enemies makes peace while destroying others. The next thing he always does is to stir up a war so that the people shall feel the need for a leader.

11. The Man Without a Face: The unlikely rise of Vladimir Putin   by Masha Gessen

1. Yeltsin was elected president of Russia in 1990. He was the only Russian leader in history to have been freely elected.

2. In August 1998 Russia defaulted on its debts.

3. On August 9, 1999 Boris Yeltsin named Vladimir Putin Prime minister of Russia.

4. The Soviet Union officially ended on Dec 31, 1991.

5. Nazi troops circled Leningrad on Sept. 8, 1941 for 872 days. It was the capitol of the empire. Depleted by WW I, when the name was changed to the Germanic St. Petersburg - Petrograd, the empire was destroyed by the revolution of 1917.

6. Leningrad became the military industrial capital of the Soviet Union.

7. On Jan 13, 1990 in Azerbaijan, the capital Buka, Armenians were killed or moved from the city. The world Chess champ, Garry Kasparov came from there. The entire Soviet economy was collapsing with food and all products were in short supply. In June 1989, tea and soap were rationed and in Oct. 1990 sugar, vodka, and cigarettes joined.

8. In 1991 an attempt to remove Gorbachev failed.

9. Baltic republics of Latvia, Lithuania and Estonia severed ties with the Soviet Union supported by Boris Yeltsin.

10. On May 7. 2000 Vladimir Putin was inaugurated as president of Russia.

11. Mandatory training for reservists included all Russian able-bodied men. This was abolished when they withdrew from Afghanistan. Mandatory military training in secondary school both public and private continued.

12. On Jan 24, 2002 Kasyanov announced 50% increase in military spending.

13. Under Putin private business takeovers both big and small were commonplace.

14. In 1991 the Soviet national anthem was changed to "The Patriotic Song" by Mikhail.

15. In 2004 governors would no longer be elected but appointed.

16. In 1998 Putin was appointed head of FSB due to allegations of corruption against previous leadership.

17. The Big Stone Bridge is the largest bridge over the Moscow River.

12. The Romanovs by Ian Grey

1. Threats to early Russia- Cossacks, Tatars, Russian brigands, Poles and Lithuanians who destroyed land, villages and robbed at will.
2. Romanov dynasty began with the election of Mikhail f. Romanov as tsar and lasted 300 years.
3. Pre Romanov's land was occupied by Mongol-Tatar for about 250 years that split into several political divisions.
4. In the 16th and 17th centuries Moscow became the capital of the nation of Russia.
5. Tsar Ivan IV (Ivan the Terrible) is the first Muscovite ruler of Russia.
6. Ivan III- his seal incorporated the double-headed eagle of the Byzantine emperors.
7, in Jan. 16, 1547 Ivan IV became the first Russian sovereign to be crowned tsar.
8. 1633- 1/3 of Moscow was destroyed by fire.
9. Drunkenness was the national vice of all classes.
10. Russia's greatest and most hated enemy was the kingdom of Poland-Lithuania. The Poles humiliated the Russians when they burned down part of their capital and occupied the capital.
11. The 30-year war lasted from 1618 to 1648. The Habsburgs led Sweden, England, Denmark and Netherland's march against the Poland and the Catholic powers.
12. In 1650 the capital taxes fell on only 1/3 of the population mostly the poor. Those exempt were the large estates or the nobles and the Church.
13. The Plague of 1654 caused shortage in grain harvest due to manpower shortage.
14. 1632-34 Sweden barred Russia from the Baltic's.
15. Peter the Great, Emperor of All Russia, was active in every area. He worked in the Holland shipyards and developed a Russian Navy. Laid foundations in May16, 1703 for the new fortress and port called Petersburg after his patron saint.
16. Peter adopted the Julian calendar on Jan. 1, 1700.

17. In 1719 Peter sent an expedition to discover whether Asia and North America were joined by land. Captain Bering on the voyage made the discovery that was named after him -the Bering Strait.

18. In Jan. 1725 Peter the Great died and Catherine was crowned.

19. 1712 Moscow declared the capital of Russia.

20. Frederick invaded Saxony in August 1756 starting the Seven Years War on Europe.

21. Catherine II 1762-96 was on the throne of the Romanovs even though she had no Russian blood. She made Moscow the center of the Government.

22. 1771-2 the plague killed many in Moscow, Kiev and other parts of Russia.

23. July 1783 Catherine incorporated Crimea into the Russian Empire. Terms were Russia's sovereign over Crimea, The Taman peninsula, the Kuban and the rights of Russian ships to pass freely to the Black Sea. The Sultan signed the treaty of Constantinople in 1784.

24. The Turks captured Constantinople in 1453.

25. 1814 Napoleon defeated the Russian and Austrian armies and this was his first battle experience.

26. Treaty of Chaumont, March 1814, bound Britain, Russia, Prussia and Austria not to make separate peace with France.

27. 1850- Crimean war arose from the claims of the Greek and the Roman Churches to Custody of the Holy Places in Jerusalem. Ended in 1852 when the Turks awarded custody to the Roman Church.

28. Alexander II eldest son of Nicholas I in 1856 increased schooling and the arts flourished with names like Rimsky-Korsakov and Borodin.

29. Military service in 1850's fell exclusively on the lower class of town dwellers and peasants, others were mostly exempt. They would serve for 6 years and be on reserve for an additional 9 years.

30. Dec. 1823, Pres. James Monroe opposed a further colonization of the Americas by European powers.

31. 1867 the sale of Alaska to the U.S. by Russia for $7.2 million.

32. Under Alexander III in 1891 the Trans-Siberian Railway started. Iron and coal industries expanded.

33. Nicholas II, 1894-1917, was responsible for the collapse of the dynasty of the Romanovs.

34. In 1914 St Petersburg received the Slav name Petrograd and it was later reverted.

13. The Burglary, FBI Secrets by Betty Medsger

1. On the Vietnam war- Ronald Reagan in March 1970 said, "If it takes a bloodbath to silence the demonstrators let's get it over with".
2. By the end of the war the US had dropped more bombs on Cambodia than it dropped in all of WWII.
3. Constructors were honored by Pres. Nixon for beating students who were protesting the war in Vietnam.
4. How could a government that claimed to be fighting a war for people's freedom in another country at the same time suppress its own people's right to dissent?
5. Vietnam War- 58,000 Americans killed, 2 million Vietnamese civilians killed and 1.1 million Vietnamese military killed. Vietnam lost about 12% of their population in the war.
6. Between 1965 and 1970 there were 170,000 conscientious objectors who refused to fight due to religious or moral reasons.
7. Woman were hired in 1972 as FBI agents two months after Hoover died.
8. FBI office in Philadelphia was broken into and all files stolen in 1971. Eventually sent to newspapers, and congressional people. The Burglars were never found or prosecuted.
9. The CIA Charter states that their activities cannot be domestic as was established by Congress in 1947. They illegally conducted domestic operations since 1959 when Helms was in charge. It got so large that they created a new branch "Domestic Operations Division".
10. Director Helms testified of their plans to assassinate democratically elected leaders of other countries and install dictators. All came out in the Media with the Burglary data.
11. FBI was building massive files to intimidate people.
12. Hoover was a lone wolf who kept all domestic intelligence work and the files for the FBI under his thumb. Those files were called COINTELPRO and revealed on May 2, 1972 the day Hoover died.

13. Stern was the first journalist to sue the Government for files under FOIA and received the files from this act.

14. There is a 5-year statute of limitation on burglary charges.

15. George HW Bush was CIA director in 1976 and lied before the Church Committee on the assassination of Richard Welch on Christmas Day 1975 then CIA station chief in Greece.

16. Recommendation of the Church Committee- 10 year limit for an FBI
director, permanent intelligence oversight committee, FISA that passed in 1978 as a court controlled surveillance authority.

17. The two FBI officers convicted of illegally breaking into homes were sent to jail. Pres. Reagan pardoned Mark Felt and Ed Miller when he was elected Pres. In 1980.

18. Administrators under Pres. Gerald Ford were Donald Rumsfeld-chief of staff, Dick Cheney-deputy chief of staff and Antonin Scalia.

19. Wisconsin FBI agents notified Washington headquarters of a threat to occur in the United States but were refused a search warrant. Then 9/11 happened. After which they got more money, more agents, and more informers.

14. The Hillary Effect by Taylor Marsh

1. Eleanor Roosevelt "To be involved in politics you have to grow skin as thick as a rhinoceros".

2. Many Senators, as did Hillary Clinton, voted for the war in Iraq to channel toughness before a general election. She tempered her words as many Senators did during election time to give the authority to Pres. Bush to attack Iraq but no harm was done.

3. Hillary co-founded Arkansas Advocates for Children and Families, helped establish the State Children's Health Insurance Program, Foster Care Independence Act, Adoption and Safe Families Act, etc.

4. Hillary was the first viable female candidate and the first to win a presidential primary.

5. Whitewater story broke March 8, 1992. The investigation cost the taxpayers $47 million. Not enough was found against the Clinton's to proceed.

6. In a 2002 speech, Hillary stated after voting for the war in Iraq "I take the president at his word that he will try hard to pass a UN resolution and seek to avoid war, if possible". All were not told about the lack of WMD in Iraq.

7. Mothers reportedly earned 79% of what fathers earned in the workplace. In 2009, 40% of women are their family's sole breadwinners. In 2007, 25.9% of wives were earning more than their husband.

8. Katie Couric was the only female nightly news anchor on broadcast TV until Diane Sawyer's role for ABC in 2009 and later others anchored on the Sunday political shows.

9. Hillary went to Wellesley College and then to Yale Law School. She worked for many civil rights organizations.

10. 2010 GAO report data showed 40% of women held management positions with an average salary that was 20% less that men of like positions.

11. Only 3% of Planned Parenthood's services go toward abortion and over 90% for preventative care.

12. In 2010 France outlawed the burqa.

13. Secretary Clinton under Pres. Obama was the first to visit the war state of Congo to view the problems of toxic environment caused by mining, and atrocities committed against women.

14. Pres. Obama defended then extended the Bush tax cuts which he said he would not do.

15. The Bush-Cheney administration was warned by Pres. Clinton of the danger of Bin Ladin and al Qaeda.

16. Under Pres. Clinton- largest expansion in America history- more that 22 million new jobs, lowest poverty rate in 20 years, the largest surplus in a number of years, lowest unemployment in 30 years, GI bill expansion for college opportunity, and lowest crime rate in 26 years.

17. Pres. Clinton was the only Democrat to win two presidential terms since FDR and go out with a superlative economic and employment record.

18. Clinton's Global Initiative – "2/3's of all the kids in the world who are alive who have AIDS got medicine from their foundation".

19. Hillary never stood up against NAFTA and was against it.

20. During the campaign, Obama spend $2.55 million to Clinton's $1.92 on polling. Pres. Obama spent more on polling in his first 18 months than G.W. Bush did in his first 24 months.

21. On Hillary being attacked as a racist- Politico stated "All the world knows the commitment of President Clinton and Senator Clinton to civil rights issues in words and in deeds".

22. By 2010 women held 90 seats in Congress- 69 Democrats and 21 Republicans.

23. Women in business 2009: 3% in Fortune 500 companies, 15% members on Fortune 500 boards, 6% of the 100 top information tech companies, 16.8% seats in the U. S. Congress, 5% of U.S. Army generals, and 19% of senior faculty at Harvard Business School.

15. The Innovators by Walt Isaacson

1. Digital is nurtured by government spending and academic collaboration with hippies that do it yourself hobbyist.

2. Digital age came from these who were able to connect arts and sciences. When Einstein was stymied working out "General Relativity" he would pull out his violin and play Mozart.

3. Lord Byron's daughter, Ada, in 1850 was impressed with punch cards used in auto weaving looms.

4. Imagination- brings together things, facts, ideas and new conceptions.

5. In1640 Pascal created a mechanical calculator to reduce the drudgery of his father's work as a tax supervisor.

6. Pascal's rotary phone became the first calculator to be patented and sold commercially.

7. Babbage's idea in 1834 was a general-purpose computer based on programming.

8. Ada Lovelace Byron was accorded the world's first computer programmer.

9. 1890 Herman Hollerith an employee of the US Census Bureau started the use of punch cards for computers. Founded the company that later became IBM.

10. Slide rule is analog, abacus is digital, clocks with hands are analog while those displaying numbers are digital.

11. British decoding machine, known as Colossus, during the war was the first all-electronic partially programmable computer.

12. All programmers who created the first general-purpose computer were women.

13. Apple and Google spent more on lawsuits and payments involving patents then they did on research and development of new products.

14. 1637 Descartes wrote: "I think therefore I am".

15. In 1907 Bell's AT&T patents were about to expire and in danger of losing monopoly on phone services.

16. The 1962 Minuteman II needed two thousand microchips for its guidance. Texas Instrument won contract to reduce this number of chips.

17. First consumer devise to use microchips was hearing aids.

18. 1972 pocket calculators cost $100. By 2014 TI pocket calculators cost $3.62 at Walmart.

19. Key lesson for Innovation- understand which industries are symbiotic so that you can capitalize on how they will spur each other on.

20. Bushnell graduated in 1968 the last in his class. He concocted schemes for turning a computer into an arcade video game.

21. Innovation requires three things: a great idea, engineering talent to execute it and business savvy to turn it into a successful product.

22. After WW II the iron triangle of military, industrial and academic companies evolved.

23. Carl Lickliter, born in 1915, pioneered two concepts underlying the internet: decentralized networks and interfaces to facilitate human machine interaction in real time.

24. In October 4, 1957 Russian launched Sputnik the first man made satellite.

25. Bob Metcalfe created a way to use coaxial cable to create a high hand with system he called Ethernet.

26. Internet was a case of collaborative creativity.

27. In 1945 Vannevar Bush had an idea of a personal computer.

28. Ken Kesey in 1958, working the night shift at a mental hospital signed up to be a guinea pig in a CIA funded series of experiments

called Project MKUltra to test the effects of LSD. He liked the drug and later wrote the novel "One Flew Over the Cuckoo's Nest." From him and LSD Flower power was born.

29. Much of the tech that makes the Internet possible was invented at Xerox PARC I in the 1970's.

30. Bill Gates III was nicknamed Trey by his grandmother, an avid bridge play. With Paul Allen he contributed to the computer revolution: Software trumped hardware" Allen explained.

31. Dan Bricklin conceived the first financial spreadsheet program, VisiCalc.

32. Gates at Microsoft working with Jobs at Apple helped with the graphical user interface.

33. The primary reason for Microsoft's success was that it was willing to license its operating system to any hardware maker. Apple by contrast opted for an intergraded approach. Its hardware came only with its software.

34. Internet and personal computer were born in the 1970's and grew up apart from one another.

35. E mail began in late 1971 started by Ray Tomlinson an MIT engineer working at BBN. He concocted a cool hack that allowed messages to be sent to a folder on other mainframes. Connection between computers and networks was called a modem. All this was slow in coming due to the near monopoly over the nation's phone system. In 1975 FCC opened the way to attach electronic devices to the network.

36. Music streaming through cable TV networks was the idea of Von Meister.

37. AOL's Case learned the trick of giving away free samples in order to launch a new product.

38. In 1992 VP Al Gore pushed the National information infrastructure Act of 1993 that made the Internet widely available to the general public. He did not say he invented the "internet". He said, "I took the initiative in creating the Internet".

39. Worldwide Web named by Tim Berners-Lee about 1990.

40. Human brain has 86 billion neurons and up to 150 trillion synopsis.

41. Neuron is a nerve cell that transmits information using electrical and chemical signals. A synapse is a structure or pathway that carries a signal from a neuron to another neuron or cell.
42. Collaboration successions: Steve Jobs built on the work of Allan Kay, who built on Doug Englebart, who built on J. Lickliter and Vannevar Bush.
43. Successful innovators and entrepreneurs cared about and deeply understood engineering and design.

16. The Snowden Files by Luke Harding

1. National Security Agency (NSA) initiated in 1952 and is located along the Baltimore-Washington Parkway.
2. SIGINT at Fort Meade employs 40,000 and is the largest employer of mathematicians in the U.S.
3. In 1970 Senator Frank Church warned that the NSA had the power to make tyranny total in America.
4. Secret sites at Fort Detrick and Edgewood Arsenal is where the U.S. develops chemical weapons. The NSA is more secret and that includes its budget and personnel.
5. After WWII intelligence sharing was known as "Five Eyes"- UK (their agency is GCHQ), Canada, Australia, New Zealand and the NSA.
6. NSA is under the Fourth Amendment that prohibits unreasonable searches and seizures against American citizens. Need probable cause and a judicial warrant.
7. MINARET scandal started FISA in 1978. NSA was supposed to steer clear of communications inside the US without a warrant.
8. Pres. Bush, instead of requesting more power, instructed Hayden to go ahead in secret with more surveillance.
9. The London newspaper Guardian started in 2011 and opened an office in the U.S.. Snowden contacted them anonymously and later gave them his downloads with strict instruction on what they could print. Actually its origin goes back to Manchester in 1821 with CP Scott. His famous words were," comment is free but facts are sacred" and this still is the Guardian's principle.

211

10. It was predicted that by 2015 all Internet traffic would be from mobile phones. In 2013 there were over 100,000 million smartphones around the world.

11. Official Secrets Act passed amid fears of German espionage in 1911 and updated in 1989 makes it a crime for British officials to leak intelligence information.

12. Cryptography was first used in ancient Egypt and Mesopotamia.

13. Putin was a KGB officer who served in communist East Germany in the 1980's and was the former head of the KGB's main successor agency, the Federal Security Service or FSB.

14. German Democratic Republic (GDR) in Berlin was the state's Security and known as "Stasi". It was a criminal investigation department from the 1950's until its collapse in 1989.

15. Eras of NSA: First- In 1952-1978 came to light due to their abuse, assassination programs and watching list of US citizens, Second- 1978-2001- where the agency operated under the parameters of Senator Church's committee, Third- current with the disclosure of the Snowden Files.

16. General Alexander, known as Alexander the Geek, headed up the NSA, Central Security Service and US Cyber Command that was set up by the DOD in 2009. After the leak he advised that the agency stopped 54 terrorist plots that were going to take place in the US. Then it changed to about 12, then he said there might have been one that could have been disrupted by the mass surveillance.

17. Clapper testified before the Senate that they were not spying on any U.S. Citizens. This was a pure lie, as he knew otherwise.

17. Westmoreland: The General who lost the War by Lewis Sorley

1. In 1954 Westmoreland said: "We will get more defense per man per dollar if we can get long-term volunteers and eliminate short – term draftees".

2. Military Academy in 1976 included females.

3. April 6, 1965, White House National Security Action Memo to introduce ground troops in South Vietnam.

4. He stated that "the enemy can't match us on a personnel buildup" which was a classic misjudgment.

5. Pres. Johnson kept Westmoreland 12,000 miles away in Vietnam to keep him out of the political arena.

6. McNamara in 1966 concluded it would take a million and a half men and 10 years to complete the Vietnam war. Westmoreland said the war will be over by mid-1967.

7. On Westmoreland's desk was a quote by Napoleon "Any commander-in-chief who undertakes to carry out a plan which he considers defective is at fault, and should tender his resignation rather than be the instrument of his army's downfall."

8. War crimes at Mi Lai, (my son), March 1968, were finally brought to light and 12 officers were charged with the cover up including the division commander, Major General Koster who was stripped of his rank and reprimanded.

9. Pres. Nixon and Sec. of Defense Melvin Laird stated there would be an all-volunteer army. Westmoreland was not interested in an army of "mercenaries. Milton Friedman said "would you rather have an army of slaves?"

10. Volunteer army rules were changed- signing out for a pass during off duty hours, reveille was eliminated in most cases, harassing young soldiers, beer was acceptable in barracks, etc.

11. Westmoreland on the eve of his retirement in June 1972 wrote to Pres. Nixon fighting against the volunteer Army.

12. He sued CBS but "the libel law does not require the publisher to grant his accused equal time or fair reply" it only requires that the publisher not slander by known falsehoods or reckless ones.

13. 1989, Kristin Baker was to be the first female Captain at West Point.

PRESIDENTS PLUS

1. A Full Life by President Carter

1. Hatch Act- removed political activity from government employees passed in 1939.
2. The State of Georgia is required to have a balanced budget but the governor could strike out any line item in the final budget bill.
3. Ford and Carter choose not to raise campaign funds from corporate or private contributors but to finance through taxpayers' contribution via taxes.
4. Carter's first official act while President was to pardon the draft evaders from the Vietnam War.
5. In January 1979 he normalized diplomatic relations with China.
6. Pres. Carter did not agree with President Nixon's decision not to deal with the PLO until after they recognized Israel's right to exist. He believed in open negotiations to bring about a desirable result.
7. To get the missionaries freed in Uganda, Carter called the king of Saudi Arabia who then influenced Amin with financial gifts and got them released.
8. In April 1977 with the help of Republican members in Congress he passed a bill to make government more simple and effective.
9. When Pres. Reagan came to office he got approval to build 100 unnecessary and unwanted B1 bombers at a cost of $200 million each.
10. Regulated businesses were discouraged from introducing better products or services. This included rail, electric power, oil and gas, trucking firms, airlines and banks. These businesses were deregulated and permitted competition in each area and were protected from abuse especially from the big banks.
11. Through negotiations the number of Soviet Jews that were permitted to leave Russia went from 5,000 to over 50,000 in 1979.
12. Concluded the SALT II agreement of nuclear disarmament.
13. The Cold War ended with the Soviet's under Gorbachev who introduced reforms.
14. Bailed out Chrysler under Lee Iacocca with a grant of $1.5 billion to prevent bankruptcy.

15. The Panama Canal, based on the advice of the military, was turned over to the Country of Panama.
16. In 1903 a treaty was signed with Colombia to take over the canal project. Then we supported the local rebels for their independence from Colombia.
17. Alaska was admitted to the Union as the 49th state in Jan. 1959.
18. Iranian militants held American hostages captive in Nov. 4, 1979. Ayatollah Khomeini and his government supported the militants. Through negotiations they were released and on a plane ready to leave Tehran airport at the time of the U.S. elections. The hostages in Iran dominated the 1980 Presidential election.
19. In June 1978 FEMA was initiated.
20. In 2010 there were more than 3,000 government organizations and private companies in 10,000 locations working on homeland security and intelligence with an estimated 854,000 people with top-secret clearance. (Washington Post study)
21. FISA Act was signed into law on October25, 1978.
22. Got Castro to release 3,600 political prisoners.
23. Soviets invaded Afghanistan in Dec. 1979.
24. The 1996 Helms-Burton bill transferred decisions on Cuba from the White House to Congress.
25. The Nonproliferation Treaty of 1970 was adopted by all nations except Israel, India and Pakistan.
26. Electricity produced by non-fossil energy: Canada 64%, Spain 42%, Germany and Mexico 25%, China 18%, France and UK 15%, and the US 10%.
27. When Carter became President AMD bought Carter's peanut warehouse to enter the peanut business.
28. After his Presidential term Carter became a distinguished professor at Emory Univ. in Atlanta. Georgia.
29. Agreement with North Korea on nuclear problem, return of international inspectors, and withdrawal of troops from the DMZ. All was calm until in 2002, Pres. G.W. Bush branded North Korea and its leader as an "evil empire".
30. Anwar Sadat was assassinated in Oct. 1981.
31. He was able to increase the auto MPG from 12 to 20.

32. Initiated the Camp David Accords with Sadat, Begin and Carter to agree on Resolution 242.

2. Founding Brothers by Joseph Ellis

1. In July 1804 Burr and Hamilton dueled. Burr shot and mortally wounded Hamilton. At the time, Burr was the second ranking official in the federal government and Hamilton was the treasury secretary After George Washington Hamilton was the most powerful figure in the Federalist Party.
2. In the 1800 election Burr and Jefferson went to 36 ballots in the House of Representatives. Jefferson became President when Delaware withdrew its votes from Burr.
3. In 1790 the financial plan was for the recovery of public credit. Problem of passing the plan was a provision of the assumption of state debts by the federal government led by John Madison. In negotiations, it was agreed that the capitol would be on the Potomac River now Washington D.C. The capitol was in Philadelphia for the prior ten years. The act was called the Assumption Bill. Washington supervised the operation and design.
4. In late 1700's the US was a tangled mess of foreign and domestic debt, and needed to restore public credit. As an example, Virginia's land class was in heavy debt to British and Scottish creditors who were compounding interest on loans faster that the profits on tobacco and wheat.
5. Madison was the first Secretary of State.
6. In 1608 John Smith first discovered the Potomac waters named by the Algonquin Indians "Petomeck" meaning "trading place".
7. The Civil War began in 1861. Virginia at that time contained about 1/5th of the nation's population and 1/3rd of its commerce.
8. The constitution imposed restrictions on the Congress's power to end the slave trade but said nothing about abolishing slavery itself. Slavery was an economic precondition of prosperity and no white man would perform the tasks required to drain the swamps and clear the land.

9. Northwest ordinance, July 1787, forbad slavery in the territory north of the Ohio River.

10. Washington assumed the presidency in 1789 with his VP John Adams. Prior to that and the Constitution of 1776, Washington's image was everywhere -an officer in the continental army and in the Constitutional Convention. He voluntarily surrendered the presidency after two terms thus setting the precedent that held firm until 1940 when FDR took on three terms. In 1951 the Twenty-second amendment was passed limiting the President to two terms.

11. Of the first six presidents only John Adams had a male heir.

12. Jefferson would not let himself get involved in policy making decisions of the Adams administration lest it compromise his role as leader of the Republican opposition.

13. It is said that history shapes presidents and not the other way around.

14. Washington and Adams were committed to neutrality at all cost.

15. Jefferson wrote Madison when Adams was president -"As to do nothing and to gain time, is everything with us in order for the Republican's agenda to win, the Federalist agenda needs to fail. Also never interfere when your enemies are busily engaged in flagrant acts of self-destruction."

16. In 1800 Adams signed the Treaty of Mortefontaine officially ending hostilities with France. In 1803, under Jefferson, US purchased the Louisiana Purchase and doubled the size of the national domain.

17. Adams – "Britain will never be our friend till we are her masters."

18. Adams stated the five Pillars of Aristocracy are: beauty, wealth, birth, genius and virtues. Any of the first three could overtake any of the last two.

19. Both Adams and Jefferson died on the same day July 4, 1826.

20. Under the Treaty of Pinckney, Spain gained access to the Mississippi River.

21. In the Treaty of Paris of 1783 English agreed to evacuate its troops from their ports on the western frontiers.

22. The American Revolution ended with Napoleon's defeat at Waterloo in 1815.

23. The Whiskey Rebellion occurred in Pennsylvania due to a whiskey tax to fund the military and pay down foreign debt.

3. Almost President by Scott Farris

1. Thomas Jefferson was the first losing presidential candidate in 1796.
2. Election ends when the loser concedes defeat.
3. Democracy works due to the restraint of the losers.
4. Telegraph invented in 1844. Newspapers increased from 300 in 1814 to 2500 in 1850.
5. Al Smith gave the first concession speech over the radio and Adlai Stevenson gave the first on TV.
6. Clay was leader of the Wig Party that was the foundation of the Republican Party in 1856. It was the first to propose a canal across Panama. He helped to compromise by reducing the likelihood of war in 1820, 1832 & 1850 to save our American history.
7. VP Aaron Burr murdered A. Hamilton in a duel.
8. Jackson's Party was the Democratic Republicans and later changed to the Democratic Party.
9. Clay died in 1852 and was the first having his body laid in State in the Capitol Rotunda.
10. Boundary of the Southern Confederacy and the Mason Dixon line was north of Washington DC.
11. April 1861 Confederates bombarded Fort Sumter outside Charleston, the first shot of the war.
12. The US went on the Gold standard in 1873.
13. Depression in 1893.
14. Smith in 1909 as Assembly leader created the first workmen's compensation Law.
15. Construction of the Empire State building began the same month as the October 1929 stock market collapse.
16. Under Pres. Nixon: wage and price controls, Environmental Protection Agency, food stamp program, affirmative action and tax reform for the poor were instituted. National debt tripled under his presidency.

17. In 1952 TV was first used in Presidential elections.
18. In 1972 there were fewer than ten million Hispanic Americans and in 2008 there were 50 million.
19. In 2008 10 million more women voted than men.
20. The 1929 depression president of the NYSE, Richard Whitney, ended up in prison.
21. Talk radio started in NYC in the 1940's.
22. Two party-system took hold in 1832.
23. Gore was only one of 12 men in his graduating class of 1100 who served in Vietnam.
24. Popular vote for the president started in 1824 and in 1876 the turnout was 82%.
25. In 1936 the nation pollsters predicted Landon would win but George Gallup predicted Roosevelt would with a smaller sample.

4. An Honest President by Paul Jeffers

1. The White House was not officially named until Pres. Theodore Roosevelt assumed the Executive Mansion in 1901.
2. Tenure of Office Act required the president seek approval of the senate for persons appointed to vacant offices if the appointment was temporary.
3. Repeal of the Bland Allison Act that compelled the government to buy and coin as much silver as could be mined.
4. Presidential Succession Act went into effect.
5. Legalized the incorporation of national trade unions. A law for federal government arbitration was passed October 1, 1888.
6. Grover Cleveland gave the speech unveiling the Statue of Liberty known as "Liberty Enlightening the World". Frederic Bartholdi, a Frenchman, sculptured the statue. No money came from either government. The statue was dedicated Oct. 28, 1886 on Bedloe Island, New York.
7. The AFL was formed in 1886 and led by Samuel Gompers.
8. A national railroad commission was formed to get control of the industry.

9. Under President Cleveland in 1887 the government had a surplus of $94 million that resulted from the collection of high tariffs.
10. Pres. Cleveland believed that immigrants had to leave their nativism behind and become Americans.
11. He supported the U.S. Supreme Court decision upholding the constitutionality of segregated schools.
12. The Republican presidential candidate spared no expense in winning Indiana by paying $15 peer vote in gold same as was done in New York via Tammany Hall.
13. The 1889-1890 Congress was called "The Billion Dollar Congress".
14. The press secretary was started in the Cleveland administration by George Parker.
15. Cleveland's running mate for his second term was Adlai E Stevenson from Illinois.
16. July 1863 was the turning point in the Civil War at Gettysburg.
17. Cleveland was the first bachelor as president, the first to get married as president and the first to have a child born in the White House on September 9.
18. "Great Panic of 1893" went into a full-scale depression. Highway construction was started to help jobs. Federally financed public projects also were under FDR- Public Works Administration in the 1930's depression.
19. J.P. Morgan coined the phrase, "If you have to ask, you can't afford it". It was said when an admiral on his yacht asked how much it cost.
20. In 1895 Carlisle was Treasury Secretary.
21. In 1895 Hawaii was proclaimed a U.S. protectorate.
22. G. Cleveland was a leader of the gold standard. Democrats and William Jennings Bryant were the champions of the free silver.
23. First president of consecutive terms in March 4, 1885 and March 4, 1893.

5. Andrew Jackson by H. W. Brands

1. Jeffrey Amherst, British commander, advocated biological warfare on the Indians by distributing blankets taken from smallpox victims and distributing them to the Indians.
2. French and Indian wars began 1754 to drive the English out. War ended in 1763 and the French surrendered all their North America territories.
3. For the British the war for America was very expensive and in 1763 banned new settlements beyond the mountains.
4. In 1765 the Stamp Act taxed the American people.
5. Most important accomplishment of the 1st congress in 1787 was the approval of the Bill of Rights- the first ten amendments.
6. Jefferson became president in 1800. Population was 5.3 million with 1 million slaves. 95 % worked on farms.
7. 1804 Burr challenged Hamilton to a duel. Hamilton died.
8. King of sports began in the Northeast in Long Island named after an English track the Newmarket. In 1804 the first community horse race from Nashville, Tenn.. Truxton, owned by Jackson, was the most valuable stud in American history.
9. Jackson and Jefferson on a political philosophy- the poor always make the best soldiers, the rich were unreliable. The poor knew hardship and danger in the lives. A republic that relied on the poor would survive, a republic that depended on the rich perhaps not.
10. Revolution ended at Waterloo and Napoleon was exiled to St. Helena.
11. 1816 Republican Congress resurrected the Bank of the United States. The bank was originally the brainchild of Alexander Hamilton. It was dominated by the richest men in the country who had controll over the financial business of the federal government.
12. Jackson wanted Spain to relinquish control of Florida. At this time the U.S. had no control over the west including Texas or California.
13. Monroe when reelected in 1820 was the only uncontested presidential race in American history.
14. Jackson said that the rich and powerful bend the acts of the government to their selfish purposes.

15. On Oct. 1 1833 Jackson declared that federal deposits would be transferred from the Bank of the United States to state banks. Biddle was its President and controlled the congress with bribery.

16. Jan. 1 1835 the government was no longer in debt. Jackson paid down the debt while in office. Jefferson believed debt was a Federalist plot to fatten bankers and subvert the Republic.

17. On Jan 1835 Richard Lawrence shot at Jackson but the pistol failed twice to ignite. Told that the president had caused his loss of occupation and want of money. He had been listening to Congress talk against him by the backers of The Bank of the United States.

18. John Quincy Adams Secretary of State consigned Texas to Spanish control in 1819.

19. 1829 Spain attempted to reconquer Mexico but failed due to General Santa Anna.

20. 1830 Texas was under Mexican rule and law prohibited immigration from the United States and banned introduction of slaves. 1835 Crockett lost reelection to congress and died at the Alamo in Texas.

21. 1838 Van Buren was president. In 1840 he lost to Harrison. Month after Harrison's inauguration he died and VP John Tyler became President. Constitution, however, only said that he had powers and duties of the vice-presidency. This changed in 1967 with the 25th amendment which said that on the death of the president the VP becomes president.

22. Bank of the United States speculated on cotton as the recovery started from the panic of 1837. The bank expired in 1841 but Biddle got out before the crash.

6. BACK TO WORK: Why we need smart government by Bill Clinton

1. Mark Twain said, "Two things people should never watch being made are sausage and laws".

2. What other presidents did: Abe Lincoln- transcontinental railroad and established public universities, T. Roosevelt- limited monopolies

power to fix prices, protected child labor laws, D. Eisenhower initiated interstate highway system with tax dollars, Nixon- OSHA and EPA.

3. Bush- first time taxes were cut while the country was waging war.

4. The U.S. fell from 1st to 12th in young adults graduating with college degrees.

5. The Glass-Steagall Banking Act of 1933 was repealed under Pres. Clinton with a dominant veto proof Republican Congress.

6. Debt: 1981-1993 debts quadrupled to 49% of GDP. By 2001 it had dropped to 33% of GDP. Between 2001 and 2008 it rose to 69% of GDP.

7. In 1960 there were 5-1 workers per beneficiary today it is 3-1 and getting smaller.

8. Medicare % of GDP about 3.6. Cost risen by 400 % since 1970 while private insurance profits rose 700%.

9. U.S. spends 17.4% of GDP on healthcare, most expensive of large countries. France spends 11.8% and some countries spend as little as 8.5%. Our spending is at 24% of GDP and we are taxing at 15%.

10. Admiral Mike Mullen- "making friends is cheaper than fighting wars"

11. Oil tax advantages cost the US. ExxonMobil 2nd quarter profits $10.7 Billion and an effective tax rate of 17.6%, well below the national American average of 20.4% and the average corporate tax rate of 23-25%. The U.S. receives 23% from corporations.

12. Main debt drivers in the past 30 years- tax cuts, wars, national security spending. We have 3 choices on the debt- live with it, raise taxes, reduce cost of government and programs, more efficient government and business. Probably need all three.

13. Most of financial managers' income tax rate at 15% due to dividend and capital gains tax rates and should be changed to standard tax rate. They that are in power change the laws to their advantage.

14. After WWII until 1980 bottom 90% earned 65% of income and the top 1% 10% of the income. Since 1980, 90% of the earners were reduced to 52% of income and the top 10% to 48% of income. Median income decreased while the top 1% significantly increased

14. Unemployment rate of college graduates is 4.5% and post-graduate is about 2%. National unemployment rate in 1981 was is at

7.6%. By 2009, 15.6 million children were on food stamps, 65% more than 10 years ago.

15. U.S. spends 1.7% of GDP on infrastructure compared with Canada 4% and China at 9% and our reluctance to raise gasoline tax.

16. Dow companies have 40% of employment here and 1/3 sales in the U.S. Clean tech jobs grew at 8.3%, 2x the rate of other industries.

17. Brazil gets 80% of its electrical power from hydropower and burns more ethanol from sugarcane than gasoline.

18. $1 billion spend on new coal plant yields 870 jobs, solar 1900 jobs and wind 3300 jobs.

19. Half of the U.S. debt is from oil imports. 25% greenhouse gas emission from transportation.

7. Bushwacked by Molly Ivins

1. Harken Energy Corporation- as CEO and company chairman HW Bush sold stock on insider information and included a fake asset swap to raise annual P&I statement. He was never prosecuted.

2. IRS auditing of rich individuals declined while the auditing of working poor increased by about 48%.

3. Cut taxes as we went into the Iraq war- first president in 140 years to do this. Mostly eliminated taxes on stock dividends.

4. Increased deficit to about $450 billion per year vs. the previous administration under President Clinton that had a balanced budget.

5. Stock market has lost value since Pres. Bush took office vs. his father and Clinton.

6. Wanted to privatize Social Security and schools. In office when the S&L scandals broke with Enron and WorldCom.

7. Restrictor requirements implemented for low-income families to obtain government benefits including housing programs, Medicaid and school lunch program.

8. Quote by Upton Sinclair "It is difficult to get a man to understand something when his salary depends on his not understanding it".

9. Ergonomics guidelines regulation- workers in repetitive work. Regulations denied through the Supreme Court under Eugene Scalia.

10. No Child Left Behind law was way underfunded giving it no chance to work. Reform under Pres. Bush had one of the highest dropout rates in the nation and included bogus test scores from schools.

11. It appeared that if one did not say what Pres. Bush wanted to hear they were fired. This happened to Larry Lindsay who advised Pres. Bush that it would cost the U.S. about $200 billion to implement the NCLB program.

12. The Bush budget for 2004 eliminated funding for rural education, gifted programs, and small and technical education schools.

13. In 1995 the Republican Party killed the Superfund Tax due mostly to the oil and chemical company's lobbies- Monsanto, Dow and Union Carbide. These were the companies that helped put HW Bush in as the Texas governor.

14. Big donors got relief from lax regulation controls as with the Pilgrim Pride Corporation's problem with some bad food. Although there were USDA rules under the Clinton administration they were relaxed under the Bush administration.

15. Wyoming produces about 25% of the nation's coal. An Environmental impact study that cost $1 million concluded that two of the nation's rivers would be destroyed along with the fish with the expanded coal and gas production. All was ignored.

16. Pres. Bush cut $300 million from the annual budget of the heating-oil and gas subsidy programs to help poor people. These people do not vote or give political contributions.

17. Enron's Lay was close to Bush. Lay got the Federal Energy Regulatory Commission chairman, Curtis Hebert, fired and replaced with his hand-picked candidate. Mr. Hebert worked toward a deregulation utility bill in Texas.

18. The number of government tax lawyers was reduced thus reducing the tax reviews on the wealthy.

19. Pres. Bush stated that he would not allow American military forces to be used in converting countries to stable democracies- that was not their job.

20. He called off American's participation with Kyoto Protocol on global warming. We were the lone holdout as 178 other nations agreed to its implementation.

21. Withdrew attempts to negotiate peace between Israel and the Palestinians.

22. Dropped a Clinton initiative to go after international money laundering as in the Patriot Act. This included offshore banks used by Osama bin Laden.

23. Backed out of both the comprehensive Test Ban Treaty to ban all nuclear tests and the Biological Weapons convention.

24. On May 2002, did not sign the Rome Treaty to establish an international Criminal Court to handle cases of genocide and war crimes. He also announced that we were no longer bound by the Vienna convention on the Law of Treaties.

25. Most U.S. Generals thought that the first order of priority should have been the Israeli-Palestinian conflict and not Iraq.

26. 90% of the first Gulf War was paid for by our allies. The U.S. paid over 90% for the Iraq war.

27. After touting WMD by the administration non was ever found.

28. The Iraq war was the first that did not have the support from the AFL-CIO.

29. The U.S. used depleted uranium (low-level radioactive waste) in weapons in the Gulf War. Health problems have now been seen in Iraq and have hit the Gulf war I vets.

30. Pres. Bush spent about 42% of his time away from the White House office. He went to Camp David, Kennebunkport or the Crawford ranch.

31. Resource-extraction industries contributed $318 million and got $33 billion in tax breaks and a weakened Superfund toxic-cleanup law.

32. Vetoed a $400 million bill passed by Congress for election reform in the wake of the Florida mess.

33. Promised to expand patrols at our borders then provided no money for this in his budget and in fact vetoed $6.25 million in pay increases for the agents.

34. The Bush administration said that there was a direct link between al-Qaida and Saddam Hussein but no link was ever found.

35. Job training programs had a 2002 budget cut of $541 million (10%) and the 2003 cut the same program an additional $476 million (9%).

8. Destiny of the Republic: President Garfield
by Candice Millard

1. Statue of Liberty was shipped to Philadelphia in pieces in the summer of 1876. Torch was 29 feet.
2. James Garfield was born in a log cabin in Ohio and fatherless before his second birthday. Eventually he was a professor of ancient languages, literature, and mathematics. To pay for his first year in college he worked as a carpenter.
3. Alexander G. Bell was primarily not an inventor but a teacher of the deaf. A job he inherited from his father.
4. The Chicago fire occurred in the fall of 1871. All buildings were made of wood including the streets that were covered with wooden planks. After the fire the Interstate Industrial Exposition Building was built of glass and metal.
5. The Democratic convention of 1860 took 52 ballots and two convention cities. But they lost to the Republican, Abraham Lincoln.
6. James Garfield became the 20th president of the US.
7. Samuel Morse developed the telegraph in 1837 and 60 other people claimed to have invented it first.
8. When A.G. Bell was struggling with an invention he would play the piano and was taught by his mother who could not hear the music. He learned to play by ear and dreamed of becoming a composer.
9. George Washington's 2nd inauguration was in Philadelphia.
10. It took 75 years to complete the reconstruction of the U.S. Capitol after the British burned it during the war of 1812.
11. 1801 was the start of the Marine band to play at the inaugural procession of Presidents. 27-year-old John Philip Sousa led the Garfield inauguration band.
12. The Secret Service was established a few months after President Lincoln's assassination and was created to fight counterfeiting not to protect the president. It became official to protect the President after William McKinley was shot in Buffalo, N.Y.
13. Charles Purvis was the first black surgeon in the country to receive his medical training at a university and only one of eight black surgeons in the Union Army during the Civil War.

14. President Garfield's second floor of his farmhouse would become the first presidential library. Garfield was shot July 2, 1881.

9. Founding Father- Rediscovering George Washington 1775 by Richard Brookhiser

1. Bunker Hill was actually Greed's Hill. The failed American defense occurred in June.
2. The first town to take Washington's name was Stoughtonham Township, Massachusetts in 1776.
3. G. Washington had wooden teeth.
4. Parson Weems made up the story that George Washington accidentally chopped down a cherry tree.
5. Washington married Martha Curtis then 27 in 1759. Martha had been previously married and had 4 children. George had no children of his own.
6. Washington was the only man to win a unanimous vote for president in the Electoral College twice. Elected when he was 43.
7. G. W. was six feet tall, liked the theater and subscribed to 10 newspapers.
8. Massachusetts opposed British policies because a British army had been occupying Boston since 1768 to present day about 1775.
9. First Congress was in 1774.
10. Washington lost more battles than he won. He fought an aggressive defensive war thus he raised the cost of victory for the British to an unacceptable level. In 1778 the French offered troops, supplies and sea power.
11. Major General Benedict Arnold resented the Congress's slowness in promoting him. He used his own money for the Quebec expedition.
12. The initial Revolution was provoked by taxes on tea and fees for stamps on legal documents. The Rebellion was again provoked by a whiskey excise tax.
13. Peace was resolved in Sept 1783 and Washington re-entered New York for the first time since 1776.

14. John Adams was inaugurated as the second President on March 4, In 1797. Washington was put in charge of the Army in case of a French invasion.

15. Benjamin Franklin as a young man drew up a list of 13 virtues he wished to acquire and a program for practicing them.

16. The words- President, Congress and Senate were all Roman terms.

17. Washington read and reread- Cato and Semaca's Morals that was a collection of moral essays. He quoted lines and phrases from Cato all of his life.

18. The back of our dollar bill has an odd little pyramid surmounted by a non-winking eyeball. It is Masonic iconography suggested by Benjamin Franklin. Masonic Lodge 22 organized a parade, when Washington laid the cornerstone of the Capitol. Washington served as the Grand Master pro tem.

19. Modern Freemasonry was invented in London in 1717.

20. Of the first five presidents only John Adams had sons that survived to adulthood.

21. Slavery was part of the Bible and Aristotle words. In 1772 in Britain any slave who set foot in the country became free.

10. Franklin and Winston by Jon Meacham

1. Frances Perkins was the first female member of President Roosevelt's cabinet and he named her Secretary of Labor in 1932.

2. Roosevelt and Churchill were sons of rich American mothers. Churchill's mother, Jennie Jerome married Lord Randolph Churchill in 1874 and Sara Delano became the second wife of James Roosevelt in 1880.

3. As young boys Roosevelt and Churchill were possessive collectors: for Roosevelt it was of stamps, birds, books and naval prints and for Churchill it was toy soldiers and butterflies. They also read the same books such as "The Book of Nonsense" by Edward Lear, Poems of Kipling and Shakespeare.

4. In 1917 Churchill said, "There are only two ways left now of winning the war and they both begin with A- Aeroplanes and the other America."

5. Churchill produced more than forty books.

6. In August 16, 1941 Churchill said, "Never in the field of human conflict has so much been owed by so many to so few".

7. Roosevelt signed the Lend-Lease for British loans on February 8, 1941.

8. Soldiers lost: Russia- 12 million, Great Britain- 400,000 and the United States- 400,000.

9. The Roosevelt's had four sons and a daughter and the Churchill's had three daughters and a son.

10. The principle of the Atlantic Charter was – the right of all peoples to choose the form of Government under which they will live.

11. On April 12, 1945 President Roosevelt died of a cerebral hemorrhage at 63.

12. Churchill died on January 24, 1965 at 75 years old on the date his father had died in 1895.

13. On April 30, 1945 Hitler shot himself in his Berlin bunker. The Germans surrendered on May 8, 1945.

11. General Ike by John Eisenhower

1. Ike loved history and was an avid reader in High School. He was an average student at West Point but appalled at how they taught history. Little attempt was made to explain the meaning of the battle, why it came about or what the commanders hoped to accomplish. However, he was number one at the Command and General Staff School at Fort Leavenworth.

2. In 1926 he was sent to Fort Benning where the primary emphasis was on a successful football team rather than a well-trained battalion.

3. Invasion of Sicily in July 10, 1943 lasted 38 days. Culminated in the fall of the Italian dictator Benito Mussolini.

4. On August 3, 1943 General Patton at a field hospital called a soldier a coward and ejected him from the tent. General Patton died in Dec. 1945 in an auto accident in Germany on his way to a hunting trip.

5. Dec.16, 1944 Hitler launched his operation Autumn Fog and was the beginning of the month long Battle of the Bulge.

6. France territory was first inhabited by the Celtic tribe, then the Romans, Huns, Goths, English, Russians, Prussians and Germans.
7. The first Air Force One Boeing 707 landed in 1956 at Orly Airport, France.
8. In July 1945, when the Potsdam conference was in session with Stalin, Churchill and President Truman, Churchill got word that he was voted out of office. Clement Atlee took over.

12. Harry S. Truman   by Margaret Truman

1. His motto: "Make no little plans. You can always amend a big plan but you never can expand a little one".
2. The destruction of a railroad- The Missouri Pacific RR had 79 subsidiaries. In 1930 Alleghany Corp., a holding company, formed by Cleveland manipulators with the money of J. P. Morgan acquired the entire RR and looted the system by declaring dividends out of capital instead of earnings. They then fired thousands and reduced maintenance and with that the RR went bankrupt.
3. Big business led Truman to conclude that tycoons and financiers dominated not only state governments and federal regulatory commissions but the Supreme Court as well.
4. May 7, 1945 was the unconditional surrender of Germany to General Eisenhower.
5. The giant manufacturing plants constructed in secrecy at Oak Ridge, Tenn. only created enough plutonium for three atomic bombs.
6. July 1945 at Alamogordo Air Base, NM was the first full-scale test of the A-bomb. It was equal to 20,000 tons of TNT and the cloud rose to a height of 10,000 feet.
7. In Sept. 1945 Truman sent a request to Congress for a universal military training though not conscription. They would be civilians in training. The plan called for one year of training for every young man. Congress did not go along with this. Although Truman thought that the Communists would not have attacked Korea or Vietnam if this had been in place.
8. The British who controlled Palestine restricted Jewish immigration to 1,500. Truman wanted to admit 100,000 of Jews displaced persons

in Europe. This came from American Jews who came to the White House and advised him that he was in danger of losing the Jewish vote if he did not act on this. He thought this personally very irritating.

9. From Shakespeare- "Who steals my purse steals trash, but who filches my good name takes that which enriches not himself and makes me poor indeed".

10. Executive Order #8802 in May 1950- abolished segregation in the armed forces.

11. Executive Order was issued that gave federal jurisdiction over all mineral resources of the continental shelf about 150 miles off shore.

12. Executive order #10310- banned discrimination with any contractor or sub doing work for the Federal Government.

13. Reagan's War by Peter Schweizer

1. Reagan signed up for the Eisenhower campaign and voted Republican for the first time. He always had been Democratic.

2. Johnson's goal in Vietnam was not to seek outright military victory but to negotiate a settlement with the North Vietnamese.

3. January 1967 Reagan was sworn in as Gov. of California.

4. Pres. Nixon- "It is when one nation becomes infinitely more powerful in relation to its potential competitors that the danger of war arises".

5. May 30, 1972 Nixon and Soviet Premier Brezhnev met to sign the SALT agreement- freeze offensive missiles construction for 5 years.

6. President Reagan promised to cut taxes, increase the military and reduce the budget deficit. He only did the first two. His main focus turned to building the military. Increased it by over 30% from Carter's Administration.

7. A strong individual against communism even from his early days when they tried to infiltrate the Hollywood union scene. Saw to it that we broadcast radio into Russia. Worked with Saudi Arabia to decrease oil prices that reduced the oil profits of Russia.

14. The Reagan Diaries- by Ronald Reagan

<u>1981</u>
1. F-15 sales to Saudi Arabia is a major Jewish concern. Concern of U.S. is the Soviet move into the Middle East. Israel bombs a potential nuclear plant in Iraq (June 1981) and France was preparing to sell them material.
2. Reagan (1981) reversed the Carter policy against selling arms to our friends as Venezuela- F16 fighter planes.
3. Saddam Hussein called for destruction of Israel, wanted to be leader of the Arab world, and he invaded Iran. This was the reason for our weapon sales to Iran.
4. Carter cut budget 40% in four years. Under Reagan and his advisors could not answer why interest rates were so high.
5. Auto industry asking for help on Japanese imports and Clean Air Act changes. Will not change but thinks current plan will work with reduced taxes. Recession in 1981 was worsening and the team wants to increase taxes to hold down the deficits.

<u>1982</u>
6. China lobby has moles in the State Department. Weapon sales to Pres Mubarak for Egypt. Leaking info on Cuba. Castro wants to make up but Reagan has a price.
7. S & L in trouble due to the high interest rates.
8. Democrats want tax cuts rescinded.
9. Lebanon wants Israel to help against the PLO then get out and help the Palestinians become citizens. Israel bombed W. Beirut for 14 hours devastating the city. Reagan angry and advised stop or relationship is in danger and he used the word holocaust.
10. Oct. 15 1982 Reagan removed the restrictive regulations on the banking institution.

<u>1983</u>
11. April 18 bomb to our embassy in Beirut by the Iranian Shiites
12. looking for spending cuts or face trillion dollar deficit over next five years.

13. Reappointed Paul Volcker. Thinks need to limit money supply and slow down recovery to reduce inflation.
14. 5 million Palestinians in Arab nations and wanting a homeland- where?

<u>1984</u>
15. Allowed U.S. to sell defensive weapons to China.
16. Budget meeting. List of proposed domestic spending cuts, defense cuts and tax revenue by way of loophole closings with no hike in rates.
17. Reduced federal employment by about 72,000.
18. Leaders of Jewish organizations continuously coming to the W.H.
19. Vetoed a 38% increase for public broadcasting.
20. Attended the festival of Our Lady of Czestochowa- the Black Madonna.
21. East Beirut embassy annex suicide bombing. PM Peres & FM Shamir of Israel are both flexible and reasonable I've known.
22. Established relations with Iraq.
23. The law of the sea permits any vessel to go into national waters on a rescue mission.
24. Jeanne Kirkpatrick handed in her UN resignation.
25. FM Rabin of Israel wants $1.8 billion since the weapon sales to Arab states.
26. 10% of the farmers involved in financial & credit crunch.
27. Russia- Cherenkov died and Gorbachev is now their leader.
28. Trying to set up a meeting with Jordan, Palestinians, and US then repeat with Israel.
29. We have been supplying the Contras with money and weapons.
30. April 4, Villanova basketball team came home as Nat. Champs.
31. Problem with trip to Germany invited by Kohl to a German Military cemetery and turned down a non-official visit to Dachau resulted in complaints from Jews in the U.S. The Jews are finding every person of Jewish faith they can to denounce me.
32. Better to use foreigners in their country as they are much cheaper - Turkey soldier $6,000 vs. U.S. soldier $90,000.

33. Israel sold Iran anti-tank weapons. Trying to get Jordon and Israel off dead center and moving on the peace talks. Jewish lobby troubled about our AWAC sale to Saudi Arabia but assured them we'll never let them be outgunned.

34. Davis-Bacon Act

35. Disco in W. Berlin was bombed. Kaddafi, the villain. Chernobyl Russia nuclear plant spill.

36. I blame the $220 billion deficit in 1986-I blame on Congress for not giving me the spending cuts I wanted.

37. Discussed oil problem and dependence with OPEC with two oilmen.

38. We will provide more money for farmers $26 billion this year than Carter provided in all his 4 years.

38. Iran paid a higher price for the same arms as we sold to them. The difference went to a secret bank account for Col. North for the Contras. This is illegal without congress approval.

1987.

39. Tried to veto the Clean Water bill.

40. Asked PM Shamir not to lobby Congress against arms sales to Arab states.

41. Sanctions lifted on Poland.

42. Chief of Staff Don Rumsfeld resigns.

43. Sold Conrail and received $1.5 billion.

44. Worried at not increasing the debt limit.

45. Greenspan accepted Paul Volcker's position of Federal Reserve Board.

1988-89

46. Israel planning new settlements in West Bank and we will try to talk them out of it. Spoke of mid-east peace plan and transition in West Bank & Gaza but PM Shamir is a hold out and is being bullheaded. Shultz is meeting with 2 Palestinians and Shamir is very upset with him.

47. Saudi Arabia will buy missiles from China. Soviet weapons going to Noriega.

48. Soviets willing to pull out of Afghanistan.
49. Setting a dividing line off Alaska in Bering Sea.
50. Iraq used Nerve Gas in driving the Iranians out of the Al Faun peninsula. Iraq gassed civilians of Kurds.
51. China has become the largest arms market to the world.
52. Saudi's are now partners in Texaco Oil Co.
53. Windfall profit tax repealed. Plant closing bill become law.
54. House defeated plan to have gun buyers checked for criminal records.
55. Peru produces 40% of the world's cocaine
56. Israel went into Lebanon-land, sea and air. Colin said I think it was stupid.

15. Team of Rivals by Doris Kearns Goodwin

1. In Springfield the capitol of Illinois, Lincoln married Mary Todd in 1860 after meeting her at a party.
2. Monty Blair represented Dred Scott, a slave. Blair investigated plans for the first Republican convention to be held in Philadelphia in 1855.
3. In May 1860 Lincoln, a virtual unknown than, served a single term in congress and twice lost bids for the Senate and had no administrative experience.
4. Before studying law Lincoln became a flatboatman, merchant, surveyor and postmaster.
5. Missouri compromise of 1820 allowed Missouri into the Union as a slave state and prohibited slavery in the remaining Louisiana Purchase Territory.
6. In 1839 New York State promoted canals and railways, the creation of treatment of the insane, and abolition of imprisonment for debt.
7. After only six months in Hew Salem, Illinois, Lincoln then 23 decided to run for the state legislature. He lost this bid. This was the only time he was beaten by a direct vote of the people. He was a Wig and joined the new Republican Party.
8. Lincoln did not drink alcohol, smoke, use profane language or engage in games of chance.

9. He studied everything he could including astronomy, economics and philosophy. Life to him was a school and he mastered every subject he studied.

10. He said, "A house divided against itself cannot stand"- quoted from the Gospels of Mark and Matthew.

11. On January 27, 1862 Lincoln issued the General War Order No.2 setting the land and naval forces of the United States against the insurgent forces.

12. At the 37th Congress, Republican majority passed the Homestead Act- free land in the West if one stayed for five years, the Morrill Act setting aside public land for land grant colleges and the Pacific Railroad Act for the construction of a transcontinental railroad.

13. Conscription Act allowed a draftee to either pay $300 or provide a substitute as his replacement to get relief from the military. This provoked discontent and was called, "a rich man's war and poor man's fight."

14. Andrew Johnson selected as VP under Lincoln.

15. Provisions were provided for soldiers to cast absentee ballots in the field.

16. The Louisiana Constitution contained the benefit of public schools equally to black and white.

17. John Wilkes booth was an actor and his brother a famed Shakespearian actor. John shot Lincoln in April 1865.

18. Seward was Secretary of State under Pres. Andrew Johnson's term and originated Seward's Folly with the purchase of the Alaska territory.

19. Andrew Johnson was under an impeachment trial in 1868.

16. The Passage of Power: The Years of Lyndon Johnson by R. Caro

1. Joe P. Kennedy sold short on the eve of the 1929 Crash then became chairman of the Securities and Exchange Commission under FDR.

2. In Jan 1967, Joe Kennedy importuned Lyndon Johnson to fill in his son, Jack, for the Foreign Relations position and he would be indebted to him.

3. Jack Kennedy in his eight years in the Senate was away from Washington about ½ the time. Most of that time he was campaigning for the Presidency setting up the background and local teams.

4. Lyndon Johnson guided Congress in 1956 & 57 to successfully passing disability insurance, minimum wage, public housing, and public works measures.

5. Ten VP's succeeded to the presidency- John Adams, T. Jefferson Van Buren, Tyler, Fillmore, A. Johnson, Arthur, T. Roosevelt, Coolidge and Truman.

6. Seven presidents died in office.

7. Article I, Section 1 of the Constitution -All legislative powers shall be vested in a Congress of the United States and the Congress shall consist of a Senate and a House of Representatives.

8. The powers of the president are not authorized to be delegated to the Vice President including: veto powers, grant pardons, and armed forces.

9. VP's offices were in the Capitol and not in the White House. Johnson tried to have his office there but Kennedy said no.

10. Cuba Crises- all Kennedy's advisors wanted him to attack Cuba but he elected to negotiate with Russia and in a letter advised Khrushchev that he would remove the Jupiter missiles based in Turkey. All was then agreed to and the Cuba missiles and base was removed. Turkey was protected with our Sub's in the area.

11. 1964 Congress has gone further than any other to replace debate and decision by delay and stultification.

12. Law of the Budget and Accounting office of 1921 stipulated that the President was required to submit his budget for the next fiscal year to Congress in 8 U.S. Constitution no government agency can spend any federal money unless it has been appropriated by Congress.

14. To end a filibuster- a closure vote can be taken to end debate and force a vote on the bill or if the sponsors voluntarily withdrew it from the floor.

15. Excise tax on luxury goods was repealed.

16. Operation "Mongoose" which approved 8 assassination attempts on Castro's life since 1961.

17. Pres. Johnson's accomplishment- tax cut, foreign aid, education, appropriation bills, Civil Rights Act of 1964- head start, and Medicare and Medicaid.

17. The Right Path: From Ike to Reagan
by Joe Scarborough

1. Book outlines the rise and fall of the Republican Party.
2. Reagan won 49 states in 1984. Raised taxes and exploded federal deficit.
3. Archduke Franz Ferdinand was assassinated in Sarajevo and ignited WWI.
4. August 6, 1965 voting Rights Act was passed into law.
5. Pres. Lyndon Johnson passed Medicare, Medicaid, Head Start and Civil rights Act of 1964.
5. Civil war ended in 1865. Dem's protected segregation.
6. President Nixon created EPA & OSHA.
7. Under Pres. Reagan, Kemp-Roth tax rate reduction bill of 1981 passes along with reduced marginal income tax rates. Pres. Clinton raised tax rates and paid for it in later elections.
8. Pres. Reagan proposed a ban on assault weapons- 1% of guns but were 10% of those used in crimes.
9. Clinton's major accomplishments- balanced budget and welfare reform.
10. President Bush increased domestic and military spending at record levels while passing a $7 trillion Medicare entitlement. Dick Cheney advised- "Deficits don't Matter."
11. Nancy Pelosi became the first female speaker of the House.

18. The River of Doubt by Candice Millard

1. This book is about Teddy Roosevelt's trip in South America down a river never fully discovered before.

2. T. Roosevelt was VP to McKinley and became president after President McKinley was shot in 1901 by John Schrank in Milwaukee, Wisconsin. Roosevelt then ran again in 1904.

3. Ran against Woodrow Wilson in 1912 and lost. He was a third party candidate along with Taft and both were Republicans.

4. Graduated from Harvard and a member of the Porcellian club. Won a boxing match in 1879 at Harvard through rigorous training. Graduated with honors and married Alice lee.

5. Alice died after the birth of their first child. He then married Edith Carow.

6. Panama Canal, a state within Colombia, was offered $12 million for the right to build the canal. Columbia wanted more money. Roosevelt encouraged a revolution in Panama assisted by the US. Navy ships in November 1903.

7. In the Amazon there is an almost transparent fish known as the candiru. This is the only other animal besides the vampire bat that is known to survive solely on blood.

8. The poison-dart frog can carry enough toxins to kill a hundred people and needs only to touch it to be deadly. Amazon Indian tribes use this toxin on their blowgun darts.

9. The word Amazon comes from the Greek word a-mazons meaning "no breast". Derived from Greek mythology of woman shooting a bow and arrow and were said to have their right breast removed to shoot effectively.

10. Marie de La Condamine, in the mid-18th century, was the first to extract a milky substance from a tall tree called "caoutehoue" and he brought a sample back to France. It was used as erasers and then called rubber. The Indians were using the material for boots and bottles.

11. When Henry Ford had introduced the Model T in 1908 the Amazon had been the world's sole source of rubber. Seeds were brought to Malaysia to grow these trees and in 1913 Malaya and Ceylon were producing as much rubber as the Amazon's.

19. Wisdom of the Presidents by Philosophical library

1. Madison most responsible for the constitution of the U.S. was not a lawyer.
2. Theodore Roosevelt- military career- colonel in the Rough Riders, volunteer cavalry unit that fought in Cuba during the Spanish American War.
3. Lincoln's advice for those who wanted to study under him- "work, work, work is the main thing".
4. Lincoln's advice- get books read and study them till you understand them in their principal features and that is the main thing. You must have resolution to succeed.
5. Lincoln's anti-slavery stance during the 1860 presidential election inflamed secession Southerners and a month after his election- South Carolina and other Southern states left the Union.
6. Southern bombardment of Fort Sumter ignited the Civil War. A quick federal victory was dashed at the Battle of Bull Run where the Union forces were routed under George McClellan.
7. Five days after Lee's surrender on April 9, 1865 Lincoln was shot and died on April 15, 1865.
8. On April 9, 1865 General Lee surrendered at Appomattox ending the Civil War.
9. In 1814 Jefferson, under bankruptcy to raise money, was forced to sell his entire book collection of about 6,700 books to Congress to replace the library lost when British forces burned the Capitol.
10. Thomas Jefferson and John Adams died within hours of each other on July 4, 1826 fifty years after the Declaration of Independence.
11. 1801 U.S. government moves from Philadelphia to Washington. Jefferson and Aaron Burr tied in the presidential election.
12. Napoleon was defeated in an attempt to defeat Russia resulting in a weakened army and then exiled to the island of Elba. He escaped and later defeated at Waterloo and died in exile on St. Helena.
13. The first impeachment of a U. S. senator was William Blount on Feb 8, 1798.

14. Libels in the press irritated Jefferson. He feared such a paper would find few subscribers without just true facts and sound principles only.

15. Jefferson while in France was fascinated with the hot-air balloons.

16. In Aug. 29, 1758 astronomer Friedrich Herschel analyzed the discovery of the new planet Uranus. He was the first to say it was a planet but not the first to discover it. Mayer saw it in 1756 and catalogued as a zodiacal star.

17. Under Pres. Jefferson in 1804, Lewis and Clark began their famous expedition exploring the Missouri river for a route to the Pacific Ocean by descending to the Columbia River.

Made in the USA
Lexington, KY
11 November 2019